D0801965

CRISIS PREPAREDNESS HANDBOOK

A Comprehensive Guide to
Home Storage
and Physical Survival

Jack A. Spigarelli

Second Edition
Updated

Cross-Current Publishing ● Alpine, Utah

CRISIS PREPAREDNESS HANDBOOK
A Comprehensive Guide to Home Storage and Physical Survival
by Jack A. Spigarelli

Published by:
Cross-Current Publishing
333 North 425 East
Alpine, UT 84004-1427 U.S.A.
(801) 756-2786
Orders@Cross-Current.com
http://www.Cross-Current.com

ISBN, print ed.   0-936348-07-0
ISBN, PDF ed.   0-936348-08-9

First Printing, 1984
Second Printing, 1984
Third Printing, 2002, completely revised and updated

Printed in the United States of America

Library of Congress Control Number: 2002090032

Disclaimer: The purpose of this book is to provide information only to help persons who want to prepare for possible future crises. It is sold with the understanding that every effort has been made to provide the most current and accurate information available to the author's knowledge when written. It is in no way intended to be exhaustive. Any errors or omissions, either typographical or in content, are unintentional. No illegal activities are suggested or encouraged. Any use or misuse of the information contained herein are solely the responsibility of the user, and the author and publisher make no warrantees or claims as to the truth or validity of the information. The author and publisher shall have neither liability nor responsibility to any person or entity with respect to any loss or damage caused, or alleged to have been caused, directly or indirectly, by the information contained in this book. Neither the publisher nor author are engaged in rendering legal or other professional advice. If legal or other professional advice is needed, the services of a competent professional should be sought.

Cover design by Daniel Ruesch Design www.danielrueschdesign.com

Contents

CRISIS SURVIVAL

OTHER PREPARATIONS

RESOURCES

1

SECURITY IN AN UNCERTAIN WORLD

We take our modern world for granted. If it's too cold we just turn up the thermostat. If it's too hot we turn the air conditioner on. If we've run short of milk we think nothing of driving our car to the supermarket to buy more. Dinner can be on the table in minutes with our microwave. We dress in the latest fashions, laundered by the newest "superpower" detergent in our five-cycle automatic washer. And merely flicking a switch lights up the room, let's us listen to a concert in stereo, or brings the evening news live, in color, from half way around the world. It's really quite a convenient life. It may not always be so.

We Are Dependent

Our conveniences are due mainly to specialization. Each of us is skilled in our own narrow field but we know less and less about everything else. This trend has made us more and more dependent on large numbers of interconnected systems for even the most basic necessities of life.

We depend on the farmer to produce our food and he, in turn, depends on having the necessary fuel, machinery, fertilizers and pesticides, favorable weather and ample water. We depend on the truckers, railroads, processors and supermarkets to transport and distribute our food, often from thousands of miles away. They depend on fuel for the trucks and trains as well as an orderly credit system.

We depend on the utility companies, with their umbilical cords continuously feeding us our heating, cooking, lighting, refrigeration, communications and water. We depend on the textile manufacturers for our clothing and the hospitals, physicians, dentists and drug companies for our health services. The oil companies supply our gasoline and the police and firemen our protection. And to pay for all this and more, we depend on a reliable source of income.

We Are Vulnerable

The multitude of vast, interdependent systems we depend on form a fragile web. Their centralization and complexity create vulnerability to disruption and breakdown. Even relatively minor incidents could interrupt the flow of food and other essential goods and services, bringing instant panic and chaos.

Consider the Possibilities

A crisis could result from a wide variety of events, both natural and manmade. It may affect only a local area, with modest disruption and inconvenience, or be a major catastrophe of global proportions causing a total breakdown and collapse of society. And even spared such a crisis, many families nevertheless face the occasional accident, illness, or unemployment. The temporary loss of income and its associated problems can create a personal crisis for that particular family.

Think about your own situation. Try to imagine what it would be like without power for refrigeration or lights to see by. What would you do without water to flush the toilets or even to drink? What if one of your children were sick and there were no doctors nor hospitals available to call for help? What would you do if you had no food to feed your family and the stores were empty and closed? Or you had no fuel to heat your home during the freezing blizzards of winter?

Dangerous Times

On September 11, 2001, terrorists hijacked four commercial airliners full of passengers and then rammed them into the World Trade Center in New York City and the Pentagon in Washington, D.C.. Passengers aboard one of the airliners overpowered their captors, preventing it from reaching its target, but over 3,000 innocent civilians lost their lives in the attack. This atrocity jolted many from their dangerous complacency, forcing them to realize that terrible destruction could happen, even in America. Many responsible, intelligent individuals think the possibilities for even worse events are more than just someone's imaginary nightmare. While a calamity of man or nature has always been possible, some believe that mankind is entering a time of unprecedented peril.

Attacks by terrorists or rogue states using biological, chemical, or even nuclear weapons could bring on major crises. Some feel that the threat from Russia and China could still trigger a nuclear holocaust, while others see the Middle East as the flash point. Scientists studying the forces of nature warn of climatic changes and forecast crop failures and worldwide famine. Many foresee societal trends that could result in hyperinflation, a collapse of the monetary system, depression, massive unemployment, rioting and a complete disintegration of society. Finally, there are potential cataclysmic events of nature that could also occur.

But, regardless of your personal view, it should be abundantly clear how fragile the threads are that hold the fabric of society together and how perilous our condition could become at any time.

Majority Unprepared

It is human nature to avoid the unpleasant. Simply thinking about the crisis possibilities is too disturbing for the majority to even consider. Having never suffered any real hardships, they find it difficult to accept the fact that they may. They feel secure in the assumption that everything will go on working tomorrow just like in the past. The many warning signs are ignored and the consequences are rejected. They go about their everyday lives sure that nothing bad can happen to them. And, if it did, they are confident that someone else would take care of them.

But the majority are often wrong. They don't realize how vulnerable they are. They are not aware of how fast a crisis could strike nor how severe it could become. They fail to recognize the true nature of their condition until it is too late.

The Prudent Prepare

The prudent realize there are no guarantees in life. They know the only security comes from being independent. They accept responsibility for themselves and their families and take steps to become as self-reli ant as possible. They recognize potential problems and do what they can to minimize their effects. In short, they prepare.

The Time Is Now

The sooner you begin preparations the more likely you are to be ready. When the crisis appears, the time to prepare is gone. If you knew for certain that a major crisis would strike next week, you would spare no effort to make whatever preparations would be necessary. How can you be positive it won't happen that fast? If you are a "someday" procrastinator or put it off because you are too busy with day-to-day concerns, you must realize the urgency. If you are waiting for a better time you wait in vain. The best time is now and you have no time to waste. The day will come when "today" is too late to prepare. Do it now.

2

MAKE THE COMMITMENT

A major commitment is required to prepare, but it can be done if you go about it step-by-step with a plan.

An Achievable Challenge

Preparing for major crises takes a good deal of thought and effort. It involves considerable expense and may require significant changes in lifestyle. The task can seem overwhelming unless you realize it doesn't have to be done all at once. First, you must start by building a solid foundation of knowledge. You will be making many decisions, and intelligent decisions require sufficient and accurate information. Then, following the guidelines in this book, devise an orderly, systematic plan. Now break the plan up into manageable steps. Since your decisions will be highly individual, naturally you should also expect to implement them at your own speed.

Develop Your Own View

It is easier to make appropriate preparations when you have some idea of the potential crises. A wide selection of possibilities has been discussed by various authors, and you can become acquainted with them by reading their books. Don't limit yourself to particular views but study diverse opinions. The views often conflict and no one knows with certainty exactly what will happen or when. Many things also happen that the "experts" never expected. You will have to make the best educated guess you can. It's your future at risk, so don't simply accept someone's view. Think through the logic. Do you agree? If not, why not? Examine the various perceived threats. Some will occur, many will not. Which are most likely to happen? Which are most dangerous? Don't ignore a possibility just because it makes you too uncomfortable to accept it.

Anticipate Consequences

Once you have developed your view, list the crisis possibilities. Think what would happen if they occurred. How would they affect you and your family? What could you do now to lessen their impact?

Does your view of the future include possible winter storms, tornadoes, or earthquakes? You may need to strengthen your home, build a storm cellar, or put in an emergency power source to ensure heat, light and refrigeration. If your area is subject to prolonged drought, you should consider alternate water sources.

Does your view contain increasing governmental control and continued budget deficits? Then you will need to plan for eventual hyper-inflation. Government may use it as an excuse to set up ineffective price controls so you'll need to read about them and their effects. You should stock up on basic commodities that the price controls would soon keep in short supply and prepare for rationing.

What about civil disturbances, mob rioting and perhaps a complete breakdown of law and order and essential services such as transportation, communications, police and fire protection and utilities? Will food production and distribution be disrupted? Will the lack of medical services and proper sanitation lead to epidemics? Will looting and violence become widespread and force you to protect yourself?

Recent events have made us much more aware of potential biological, chemical and even nuclear attacks by terrorists or rogue nations. There is also still the possibility of an all-out nuclear war. Whatever their motives, some claim a nuclear war would annihilate the whole earth and entirely destroy civilization. They state flatly that it is ""unthinkable" but we now know that the "unthinkable" can happen. The Russians continue to amass their ICBM arsenal, devise new ways of protecting their industry and build shelters for their people. China tries its best to increase its nuclear capabilities. Misinformed, we continue to believe that nothing can be done to prepare for it and therefore do nothing. The truth is there are a number of things you can do to greatly increase your chances of surviving a nuclear war. Chapter 27 tells you the minimal preparations you should make and where to learn about more extensive ones.

Extent Of Crisis

Obviously crises come in all dimensions and durations. Likewise, it is obvious that if you prepare for the worst you will also be prepared for everything less. In many parts of the world, if a crisis prevented the food crop from being harvested, it would be at least a year before substantial replacement food could be grown. Thus, I recommend a one-year period as the minimum that should be considered and this book is based on that premise. Whether you decide to plan for more or less is up to you.

What It All Costs

Depending on perceived needs and desires, costs can vary tremendously. A one-year food supply for an adult, for example, can cost anywhere from less than $300 to more than $3,000. Some may already have a good share of what they feel is needed while others must start from scratch. If you feel comfortable with just the basics, you can probably prepare for less money than a decent automobile would cost. If you see it necessary to establish a full-blown retreat in the wilds of Canada complete with a jet helicopter to take you there you can spend millions.

There are many ways to keep costs to a minimum and some of them are listed under Budget Basics in the following section. Other budget tips are included where appropriate throughout the book. Keep in mind that most preparedness items can nearly always be used at some time or another no matter what, and they are likely to cost more as time goes by. But whatever the costs, the price of doing nothing may be much higher.

How To Get The Money

If you have limited funds like most people and are just beginning to prepare, at this point you are probably looking at your already-strained budget and wondering where the extra money is going to come from. You may even be thinking you can't afford to prepare. The truth is you can't afford not to. Maybe you won't be able to prepare exactly as you'd like nor as quickly, but that's no excuse for not doing what you can.

So where does the money come from? My observation is that most people can nearly always find money for the things they really want. It's a matter of priorities. It often takes imagination and sacrifice, but they do it. And so should you.

Start by getting the most for your money with the Budget Basics. Compare prices and shop the ads, special promotions, liquidations and close outs. Don't forget quality often pays in the long run. Check out discount stores, wholesalers, factory and freight damage outlets. Buy directly from the producer if possible. Get discounts by buying in quantity. Join a co-op or set up your own with family, friends, or neighbors. Shop garage sales, flea markets, swap meets, nickel ads and newspapers for second-hand items. Buy military surplus. Use your own labor by growing a garden and preserving the food, preparing storage foods from bulk and making items from kits. Make do with scavenged goods.

Examine your budget for any excess. If you regularly save a portion or put some into investments, realize that preparedness is the most tangible form of savings and the surest investment. Good storage food costs half what the average family spends for food. If they ate similarly to the storage food, each month they could store a month's supply from the savings. You may find it necessary to temporarily reduce your standard of living. Eat cheaper cuts of meat and less prepared food. Eat out less. Cut back on recreation, make fewer trips and take less expensive vacations closer to home. Make do with what you already have by repairing and using items longer. Give preparedness gifts for Christmas, birthdays and other occasions.

If you can't cut expenses enough, get more money coming in. Do family fund-raising projects, take a second job, or upgrade your present employment. Have a garage sale and sell those items you seldom use. Perhaps you should get rid of luxury items such as boats, waverunners, snowmobiles, campers and summer cabins.

In the end, you must decide how important it is to be prepared for possible crises. If you are committed, you will prepare.

3

A FRAMEWORK FOR TOTAL PREPAREDNESS

Total preparedness means being able to provide for your own needs as much as possible. It consists of three areas: material provisions, personal preparation, and financial resources. This chapter looks at each and then shows you how to integrate them into a workable plan.

Material Provisions

Having space for a garden and orchard, acquiring animals, securing a reliable source of water, building a root cellar, and modifying your home for a wood stove are all part of material provisions. So is stockpiling supplies, tools, and equipment. These aspects and others are covered in detail in upcoming chapters. As you read each chapter and your family's individual needs become clear, make a list of the provisions you want with amounts where appropriate. One item in particular you shouldn't overlook is a good reference library (see Chapter 31). Don't skimp in this area because information may be your best investment.

Make sure you plan adequately. People have a tendency to underestimate their needs and overestimate their provisions. Many "year's supply" would be gone in a few months! Although it is true that you might get by with a lot less than you thought possible—you may also need a great deal more than planned for. Extra can't hurt and you may want some for barter. It's also best to begin a crisis with fresh, up-to-date equipment and supplies. This is accomplished by rotation—using the oldest and replenishing with new. A sensible idea is to store more than your anticipated needs, use it down to a minimum level and then stock back up.

Include whatever you will need. Many items are mentioned in this book but you may also want to double-check by going through your home and making a list of all consumable items you find that would be difficult to live without. Look for items that could be damaged and would need replacing. While it may become necessary at times to "make do" during crisis, it is best to prepare in advance.

Have redundant systems so if one fails you have a backup. For example, store food as well as grow a garden and raise animals. While food can usually be securely stored it will eventually run out. Gardens and animals are "renewable" on the other hand but are quite vulnerable to drought, disease, and vandals. Using both increases your odds.

Personal Preparation

There is more to preparedness than the mere accumulation of material goods. Personal preparation, although requiring more time and effort than stockpiling, can often be the difference between being a survivor or just another casualty. Some of the preparation must take place prior to a crisis to be effective so you should start working on it as soon as possible. The most profitable investment is in yourself.

Knowledge and Skills

The more skills and knowledge a person has about a wide variety of situations and problems the better he is able to cope with whatever may confront him, the less likely he is to panic, and the more confident he will be. However, you can not buy the knowledge and skills that may be necessary to survive as you can stockpile goods. They come only through study, practice, and adaptation to your needs and circumstances. And although they may take years to develop, once mastered they can't be taken from you.

One way of learning a skill, perhaps the cheapest and most convenient, is from a good book. Many are guided by the motto: "if I can read it I can do it." The surest way is to become an apprentice to a practitioner who is willing to teach you. A third method is to take a class or seminar through a university, community college, adult education program, special interest club, or from a private source. But learning a skill is just the beginning step. Practice is essential to build efficiency and familiarity. If this sounds as if it might take a lot of your time, just remember during a crisis there may not be a great demand for skills such as watching television, golfing, or playing computer games.

Table 3-1 has a list of skills you may want to consider. It is not exhaustive but should get you started. Use it to make your own list of skills you think may be necessary. Divide your list into two categories—essential and desirable—and then mark the ones you already have. Now plan to acquire the remaining ones. Don't feel you must master all of them immediately, but pick one or two to begin with.

Physical Health

Survival both during and after a crisis may depend on your physical health. Build up your general physical condition and stamina now by eating a balanced diet, getting adequate rest, and exercising properly. Have regular medical checkups and keep immunizations current; diseases that are "controlled" now may not remain in that state. In particular, be sure to have diphtheria immunizations and have a tetanus booster every five to ten years. Get preventative and corrective surgery and dental work done. Have regular eye and hearing examinations. Minimize your dependence by relying as little as possible on drugs and medication, including alcohol and tobacco.

Mental Health

Perhaps more than any other one thing, your survival may depend on your state of mind. Major crises create stress for all, but reactions differ markedly. Many react with excessive fear that quickly turns to panic and sheer terror. If not completely paralyzed by the overwhelming sense of weakness and vulnerability, they act ineffectively and even downright dangerously. Others become deeply depressed and apathetically give up. But some, although facing the same difficulties, cope with an inner strength born of being mentally prepared. With an emotional stability unknown by the rest, they function with a clear head and a calm mind. Any eventuality is less threatening to them.

Preparing requires exercising your mind by expanding its perspective and increasing its adaptability. Try new things and put yourself in different situations. Accept the fact that conditions could change abruptly for the worst and be aware of what to expect. Your mind can be acclimated to the possibilities by reading real or fictional accounts of survival experiences. Use worry constructively by planning out exactly what actions you would take in various crises. This will not only increase your confidence but also tend to reduce anxiety, confusion and disorientation if and when it happens. Learn how to reduce tension through relaxation and venting of feelings harmlessly with physical activity. Keeping a sense of humor also builds resiliency.

Finally, don't ignore the strength of spiritual anchors. All is lost without hope for the future. Consider who you are and what you stand for. Think about and discuss your ethics and moral values, your beliefs and your relationships with others and God. You've got to want to be a survivor and believe you can be one before you will be.

TABLE 3.1 PREPAREDNESS SKILLS

☐ Grow a garden, cultivate an orchard, and plant field crops. It's not as easy as it looks so doing it now is important. You must gain experience working with your particular soil, water, climate, insect, and disease conditions. Building up the soil can also take years.

☐ Raise some rabbits, chickens, goats, or other animals permitted by space and local zoning laws. Learn the techniques of animal husbandry and accumulate the necessary equipment and supplies.

☐ Process and preserve food by dehydrating, canning, smoking, curing, and pickling.

☐ Make your own cheese, butter, and yogurt.

☐ Plan and prepare nutritious, appetizing meals using the same foods and methods of preparation and cooking you would use during a crisis. You'll find cooking on a wood stove is a lot different than using electricity or gas.

☐ Sew, mend, and remodel your own clothing. Learn to quilt, knit, crochet, weave, spin, and dye wool. Make and repair your own shoes and emergency footwear. Tan leather and do leather craft.

☐ Make your own soaps and candles.

☐ Make your own gifts, toys, and household furnishings and decorations.

☐ Learn how to repair and maintain your home. This includes carpentry, painting, plumbing, electrical wiring, masonry, and woodworking. Know how to survey and clear land, drill wells, dam streams, and how to build using rammed earth and other construction techniques.

☐ Cut your family member's hair.

☐ Learn metal-working skills such as welding, casting, and black smithing.

☐ Learn basic auto mechanics and repair and do your own tuneups and maintenance. Learn to fix appliances, machines, and small engines.

☐ Learn about radio and communications. Understand police and fire codes and CB lingo.

☐ Take the beginning and advanced first aid classes from Red Cross or other service group. Best if every teenager and older knows at least the basics. Take Cardiopulmonary Resuscitation (CPR), paramedic, and Emergency Medical Technician (EMT) courses. Learn practical nursing skills and how to handle emergency childbirth. Get practice and experience if possible.

☐ Learn and practice wilderness and primitive survival skills. These include foraging for edible plants, snaring wild game, starting fires without matches, cooking without pots and pans, finding water, making emergency shelters, map reading and navigation, weather prediction, knot tying, and making primitive tools. You don't really have the skills until you can survive on your own in any weather, including winter, in a variety of terrains and climates.

☐ Participate in outdoor sports to learn survival skills and to keep in shape: camping, backpacking, hunting, fishing, trapping, tracking, mountaineering, snowshoeing, downhill and cross-country skiing, archery, canoeing, rowing, sailing, and swimming. Learn to field dress and butcher game.

☐ Learn about weapons and practice marksmanship and practical defensive shooting. The National Rifle Association (NRA) and local gun and archery clubs can help.

☐ Learn practical unarmed self-defense. The martial arts are often offered by local clubs or schools.

☐ Learn to barter. You can hone your techniques as a member of a barter club or by trading goods and services locally among friends and neighbors.

Financial Resources

The first rule of financial preparedness is to preserve what you already have before seeking to accumulate more. Pay off your mortgage and get out of consumer debt as soon as possible. Financial independence requires solvency and you should have enough cash and savings reserves in Treasury bills—or money market funds invested in T-bills—to cover necessary expenses for at least six months. Have a current will and use tax avoidance and estate planning to maximize your net worth. When trying to increase your worth, don't forget that large returns are always accompanied by large risks. Greed and speculation often result in losing all you have.

Realize that paper money has value only in a working economy that accepts it and that it may be absolutely worthless in the future. Then your storage of real goods for barter will be crucial. Among the best trade items are the basic foods (particularly oil), garden seeds, toilet paper, hand sewing needles and thread, .22 Long Rifle ammunition, matches, razor blades, wire, and cloth. I wouldn't store anything my family couldn't use itself and I'd diversify and keep a balance of items. While gold and silver can be transporters of wealth to a more normal economy, their intrinsic value is low in a basic society. I'd be wary of diamonds, other gemstones, rare coins, and collectibles.

Unless you already perform a basic service or produce an essential good, now is the time to develop an alternate livelihood that would

TABLE 3.2 MATERIAL PROVISION PRIORITIES

PRIORITY 1: The most essential storage items to sustain life.

☐ Basic food plan for one year with recipes	Chapter 8
☐ Water for two weeks (14 gal/person) and purifier	Chapter 11
☐ Garden seeds for one season	Chapter 13
☐ Manual grain mill	Chapter 10
☐ Basic medical supplies and medicines	Chapter 24
☐ Minimal sanitation needs	Chapter 25
☐ Clothing to last one year	Chapter 22
☐ Bedding to keep warm without additional heat	Chapter 22
☐ Method to cook and heat with fuel for one year	Chapter 23
☐ Basic survival library	Chapter 31

PRIORITY 2: Portable Storage for minimal needs for 72-hours.

☐ Emergency Evacuation Kit (EEK)	Chapter 20

PRIORITY 3: Storage and other items necessary for a more normal lifestyle. This priority includes equipment, tools, supplies and other items including a self-sufficient homestead or a survival retreat. Among the first items to be considered are an advanced food plan and additional clothing, bedding, medical supplies and fuel.

---

remain in demand. Look over the list of goods and services you would need, compare with your interests and abilities and then choose a suitable trade. Perhaps it could be a hobby or sideline for now.

Your Master Action Plan

As you assess your needs, guided by this and following chapters, you will develop lists for each of the three areas. This is the first step in making up your own **Master Action Plan (MAP)**. Next you should establish priorities among the listed items. Needs and desires vary widely, particularly in the personal and financial areas, and you must decide your own priorities. However, as a possible help, Table 3-2 lists some suggested priorities for the material provisions area.

Once your priorities are determined you need to set specific goals. Naturally you would like to do everything immediately. Realistically, however, your timetable will probably be a compromise between urgency and available resources. Guided by your timetable, set a target date for each item on your lists. Items to be stockpiled should be listed together on an **Inventory Planning Checklist (IPC)** with the amount needed, the target date, a space for marking when achieved and the storage location. Buy to complete the **IPC** consistent with your needs and means. Using the amount allowed by your budget, build a **Master Shopping List (MSL)** showing your planned month-by-month purchases.

Now the most important step of all: implementation. The best plans are useless unless acted upon and the longer you put it off the less likely you are to do it. It takes most families months and even years to build an adequate program and to learn the skills to use it effectively.

Keep Track and Update

With time your stockpile will grow and your preparations will take shape. You will need to keep track of your material goods with an inventory control system (see Chapter 5). Establish a regular schedule for taking a physical inventory to make sure it is all there and in working order. Any worn out or malfunctioning items should be replaced. As perceived threats and needs change, examine your plan and update it.

Trial By Fire

When you have completed enough of your preparations that you feel you could handle most anticipated crises, it is time for the Preparedness Test. This simulated experience is the best thing, short of an actual crisis, to check your program and point out any failings.

The test lasts seventy-two hours and consists of getting by as though you were deprived of all outside assistance and services by some crisis. (Your food plan requires more time to test sufficiently and a separate test is outlined in Chapter 8. The first three days of the food test could take place during the Preparedness Test and continue afterwards until complete.) The ground rules are simple: start the test without warning other members of the household to preclude any last-minute preparation, turn off or otherwise prevent use of all electricity, gas and water, and do not use any item or service you did not have at the beginning (no buying, bartering, borrowing, or begging, please). The survival "atmosphere" can be increased by limiting your outside contacts during the period (turn off the phone?) And the most revealing test will be one undertaken during the worst weather.

Once started, don't back out. It can seem very trying after a day or so but you can certainly survive for the remaining time. If you have any doubts about the need to prepare, you'll be surprised how effectively this test will convince you. Problems most likely to appear are in the areas of water (toilet won't flush, no baths or showers, no hot water to wash or clean up with) and cooking (now just how do you cook in that fireplace?) One important precaution: be extremely careful of fire in any form and have fire extinguishers handy. Make sure that fuel is burned only in well-ventilated rooms and be especially careful, particularly with children, that no lamp, heater, or stove gets tipped over.

4

ANSWERS TO COMMON QUESTIONS

Q.   Don't you think it's being overly pessimistic to expect major catastrophes requiring such a level of preparation? Isn't it a bit paranoid?

A.   I think recent events have answered this question pretty well. We now know that the "unthinkable" can actually happen, even in America. Actually, I think it's quite irrational and irresponsible to ignore obvious threats to one's security and to ridicule those with more foresight. It's just common sense to prepare. The prudent protect themselves with life, home, car and health insurance and no one calls them paranoid. Yet crisis preparedness is the most concrete form of insurance possible. I'd much rather be prepared for some eventuality and not have it happen than the reverse. Only a prepared pessimist can afford to be optimistic about the future.

Q.   Isn't it immoral to store food when so many people in the world go to bed hungry each night and many are starving? Isn't that hoarding?

A.   The negative connotation of hoarding comes from those who attempt to get more than their fair share of a scarce good. But, as I write this, we are in the midst of yet another year of record and near-record crops. Food prices at the farm level are depressed and many farmers are being forced into bankruptcy. The government is actually paying them to not grow food. They are simply producing more than the market needs. Over the years we have seen excess cattle and pigs dumped into pits, grain piled high to rot and even half of the orange crop destroyed to keep prices up! And according to a Department of Agriculture study 137 million tons of food is lost, wasted or destroyed each year by Americans. Most of it is simply thrown out.
    What person could honestly claim that storing food during a

time of such surplus is immoral? Even outside the United States, in Africa and Asia where famines are common, starvation is not really a problem of scarcity. In India, for example, one-fourth of the food supply is destroyed by rats while the nation spends hundreds of millions of dollars developing nuclear weapons. This is not to say there aren't starving people in the world today. There certainly are. But whether or not you store food for leaner times won't affect that at all. And the more you store now, the less the competition will be later. The immoral are those who reject stocking up now but will demand a share of other's storage when shortages appear.

Q.   Wouldn't it cause a shortage if everyone decided to prepare?

A.   If everyone sought to do so all at once it would. In reality, only a small minority will even buy a book like this in the first place, fewer still will read it and only some of them will actually follow through. Stockpiling is normally a gradual process that allows producers time to adjust. Another thought is that if a majority of the people were sufficiently aware of the possibilities and concerned enough to prepare, many of the predicted crises could be prevented.

Q.   If times do get as bad as some predict, wouldn't I either have to share my storage with others who failed to prepare or protect it with force?

A.   If it gets as bad as some predict the answer is certainly yes. It may be a time of real moral decision. Some will choose to share while others may exercise their right to protect their lives and property with force. But isn't either choice better than being unprepared? The truly prudent will store extra and try to convince their family, friends and neighbors to do likewise.

Q.   Should I keep my preparations secret?

A.   It's a real dilemma. By letting others know you can possibly recruit them to the cause and reduce the impact on everyone later. Or you just might be inviting them to steal your stockpile. I think I'd be a bit cautious but I wouldn't try to keep it top-secret, either. If you are afraid that the minute something happens your neighbor is going to stick a gun in your face, then perhaps you live in the wrong neighborhood. In any major crisis, you'd have to move out fast. You might as well think about moving now.

Q.   How can I convince my skeptical friends and loved ones to prepare?

A.   This can be a real problem that is not always easy to solve. You can start by not being overly aggressive in your attempts to convince. Set a good example by carrying out your own preparations. If you have additional resources, perhaps you could set extra aside for them in case they change their minds. Sometimes people respond better if they hear the message from a stranger; you might give them a copy of this or another book that explains what could happen in the future. You can also give them other gifts of practical survival value when the occasions arise. Allowing them to help you in your planning and preparation may spark an interest in their own. Be patient and remember that after all you can do, each individual is responsible for himself.

Q.   How can I answer those who reject preparing with the comment: "I wouldn't want to live in a world like that"?

A.   It's easy to make such comments with a full stomach and a warm bed in a relatively secure society. However, the reality of a situation can rapidly change minds and morals. Actually in dire circumstances, most people will do whatever they have to do to stay alive. But, even if not concerned for themselves, how about their loved ones? Death by starvation or disease is neither quick nor painless. Could they really just stand by and watch them die?

Q.   We've survived bad times before, why not again?

A.   Admittedly, humans adapt well and we've been able to survive many trials in the past. However, we've never been anywhere nearly as dependent as we are now on a fragile, technological system built on energy and other strategic supplies from unreliable sources. Never before have there been the tremendous forces of destruction in man's control. And people are also changing. The first blackout of New York City in 1965 was followed by an increased birth rate but the second one in 1977 by looting and burning.

Q. Things don't seem that bad right now. What makes you think they'll get worse?

A. It's simply the calm before the storm. Problems normally don't just get progressively worse but respites are to be expected. Don't be lulled into thinking they've gone away—because they haven't. A period of relative calm is the best time to prepare simply because so many others are no longer concerned.

Q. This handbook covers a lot of areas to prepare for, and it can look like an insurmountable task to prepare for everything covered here. Can anyone possibly do it all? Should I even try?

A. There are a lot of potential crises. It is a monumental task to prepare for everything and, almost regardless of the amount of preparation, no one can be prepared for them all. However, every thing you are prepared for makes one less thing to worry about. Just do what you can.

This book wasn't written with the idea you must do everything in it. It gives you ideas to think about and then tells you how to prepare for each idea. The choice of which to do is yours.

5

THE FUNDAMENTALS OF SUCCESSFUL FOOD STORAGE

It would certainly be a tragic waste of time, money and effort if, when needed, you found your stored food unusable. Following certain essential principles helps prevent this.

Store What You Eat—Eat What You Store

Many people store large quantities of foods they seldom, if ever, eat in their normal diet. Often they don't even like the particular foods but store them because others have told them to. They seem to think that when the time comes they'll simply change their eating habits. Let's take a look at some of the problems they might find.

People Won't Eat Anything

A common belief is that people "will eat anything" if they are hungry enough. While this is obviously true of many, experience shows that a substantial proportion will go without, even starve, rather than eat unfamiliar or distasteful foods. This is particularly true of the young, ill and aged. The stress of crisis tends to increase rejection of strange foods even more than during normal times. The solution is twofold: store foods as similar to your normal eating habits as possible and acquaint your family with and cultivate a taste for the foods you store.

Sudden Diet Changes Harmful

Your body's digestive system is used to your regular diet. It takes time to adjust to changes. In what is likely to be an already stressful situation, a dramatic change can cause additional stress as well as severe discomfort, illness and possibly death. Changing suddenly to a diet of high fiber, for example, will have a laxative effect accompanied by intestinal gas and a bloated, stuffed feeling. Severe diarrhea and even dysentery can follow. A family I know switched to their food storage and within days the wife was hospitalized. She was unable to either eat or drink for two weeks. The Benson Institute at Brigham Young University showed the same results when they asked a family to live solely on their food storage. The food, largely dehydrated, put a couple of the family members in the hospital within weeks.

This problem can be avoided by slowly building a tolerance now for the foods you store.

You May Be Allergic

Many people find they are allergic to particular foods. Unfortunately, a number of these are some of the best storage foods.

The father of one family attempting to live off it's storage found he was allergic to wheat. This allergy is usually to the gluten which is contained in all cereal grains except rice and corn. Approximately 10% of the adult white population and up to 90% of some ethnic groups suffer from an intolerance to milk. Their systems lack the enzyme lactase needed to break down the milk sugar, and they suffer gas, abdominal pain and diarrhea. Others find they are allergic to egg whites or that they can't easily digest beans.

Being allergic to the foods you store isn't a problem you want to discover later. Now you can make the necessary adjustments.

Foods Don't Keep Forever

All foods deteriorate with time. This fact is examined in detail in the next section. Although possible to a limited extent, it is difficult to just "store and ignore" your food storage. You will find it to your advantage to rotate your food by eating the older and replacing it with new.

Other Factors

If you store food you don't normally use, you may find when the time comes that you lack the culinary skills to prepare appetizing and acceptable meals from it. Learning is a trial and error process and you will be wise to develop the necessary skills now. In addition, storing what you now eat will automatically tend to increase the variety in your storage plan while using the more readily available and affordable foods.

Getting There From Here

The ideal is to live off your food storage daily, but there is a considerable gap between what most people normally eat and what they store. Although you can still eat foods not in your storage, you should make adjustments to bring the two closer together. You may need to become accustomed to some of the storage foods. Start by incorporating small amounts of the particular foods into your menu and gradually increasing them. Don't store the foods in large quantities until you are comfortable eating them. Never store foods you absolutely can't stand.

Storage Life of Foods

As mentioned, no food is entirely static during storage and all eventually become inedible. The length of time a food takes to become inedible is called its storage or shelf life. Shelf life figures for the various foods are easy to find. Nearly every food storage book and advertisement has them. The problem arises because the figures often don't agree. One source may claim a shelf life of less than six months for a particular item while another states it lasts indefinitely. Which is right? The answer often lies in what is meant by a food being "no good".

What "No Good" Means

A food can become "no good" in four different ways:

1. Loss of nutrients. Once a food has lost its nutritional value there is no reason to eat it. Chemical deterioration causes a loss in vitamin potency with the water-soluble vitamins being most susceptible. The losses are usually greatest during and soon after the processing and packaging, tending to decrease substantially with time. Proteins break down and become insoluble. Minerals gradually oxidize.

2. Spoilage and contamination. Microorganisms are found nearly everywhere and, given the proper environment, grow rapidly. Bacteria cause botulism, salmonella and other food poisons, while the fungi—molds, yeasts and slimes—produce many dangerous toxins, some deadly. Enzymes, either microbial or natural such as bruising or darkening, spoil food. Additional spoilage and contamination comes from infestations of weevil, mites, other insects and rodents, and the environment adds foreign odors, dust and even radioactive fallout.

3. Loss of palatability. Food may develop a terrible or offensive smell. Oxygen causes fat to break down and become rancid. Vegetables become "musty", and starch products become stale. Crystallization and colloidal modification causes food to soften, curdle, turn grainy, lump, cake, oil-out and cast off layers. Color pigments oxidize, fade, darken and otherwise discolor.

Loss of palatability is very subjective. Some people are extremely sensitive to off-flavors and odors, while others will eat just about anything placed on their plate. Even the freshest foods don't satisfy every taste preference. A useful fact to keep in mind about palatability is that most studies show food tends to loose its aesthetic appeal before losing appreciable nutrients.

4. Loss of functional properties. Some foods simply loose their ability to function as required. They may no longer leaven (yeast, baking powder and soda), thicken (corn starch and sauce mixes), whip, gel, or "set" (gelatins and instant puddings).

Clearly a shelf life based on one of these meanings may differ markedly from that based on another.

Determining Shelf Life

Predicting shelf life is made difficult by the many variables in four areas:

1. Food characteristics. Each component of food (fats, proteins, carbohydrates, vitamins, minerals and color pigments) undergoes its own forms of deterioration. Individual foods have their unique physical and chemical properties, giving each definite storage potential. Storage also tends to magnify whatever weakness there was in the quality of the original food as well.

2. Processing methods. A variety of methods are used to preserve food, each with a significant influence on product stability and shelf life. The method chosen greatly affects the nutrient retention, particularly of the water-soluble and heat-susceptible vitamins.

3. Packaging methods. The packaging may be anything from a thin paper sack or plastic bag to a hermetically-sealed metal can double-coated inside and out with a food-grade enamel and containing a special nitrogen atmosphere.

4. Storage environment. The shelf life depends heavily on where the food is stored. Much more will be said about packaging and the storage environment in the next chapter.

Limited Hard Data

You would think that with all the shelf life claims for various foods that there would be a large body of knowledge in this area. But the fact is there has been relatively little scientifically-controlled research on shelf life. Foods usually have not been analyzed at the time of storage but have been attributed nutritional values based on fresh foods prior to processing. There is even a greater lack of believable data on nutritional values after long periods of storage. Although some testing has been done, mainly for the military and NASA, in large part we are reduced to using extrapolations and making educated guesses.

All stated shelf lives are estimates. Even those recommended in this book are only based upon the best currently-available data modified by my own years of experience under various conditions and climates. And, because they may not have been determined using exactly the same foods and conditions as you have, they are only guides. The unique shelf lives you will experience can only be established by frequent sampling of your particular storage.

Recognizing Spoilage

Medical care will likely be limited during a crisis but, because of shortages, food poisoning is more likely. To keep your family safe there are some precautions you can take.

Don't taste an item as soon as you open it but examine it carefully for any signs of spoilage. An unbroken seal generally means it's safe but it's probably spoiled if the can end or jar lid is bulging or leaking. Gas bubbles, foamy or spurting liquids, visible molds or slimes, emulsion separation, cloudiness—if not caused by starch from overripe vegetables or minerals in the water—and discolorations other than iron and sulfur blackening of meats are all signs of spoilage.

Smell the item. It's likely to be spoiled if it smells acidic, cheesy, fermented, musty, putrid, sour, or like rotten eggs. If in doubt, remember that heating brings out the characteristic smells of spoilage. Heating in a covered pan will also increase the odor.

Lastly, taste a small portion of the food. Off-flavors do not always indicate spoilage but should be considered suspicious. If a bland food has a sour or bitter taste spit it out immediately. Unusually soft or mushy foods may also be bad.

Some foods can be salvaged. Mold can be cut off apples, cheese, bacon and meat products. If mold is found on butter, other fats, breads, grains and other fruits and vegetables, the product should be thrown out. As an extra precaution against botulism, home canned meats and vegetables other than tomatoes (tomatoes are technically a fruit but are used as a vegetable and will be listed as such in this book) can be boiled for ten to twenty minutes before taste testing. Botulism may be present without any signs of spoilage. If a food is suspected of being spoiled, immediately destroy or bury it with its container where it won't accidently be eaten by children or animals. Radiation does not harm a food unless the actual fallout particles get on it. Clean the outside of intact cans before opening them if fallout contamination is suspected. Fruits and vegetables can be peeled and the peeling discarded.

Rotating Your Storage

By far the best results come through rotating your food storage. Rotation insures that the foods are as fresh as possible, are used in your daily diet and are sampled on a regular, automatic basis. It also minimizes loss of food value and flavor as well as reducing chances of loss due to spoilage, contamination, or damage.

The first consideration for rotating your storage is to have easy access to the storage area. Then, each time you purchase or store an item, label and date the container with the month and year. You can use self-adhesive labels or adhesive tape with permanent ink felt tip markers or grease pencils for glass and other slick surfaces.

Finally, you need a rotation system. You can develop your own to fit your circumstances, but it should take into account the approximate shelf lives of the food you store and rotate all of it within the recommended periods. Replacement dates could be marked on the label, and the foods separated into different locations according to the dates. Another system would be to use different shelf rows. Commonly this is done by placing fresh items at the back while the older gets pushed to the front. A second method is to assign rows of space for each item with additional rows for the new. For example, you might have rows A, B and C for the regular product with row D for new additions. You would use row A first, while adding new to D and go on to row B while adding to row A.

There are also physical helps you can build or buy. These include a slant shelf unit for cans (see illustration 6-3), a can dispenser, or even an entire built-in wall where cans are put in at one point and taken out at another.

Inventory Control

Once you have some storage, it is important to know exactly how much of which items—food and non-food—you have on hand at any particular moment. For this you need an accurate, written record that is kept current. Don't estimate or guess. Many people get a year's supply and think they still have it when in reality they've used a good part of it up.

Your inventory control record needs to tell you the following information about each item:

1. How much you need (your goal).
2. How much you now have stored (on hand).
3. Your rotational schedule for the item (replacement date).
4. Where it is stored (location).

There are many methods you can use and you should pick one or a combination that best suits you. Whatever method you choose, however, keep it as simple as possible or you won't use it and that defeats the whole purpose. Here are some sample methods:

1. Set up a card file using 3x5 or 4x6 cards with separate cards for each item or category. List the item, shelf life, replacement period, storage location, item size, purchase date, replacement date, amount purchased, amount on hand and storage goal. Cards can be filed in related categories, alphabetically, separated into food and non-food, etc. They could also be color coded by category or source for the item.
2. Use a looseleaf binder. Separate lines could be used for each item with a sheet for each category.
3. The **Inventory Planning Checklist (IPC)** of Chapter 3 could be used although this is harder to keep current with rotation. This can be done by:
    (a)   keeping a sheet—taped up or on a bulletin or clipboard near storage area. Write down every item removed and use as shopping list to replenish.
    (b)   use blackboard. Write down as removed and erase when replaced.
    (c)   cover the **IPC** with acetate and tack up or put on clipboard. Mark with grease pen or washable marking pen.
4. A particularly convenient and easy way to keep track of your storage inventory is to make an inventory card for each unit of every item stored. On each card list the item, its size or amount, its purchase date and its replacement date (the dates can be changed when you replace the item). Then make a board (poster board will do nicely) with a pocket on it for each type of item in your storage. Label each pocket by the type or category of item,

its shelf life, replacement period and the total amount needed
You could also list the size of each unit and the number of units
needed to make up the total needed if the size is uniform.
Whenever an item is used, take the corresponding card and place
in a pocket, envelope, or other place to keep until buying the
replacing item. A quick inventory can be taken of each item by
simply counting the appropriate cards.

Don't forget to store extra so that you can use some before replacing
without going below your minimum level. A physical inventory should
be taken at least once a year—every 3-6 months would be better—to
correct any mistakes that may have sneaked in.

SUMMARY

1. Store what you eat and eat what you store.
2. Store the best quality possible.
3. Inspect regularly for possible spoilage and contamination.
4. Rotate storage by consuming within recommended period and
   replacing.
5. Keep track of what you need and what you have stored.

6

HOW AND WHERE TO STORE

How and where foods are stored greatly influences their shelf lives. Although their deterioration can't be stopped entirely, it can be minimized by providing the proper packaging and storage conditions.

The Storage Environment

To maximize shelf life the adverse effect of environmental factors must be avoided. Each factor not only has its own effect but, together, they multiply the rate of deterioration.

Heat

Heat is a powerful destroyer of food quality. The rate of a simple chemical reaction roughly doubles with each 18^0 F (10^0 C) rise in temperature, but reactions in food often increase at a far greater rate because of their biochemical and enzymatic natures. These reactions affect the color, flavor, texture and nutritional value of foods. Heat increases the growth rates of both microbes and insects. It dries out some foods and generates moisture inside containers, also increasing microbial activity. At the other extreme, freezing can bulge and break containers as well as damage texture and flavor.

Moisture

A certain amount of moisture is necessary to maintain quality in most foods but too much moisture—above about 10%—promotes the growth of yeasts, molds, bacteria and insects. It also increases non-enzymatic browning and the break down of fats, provides a medium for chemical reactions and corrodes containers. Foods prepared for long-term storage normally contain the correct amount of moisture after processing, and the task for prolonging shelf life is to keep that level constant. This requires a dry storage environment so containers won't corrode and suitable packaging to keep the right amount of moisture in and additional moisture out.

Oxygen

Oxygen is essential for the growth of fungi—yeasts and molds—and some bacteria. Even small amounts of it will oxidize the fat contained in nearly all foods, causing rancid odors and flavors, changing colors and destroying vitamins. Oxidation is increased by slicing and grinding foods and by the presence of heat and light. Foods high in fat are particularly affected. The effects of oxygen can be reduced by using anti-oxidant additives and airtight containers filled to the top and processed with either a vacuum, an inert atmosphere, or absorbers.

Light

Although light does inhibit the growth of molds, it is best to shield your storage from both artificial and sunlight. Ultraviolet is the primary culprit. It bleaches color pigments, damages flavor and texture, increases rancidity and destroys vitamins. Highly pigmented foods are especially susceptible. Light-penetrating containers can be shielded by keeping them in their original cartons, placing them in a closet, or by covering with an opaque material.

Odors and Dust

Some foods, particularly grains, flours and milk, absorb odors from their environment. They should never be stored around strong-odor substances such as garlic, onions, soaps and petroleum-based products like gas, oil, kerosene, paint, paint thinner and pesticides. Dust should be kept to a minimum to avoid contamination of your food.

Insects and Rodents

Concern for these pests is obvious. Insects need oxygen, moisture and the proper temperatures to survive. Rodents come looking for food. Both can be excluded from your storage by the proper containers and environmental control.

Storage Containers

A suitable container retains the proper moisture and natural food odors while keeping out additional moisture, air, light, dust, foreign odors, insects and rodents. They can be made from a variety of materials in different styles and the "best" is whichever meets your particular needs.

Metal

Airtight metal containers are excellent barriers to air, moisture and light. Rodents can't chew through them and they are resistant to earthquake damage. However, they are usually a bit more expensive, have a tendency to react chemically with some foods, and are best used in dry areas to prevent rust. When placed in a location subject to atmospheric pollution—such as heavy smog, industrial chemicals, or near the sea—they are highly susceptible to corrosion. The seams frequently are not airtight and even the seaming compound will deteriorate.

They come in a wide variety of sizes and shapes. For those desiring to prepare their own foods, the round or square five-gallon cans with either the "paint-can" or a small screw-on lid are good choices. They may be purchased new or possibly from a local bakery or restaurant that buys lard, shortening, or other foods in suitable containers which they discard after use. Clean used containers well with a detergent (the fat in soaps attracts weevil) and you have a good, inexpensive container. Galvanized garbage cans are not airtight. The seams in the side and bottom may only be soldered in a couple of spots—leaving the rest open—and the lid is another problem.

Some sources offer a similar container made of spiral-wound aluminum lined with a moisture-proof fiber material. They claim it costs less to produce than all metal, weighs less, is more dent resistant and seals better than regular metal cans.

Lining and Liners

To prevent the metal from reacting with food, the inside of the can may be commercially lacquered or enameled or you can line it with a food-grade polyethylene bag. Enamel sometimes flakes into the food and only clear or white plastic bags should be used since color pigments can migrate into the food.

Sealing Lids and Seams

Two methods, neither particularly convenient, can be used to seal seams and lids. Hot paraffin wax does a fair job sealing lids but is generally harder to use for sealing seams. Friction-type twist-on lids that don't otherwise seal well can have wax poured over their contact points. The second method uses sodium silicate or "water-glass" available from drugstores. Prepare the water-glass as directed, turn the container upside down and then fill the gap around the lid and along the seams using a small paint brush or medicine dropper. This is an ideal sealant to fill small gaps and make openings airtight but it also has a drawback. After hardening it can only be dissolved in boiling water and that's hard to do with a large filled can!

Masking tape, heat duct tape and other heavy tapes can be used to help seal lids but shouldn't be counted on by themselves. Even overlapping two or three layers probably won't make it absolutely airtight and will permit the escape of fumigants and possible infestation over time.

Rust Prevention and Inhibition

There are a number of coatings that may be applied to prevent or minimize corrosion due to excessive moisture or pollution:

1. Rub the outside with automobile wax or polish.
2. Lacquer the entire outside with varnish or lead-free oil-based paint.
3. Coat small cans with a very thin layer of paraffin wax or dip in a solution made from two ounces of wax dissolved in a quart of warm mineral spirits. Place the can on a wood block to dry.

    Prepare the cans for coating by first removing any rust spots with steel wool, wiping them with an alcohol-soaked cloth and then drying with a clean cloth. Keeping small cans in cardboard boxes on shelves will also significantly reduce rusting.

Plastic

Rigid polyethylene buckets are inexpensive, won't rust or corrode, are seamless for easy cleaning, are lightweight, stackable and quite resistant to damage by rodents and earthquakes. The negative aspects are that after many years they become brittle, crack and emit odors, especially in high smog areas. Rodents have been known to chew through the thinner walls of plastic garbage cans and sunlight also deteriorates plastic. They let some light in and are somewhat permeable to water, oxygen and hydrocarbon vapors.

Again they are available in a wide variety of sizes. The best for home storage are the two to six-gallon buckets made from thick high-density food-grade polyethylene with molded lids—even better with rubber gasket seals—and wire handles if possible. A rubber mallet is handy to close them air-tight and a special lid tool is nice to open them easily. (Some types have lids that are meant to be cut off and are very hard to open without permanent damage to the lid.) Used buckets can be obtained from some sources but be sure they are FDA-approved for food.

Glass

Glass is easily sterilized, won't corrode, is the least reactive with food and is impermeable to air, water and rodents. Its major drawbacks are that it is expensive, heavy, lets in light and breaks easily. The last two problems can be overcome somewhat by storing the jars in their original cartons and tightly packing the spaces around them with wadded newspapers, cardboard, excelsior, or other packing material. Glass jars also do not stack well and their lids can corrode.

Other Materials

Other materials can be appropriate under certain conditions. Some sources offer items in polypropylene bags with a liner of metalized plastic. Cardboard boxes seldom protect enough but some are impregnated with a plastic-wax compound and may suffice in particular situations. Both the bags and boxes would need protection from rodents.

The cellophane, thin plastic, heavy paper and cardboard containers commonly found in supermarkets are not for long-term storage. They are not airtight, are easily punctured and are quickly penetrated by insects. Even the heavy-duty ten to twelve-mil polyethylene used to package the MRE military rations is easy game for the little Rhyzopertha dominica beetle! Of course, they could be placed inside larger, more protective containers.

Size Considerations

When choosing sizes for your containers there are a few things to keep in mind. Smaller containers reduce the possibility of contamination of large amounts, are easier to rotate and can often be stored in spaces too small for larger containers. They may also be more portable in mobile situations and for evacuations. I know people who have 55-gallon drums of wheat in their basements that weigh over four hundred pounds and would require a forklift to move. Larger containers, on the other hand, can be much more economical, particularly for items not costing much per pound. Wheat, for example, can be purchased in six-gallon poly buckets for about half what it costs in #10 cans. Dehydrated fruits and vegetables cost about one-third more in #2½ cans compared to #10 cans.

Vacuums and Inert Atmospheres

Excluding oxygen can significantly increase the shelf life of some foods by retarding oxidation. For example, it's a necessity with most freeze dried meats. However, it doesn't seem to make much difference with powdered foods such as tomato powder where the oxygen is apparently trapped by the small particles. Lack of oxygen does prevent the growth of insects, their larvae and microbes.

The simplest method to remove the oxygen is by creating a vacuum and then hermetically sealing the container. A second method is to replace the oxygen with an inert gas like nitrogen or carbon dioxide. A third method is to use oxygen absorbers. Oxygen absorbers are quick and easy to use with dry ingredients, but don't replace as much of the oxygen as using nitrogen. There is also some indication that the absorber ingredients might combine with the food, contaminating it.

You can save substantially by preparing your own with dry ice (see the fumigation section of this chapter for instructions), vacuum-packing your own at home with readily available systems, or using oxygen absorbers. Complete directions for using oxygen absorbers are available at waltonfeed.com./self/upack/oxyintro.html. Sources for the packets are listed in Chapter 32.

Packaging Your Own

As noted above, you can save large amounts of money by buying bulk grains, beans, sugar, powdered milk and other food items to re-pack in your own containers. The commercially-packed are ready to store and if you have the money and don't want to mess with it perhaps that's the way to go. On the other hand, you should at least be aware just what you're paying for that convenience. Buying the basics in #10 cans will cost about two to five times as much as doing your own in five-gallon poly buckets. That's about $300 to $500 extra per person! Even getting them commercially prepared in five to six-gallon poly buckets will cost about 50% more than if you did it yourself.

Powdered milk can also be canned at home and keeps as long as the commercially-canned (7 years or so). Doing your own can save lots of money and it is not difficult to do:

1. Obtain the proper number of suitable containers. Table 6-1 can help you determine how many you will need.
2. Obtain the food items and re-pack as soon as possible. This is best done on a low-humidity day with no wind if doing outside.

3. Make sure the containers are clean of all foreign matter, contaminants and condensation. If necessary, clean with detergent, let dry thoroughly and then wipe with a clean, dry cloth.
4. Line, if necessary, with a heavy-duty white food-grade bag.
5. Add food item to container and fumigate if desired (instructions in following section). The amount you get in each container depends a lot on the particular item but can be increased by vibrating and tamping down.
6. Put any desired desiccant or oxygen absorber on top of the food.
7. Seal tightly. This step is critical and you should make sure the rim is not contaminated with dust or other matter. This is best assured by wiping with a clean, dry cloth after filling.
8. Label container with contents and date prepared (month and year).

Fumigation

The need for fumigation depends on your situation. If you start with properly cleaned, low-moisture grains, store them in suitable containers and live in a dry climate, you probably don't need to go to the bother of fumigation. If you live in a high-humidity climate or have had infestation problems before, you will want to fumigate In either case you'll want to inspect regularly and take appropriate action if needed. Generally, legumes do not need fumigation.

Dry Ice

Dry ice is the most widely used method for home fumigation of grains, pasta and dehydrated fruits and vegetables. It is inexpensive, generally costing less than a dime per five-gallon container, safe and easy to use, and the method I recommend. Because it is solidified carbon dioxide that creates tremendous pressures when it returns to its gaseous state, it should never be used with glass containers. It does not affect the sprouting capabilities of grain other than perhaps of that very near the dry ice as it vaporizes. Adult insects and larvae are suffocated by the lack of oxygen, but their eggs and pupae remain dormant in the food.

You will need about one pound for each thirty gallons of containers (four grams per liter). Dry ice is sold at many grocery stores or look in the Yellow Pages under dry ice or beverage companies. Although non-toxic, dry ice is very cold—as low as -100^0 F (-73^0 C)— and you should use folded newspapers, tongs, or heavy gloves to avoid being "burned".

TABLE 6-1. PROXIMATE WEIGHT PER CONTAINER VOLUME

The following list can be used to estimate how many 5-gallon containers are needed to store a particular amount of an item. Other sizes can be calculated from the 5-gallon size. The actual amount possible per container depends on the actual food particle size, its moisture content, the grade of the product and how well it is tamped or vibrated down when put in.

Food Item	Pounds per 5-gallon container
GRAINS	
wheat, rice, popcorn	34-36 lbs
corn, barley, rice	32-35 lbs
buckwheat, millet, triticale	30-33 lbs
cracked wheat	25-28 lbs
cornmeal	22-27 lbs
flour	23-25 lbs
macaroni	16-23 lbs
rolled oats	15-19 lbs
BEANS	
small white (Navy)	35-38 lbs
baby lima, Great Northern, black, whole and split peas	33-35 lbs
pinto, garbanzo, large lima	31-34 lbs
soybeans, lentils, light red kidney, black eye peas	30-33 lbs
MILK	
regular non-fat dry	22-25 lbs
instant non-fat dry	13-17 lbs
SUGAR	
granular	29-34 lbs
brown	30-36 lbs
SALT	36-38 lbs

Follow this process to fumigate:

1. Brush off any water vapor that may have condensed on the dry ice from the atmosphere. This prevents additional moisture from being added to the food.
2. Use two to three ounces (about two to three cubic inches) for a four to six-gallon container (two cubic centimeters per liter) and place in the middle and as low as possible in the container. That can be directly on the bottom of metal containers but, because the intense cold may crack the bottom of a plastic one, first place an inch or two of grain in a plastic container and set the dry ice on that.
3. Finish filling the container. After the visible fumes have disappeared, loosely place the lid over the top. Do not seal the lid until the dry ice is entirely evaporated or the pressure may cause the container to explode! Depending on the container size, this may take thirty minutes or longer. If any bulging should occur quickly remove the cover, wait a few minutes and then replace it.

Unlike nitrogen, carbon dioxide is heavier than air and will tend to remain in the container even after opening. Much of it will stay in the container if you scoop the food out rather than pour it.

Other Chemical Fumigants

There are many chemical poisons that can be used as fumigants but they are often hazardous, toxic when used improperly and may be regulated or illegal in your area. Many will even kill insect eggs, but they also usually destroy the sprouting capabilities. If you desire to use any of these compounds, I strongly suggest you call or visit your local county extension agent or a reliable commercial firm for complete directions on how to do it properly and safely.

Dusts

Grains and seeds may be preserved by coating them with a small amount of fine dust. The dust suffocates and scratches the insect bodies, causing them to dehydrate and the insect to die. Although a variety of dusts can be used, diatomaceous earth is the most common. It is a very fine dust made from the ground-up silicate shells of a pre-historic, microscopic algae called a diatom.

You will need about one cup for each five-gallon container. A protective mask should be worn to prevent irritation of the lungs. To be sure every kernel is coated, it can be mixed in small quantities or placed between alternating layers of grain, finishing with dust on top, sealed and then shaken or rolled to mix thoroughly. Small amounts of the dust are not harmful to the digestive system and, as it is quite difficult to remove, you will probably simply eat it. It does not affect the milling, baking, nutrition, or germination of the grain. However, if you desire to remove it, either shake thoroughly in a fine mesh bag or rinse with clear water. The kind of diatomaceous earth sold by swimming pool maintenance firms has been heat-treated and crystallized for water filtering, is inedible and not what you want. Suitable dusts are available from Diatect and WholeWheat (see Chapter 32).

Organic Insecticides

Pyrethrum is an insecticide made from the flower of the pyrethrum chrysanthemum. It is generally safe for humans and readily breaks down when exposed to heat and light. It is quick acting and is usually combined with piperonly butoxide or sulfoxide to increase its effectiveness. Use it the same way as dusts. It is sold in garden supply stores in aerosol cans or powder form. Food that has been treated with it should be washed or exposed to light for a few days before eating.

Ineffective Methods

Methods you should not count on, but recommended by some, include bay leaves, chewing gum and ten-penny nails. Salt is also poor because it concentrates the moisture.

Desiccants (Dehydrating Agents)

Dehydrated foods, including grains, tend to attract moisture from the air, which may result in spoilage or infestation. If there is doubt about the stored foods being dry enough, or you will be opening the container regularly to use the contents, you may want to use a desiccant to keep the food dry. They are available commercially or you can make your own. Besides those mentioned below, calcium oxide is also used extensively by the U.S. Army.

Silica Gel

Silica gel (also alumina gel) is the desiccant used by the government and industry to protect fine guns, new cameras and delicate electronic equipment from moisture. It is relatively expensive but its reusability makes it practical for keeping dehydrated foods dry. It should be desiccant grade and is available from most general chemical supply stores. Often it can be bought with an added moisture indicator that makes it look like small grains of sharp blue sand when dry. As it becomes saturated it then turns pink, white, or clear.

Although an ounce will protect about two cubic feet of space when used with equipment, because of the high moisture content with food you will need about 2½ ounces (about a quarter cup) per five-gallon container. The silica gel can be placed in a porous cloth bag or you can make a bag from a cloth approximately one foot square by tying with a wire or string.

The bag should be checked every month or so. If the color has changed, indicating it is saturated with moisture, it should be removed for reactivation. This is done by heating in an oven at 300^0 F (150^0 C) for about ten minutes. Overheating—about 450^0 F (230^0 C)—will destroy its dehydrating ability. The blue color will return when it is dry. Let it cool before returning it to the container for re-use. Unused gel should be stored in well-labeled, airtight containers.

Prepackaged units with built-in indicators are available from the Hydrosorbent Company.

Calcium Chloride

Calcium chloride—that's $CaCl_2$ and not calcium hydroxide or slaked lime—is not reusable but is quite inexpensive (less than $10 for a twenty-five pound sack) and can be used in the final drying of large quantities of food. It looks like pieces of chalk, is available from some building supply stores and is used to keep icy roads from freezing and in construction work as an additive to set up concrete. Pharmacies also carry pellets in smaller quantities at higher prices.

You need about an ounce (one-fifth cup) per gallon of container. Fill an open glass or plastic container half-full or less with the chips or pellet and bury it upright in the grain almost to the top so it won't tip. Make sure the lid won't touch its top and then seal. Check every few months and replace if it is quite moist or has turned to liquid. Although not highly dangerous, it should be kept in airtight jars out of the reach of children.

Decontamination

Three methods can be used to destroy or prevent infestations in new or salvaged storage foods:

1. Cold. Place small bags—ten pounds or less—of infested foods in the freezer. Two or three days at or below 0^0 F (-18^0 C) will kill the adult insects while the same time at -10^0 F (-23^0 C) will destroy the eggs and larvae as well. Upon removal, wait twenty-four hours and then dry off any condensation prior to storing.

2. Heat. All stages of insects can be killed by heating the internal temperature of the food to 150^0 F (66^0 C) and maintaining for four minutes, 140^0 F (60^0 C) for ten minutes or 120^0 F (49^0 C) for twenty minutes. Higher temperatures or longer periods of time may reduce the germinating abilities and affect the qualities of flours subsequently milled from the grains. Small packages may be heated directly while the contents of larger packages should be placed on a shallow pan to a depth not greater than ¾ inch to assure complete penetration of heat. The oven door should be left slightly ajar to avoid overheating and you may want to stir the food occasionally at the higher temperatures to keep it from scorching. Check oven temperature prior to use with an accurate thermometer. Food should be placed in insect-proof containers before it cools to avoid re-infestation. This method can also be used to reduce the moisture content of foods.

   A variation of this method, for use with lightly infested raisins, prunes, or home-dried fruits, is to place the food in a small cheesecloth bag and dip in boiling water for one minute. Then thoroughly dry the contents before storing.

3. Mechanical. Infested grains can be submerged in a container filed with cold water and the bugs will float to the top where they can be skimmed off. Then either use the grain quickly or oven dry with the above method until hard for milling or storage. Flours can be cleaned by sifting through a #64 wire screen.

Keep for Reuse

Don't throw a container away just because you've used its contents. It can often be recycled for other uses limited only by your imagination and needs. For example, glass jars and jugs can be used to store grains, beans, powdered milk, salad dressings and pickles. Canning jars you're saving for the next harvest can store water in the meantime. The #2½ and #10 cans can store home-dehydrated foods, be used to save wax and lard in, or even made into emergency stoves or homemade water filters. A five-gallon bucket can store water or be used as an emergency toilet.

Storage Areas

Your storage areas should be orderly and readily accessible to accommodate rotation and inventory control. You may also want to spread your storage among a number of locations rather than have it in just one place to decrease the chance of it all being affected at one time by flood, theft, or other mishap.

Ideally you will want two different types of storage areas, one with high humidity for storing fresh produce (see Chapter 16) and one with low humidity for storing preserved foods such as canned and dehydrated foods, grains, legumes, milk, sugar, salt, etc. This latter area should be:

1. Cool. As close to 32^0 F (0^0 C) as practical without freezing. About 40^0 F (5^0 C) would be ideal but $50\text{-}70^0$ F ($10\text{-}21^0$ C) is acceptable and attainable by most. Avoid extremes if possible.

   Lower locations are normally best—basements as opposed to attics—while north and east walls minimize the heat from the sun. Insulating food by storing in closed cardboard boxes stuffed with newspapers can keep foods about five degrees cooler than the surrounding air on hot days. Good ventilation will help control temperature as well as moisture. Locate storage away from heat sources such as furnaces, heaters, heat ducts and vents, steam and hot water pipes, radiators and hot water heaters, dishwashers, dryers, ovens and stoves. Placing sensitive foods like milk, eggs, fats and oil near the bottom of a seven foot stack can keep them five to ten degrees cooler on a very hot day.

2. Dry. Locate away from water sources such as steam and water pipes, cooling vents, radiators, dishwashers, clothes washers and unvented dryers. Never store containers directly on concrete or dirt floors but place on wood slats, racks, boards, blocks, plywood, cardboard, or even rolled newspapers. Keep containers one inch from walls to prevent picking up moisture and to improve circulation. Keep humidity below 60-70%.

3. Dark. Keep out of direct light, particularly sunlight.

4. Away from dust, smoke and strong odors.

Space Needs

Obviously, the amount of space needed depends on how many people you are storing for, how long you're storing for and types of food. This book's basic plan—and similar plans—will take about seventeen cubic feet (thirteen in square cans) per person for a year's supply. The advanced plan takes about thirty cubic feet, less with air dried fruits and vegetables and more if extensive freeze dried is used.

Finding the Space

Finding the needed space is never easy, particularly for those in small apartments or a highly-mobile situation. A survey showed that nearly three out of five families felt they had inadequate storage space in their homes. However, by being creative you can probably find it. Here are some ideas to get you started:

1. Make space for food items by re-arranging present storage and placing items such as clothing, bedding and other items not affected by temperature in un-insulated garages and attics. Foods like salt, sugar and whole wheat could be placed there.
2. Make better use of cupboard, pantry, or closet space.
3. Use "dead space" behind furniture placed across corners, on balconies, under stairways, beds, sofas and tables.
4. Make furniture, such as bookcases, beds, coffee and end tables, from the storage containers.
5. Partition part of a large room with a false wall, room divider, decorator screen ,or curtain and use the space for storage.
6. Use "hidden space" between studs on inside walls or between the joists under floors.
7. Crawl space under a house or mobile home can be used if you can keep it dry and safe from rodents. Coated metal or plastic containers covered with plastic and set on a plywood sheet up on concrete blocks may work.
8. Store outside in a well-ventilated shed, a large weather-resistant drum, or in an air and watertight underground fiberglass tank.
9. Rent space in a mini-warehouse or maybe you have friends or relatives that can find space they don't currently use.

Shelving, Racks and Bins

You can buy or build shelves. Most of the commercial variety are three feet wide and can be equipped with shelves twelve to eighteen inches deep. You can also make your own with normal shelves or with slanted shelves that automatically rotate the cans as they roll from the loading end to the other for removal as needed (see Figure 6-3). If you build your own, remember to leave two inches of head space and use vertical supports at least every three feet. A half to one inch strip can be placed on the outer edge for security and ¼ by ½ inch molding can be used to separate cans.

Minimizing Earthquake Damage

If you live in an earthquake-prone area there are some simple precautions you can take:

1. Use unbreakable containers as much as possible. Glass jars can be stored in their original cartons and cushioned with newspapers.
2. Store heavy, large items near the floor to minimize breakage. Plastic and even metal containers filled with heavy foods have been known to split open when falling several feet or more.
3. Either don't stack storage or stabilize the stack against tipping.
4. Use sturdy shelving and anchor at top to wall by bolting or tying down securely. Portable shelves are especially easy to tip over.
5. Enclose cupboards with sliding doors, sturdy latches, or hooks so they won't dump their contents if tipped or jarred. Open shelves can have "lips" or guard rails installed all around (use piano wire, strong fish line, or nail dowels or lath a couple of inches above each shelf). Metal shelves can be installed upside down to give a small "lip" that will help.
6. Locate the storage areas in the sturdiest part of the home.
7. Have an outside entrance so you can still get to it if your home happens to collapse over the storage area.

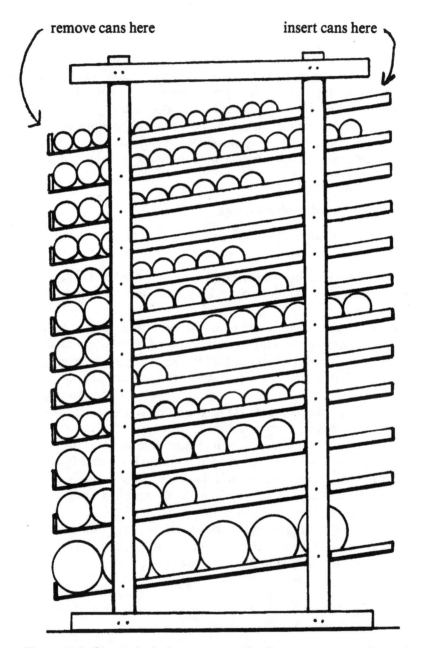

Figure 6.3. Slanted shelves automatically rotate canned goods.

TABLE 6-2. CONTAINER SIZES

Size	Proximate Contents		Normal Case	Proximate Case
#300	14-16 oz	1¾ cups	24 cans	12 x 9 x 9
#303	16-17 oz	2 cups	24 cans	12¾ x 9½ x 8¾
#2	20 oz	2½ cups	24 cans	14 x 10¼ x 9¼
#2½	27-29 oz	3½ cups	6 cans	12¼ x 8½ x 5
#3	46 fl oz	5¼ cups	12 cans	17 x 12¾ x 7¼
#5	56 fl oz	7 cups	6 cans	16 x 11 x 6¼
#10	112 fl oz	13 cups	6 cans	19 x 12¾ x 7¾

Pest Control

Cockroaches, silverfish, ants and rodents ruin billions of dollars of food each year. They contaminate far more than they eat. They also carry diseases such as bubonic plague, dysentery, infectious hepatitis, rabies, trichinosis, tuberculosis, tularemia, typhoid fever and typhus. During an extended crisis, with poor or nonexistent sanitation and a buildup of refuse, pests could be a major problem. Prepare now to minimize it.

Prevention starts by building out pests. Inspect your storage area for places where pests can get in or hide. Fill cracks in foundations, close off spaces around doors, windows, wires and pipes, and put adequate wire mesh screening over air vents and other openings. Eliminate dark, humid and warm places where they love to hide and don't bring pests in with already-infested foods. Prevent their access to food by using insect and rodent-proof containers and cleaning up any food spilled. It is extremely important to keep the area clean and to prevent trash from accumulating. Walls and floors can be washed and disinfected.

If infestations occur, destroy the contaminated food immediately, clean the shelves and then use pyrethrum dust (see fumigation section) or two tablespoons malathion in a gallon of water. Dust or paint the solution on and under shelves, floors and baseboards. Spray carefully into hard-to-reach places such as cracks, crevices ,and behind the baseboards. Don't spray on food or near open packages. After the solution dries the shelves may be covered with clean paper or foil. Applications may be repeated every few months if needed.

You may want to use stronger insecticides such as diazinon or ronnel in smaller, restricted areas—such as behind radiators—to kill ants, earwigs and silverfish. Read label instructions for details. One form of diazinon, KNOX OUT, is in time-release capsules and is less likely to be inhaled by humans or pets than a spray. Recommendations of pesticides for use around food are constantly changing and even the available pesticides change according to EPA edicts. Check with the local county extension agent before buying for use or storage. Chlordane, lindane and methoxychlor are not currently recommended around food, and diazinon is being totally phased out.

The best solution for cockroach problems is to deposit boric acid dust—no more than half teaspoon in any one spot—into the dark, narrow and inaccessible places that roaches hide in. Wear a dust mask because boric acid is poisonous to people, too. It acts as a nervous system and stomach poison, killing in one to two weeks. Some drugstores carry it. Ants can be controlled by placing small bottles of Antrol or ant stakes in ant runs and around foundations. These are very toxic and should be kept out of the reach of children and pets.

Store a supply of DECON or similar poisons containing warfarin and a dozen or so traps to control mice, rats and other rodents. Traps are often preferred to poison grains and other toxic baits because it can't be mistaken for food by children or useful animals. You may even want to store a few larger traps for possible problems with wild dog packs. A cat or two may also come in handy. Females are best because of their stronger hunting instinct.

Local Problems

If you have a storage condition or problem peculiar to your particular geographical area, contact your local county extension agent for advice. Other information sources include government agencies, colleges and universities and those engaged professionally in the food storage business.

SUMMARY

1 Use durable, airtight containers in convenient sizes that are impermeable to moisture and resistant to pests.
2. Store food in cool, dry and dark locations away from strong odors.
3. Keep the storage area clean and store disinfectants, pesticides and traps.

7

THE MODES OF FOOD

Foods can be stored in different modes, from fresh to freeze dried. This chapter examines the characteristics of each mode so that you can make intelligent choices for your food storage plan.

Keep in mind that individual foods may be superior in a particular mode while completely unsatisfactory in another. The best plan will consist of a combination of modes appropriate to your needs. Considerations affecting your choices are: (1) budget limitations, (2) desired convenience and (3) personal preferences. Combination foods (casseroles, stews, etc.) are almost always more expensive, regardless of mode, than buying the separate foods. And you really should sample all foods before including them in your storage.

The Basics

The majority of every adequate food storage plan consists of the basics: grains, flours, pasta, dried legumes, powdered milk, sugar, honey and salt. They are available conveniently packed in cans and poly buckets, or you can prepare your own by buying in bulk and repackaging. Doing your own is by far the least expensive, and you'll know exactly what you have. You may also choose to buy some commercially prepared while doing the rest yourself. Besides some of the sources listed in Chapter 32, many of the basics can be purchased in bulk locally from feed and seed stores.

Canned Goods

Although given a bum rap by some, canned foods deserve consideration for your plan. They are familiar to all, readily traded and can be consumed right from the can without heat or additional water if need be. Foods that are usually cooked thoroughly are especially suited to canning, and most people consider them much tastier than their dehydrated counterparts. Industry and military research shows that at 70^0 F (21^0 C) most canned goods keep anywhere from two and a half to more than seven years (see Chapter 9 for specifics on individual foods). A system rotating fruits within two years and other items within four would be adequate.

Nutritional Value

Undoubtedly the processing of canned goods causes them to loose some of their original nutritional value, but this is certainly not unique to them. Losses occur during the preparation of all foods, and even fresh foods suffer losses soon after picking. The blanching process is responsible for a large portion of nutrient loss, but it is an essential step for many frozen or dehydrated vegetables. Major losses occur during the final preparation and cooking in the kitchen, no matter what the mode. For example, approximately 50% of the vitamin C originally in fresh beets is destroyed when they are peeled and sliced! The Benson Institute at Brigham Young University finds that canned goods effectively retain 70-90% of their vitamins and all their protein, carbohydrates, fats and minerals. And a 1983 study by Del Monte showed that forty-year-old canned creamed corn, fruit cocktail and green peas was essentially nutritionally equal to fresh-canned.

Compared with frozen—generally credited with being the most nutritional of all preserved foods—canned fruits and vegetables both retained vitamin A equally well. One study of ten canned vegetables showed no significant loss of vitamin A after three years of storage with an average of 61% of the vitamin C remaining. In fact, after five to six years there was still 50% of the original vitamin C left.

Most fruits and some other canned goods have sugar added during processing, but sugar is an important energy food. If you don't want the extra sugar, you can buy or can your own in lighter syrups or juices.

Costs

Canned goods are quite inexpensive when compared with dehydrated (see actual comparison under dehydrated foods). Studies have shown that about 60% of commercially canned goods are even cheaper than comparable fresh. Various canned items are nearly always on sale, and you can save considerably by price shopping. One thing to avoid, though, are the case lot sales in late summer and early fall that are closing out old product to make room for the new. The lower prices are accompanied by shorter shelf lives. Further savings are possible by canning your own with in-season or home-grown produce.

Retort Foods and MREs

Retort foods, a fairly recent development in food packaging that requires no refrigeration, have been sold outside the United States since 1967. The Japanese purchase over one and a half million of them each day and they are widely used throughout Western Europe and Canada. They were used as early as 1969 by NASA for the Apollo mission to the moon. The Department of Defense calls them MREs (Meal Ready to Eat) and they are used now for all combat rations.

The food is placed in a thin, flexible "pouch" made from a three-layer laminate. The air is then evacuated and the pouch is sealed. Next, it is placed in a special pressure cooker called a retort oven where it is sterilized at temperatures of $240\text{-}250^0$ F to prevent deterioration.

Because the thin pouch requires less processing than metal cans, the food undergoes less deterioration and has the potential of being superior in quality to even frozen food. Foods remain moist, and their colors, textures and flavors compare favorably with canned and frozen. It contains no preservatives and can be eaten directly from the pouch. The pouch is lighter than metal cans and requires less time to heat. The sealed pouch is simply placed directly into boiling water for three to five minutes. Shelf life is approximately equal to or a bit longer than canned.

Now the bad news. Current prices, at $3-6 per pound for mixed entrees, are substantially more expensive than frozen and in the same range as freeze dried. The pouch is also susceptible to puncture and rodent damage. In its carton it takes up more space than canned.

It is highly unlikely that retort foods will ever entirely replace canned goods or make them obsolete for crisis storage as some have claimed. However they are a good alternative to both canned and dehydrated foods and certainly have a place wherever refrigeration is an uncertainty.

SAP Foods

Sterile Aseptically Packaged (SAP) foods are similar to retort in that they are also very rapidly sterilized at high temperatures to allow non-refrigerated storage for periods up to one year. The container, a flexible bag or rigid carton, is sterilized in hot hydrogen peroxide, blown dry with sterilized air, filled, vacuum packed and then sealed. Fruit juices keep about six months, and milk keeps about eight months. There is come controversy whether the milk tastes canned, cooked and chalky or is "indistinguishable" from regular pasteurized milk. Other milk products, margarine and peanut butter are also available.

Again, costs are high and, although expected to come down over time, are anticipated to remain 20-30% above conventional items. Once the container is opened the foods must be treated as fresh. That means refrigerate the milk!

Dried Foods

As the term is used here, dried foods refer to those whose moisture content has only been reduced to the 20-25% level. These foods include raisins, prunes, figs, dates and slices of apples, apricots, peaches and pears. They feel moist and soft to the touch and are available from supermarkets, usually packaged in a plastic or cellophane bag or in a box. Because of their relatively high moisture content, dried foods tend to mold easily and are not particularly suited for long-term storage. However, if placed in an airtight, pest-proof container and kept in a cool, dry and dark location they may keep one to two years. If they become overly hard they can be soaked overnight in warm water or stewed.

Dehydrated Foods

Dehydrated foods—also called low-moisture foods—have had the moisture level reduced to only a few percent. They are produced by two different processes:

1. Air dried. The foods are dried by heated air at temperatures anywhere from 140^0 to 400^0 F in large ovens or drums. The foods shrink and become hard and brittle. After reconstitution they look similar to cooked foods.
2. Freeze dried. The foods are flash frozen at temperatures as low as -50^0 F and then radiant heat is used to turn the ice crystals directly into water vapor which is drawn off by a vacuum. The cellular structure of the food is unchanged and results in a sponge-like, porous food that basically retains its original size and shape.

Both types result in reduced weight. Dehydrated fruits weigh about one-seventh of their original weight, while vegetables average about one-tenth. Freeze dried meats, not containing as much water to begin with, weigh about one-third of their fresh weight.

A wide variety of foods are available in dehydrated forms including most popular fruits and vegetables as well as meat, fish and poultry. They are widely used by backpackers, campers, other sportsmen, schools, restaurants, hospitals and by the armed forces. Many are commonly sold as "convenience foods" in the supermarket: instant potatoes, powdered milk, dry soup and cake mixes, cereals and instant puddings. They come in heavy-duty metal foil pouches for short-term use as well as in #2½ and #10 cans with inert atmospheres for long-term storage.

Store dehydrated foods in their original cartons in a cool, dry location. Because they contain almost no water, freezing doesn't affect them, and dented cans are okay as long as the seal remains intact.

Shelf Life

Foil pouches will keep up to two years if stored properly while the food in metal cans will last from about four to more than ten years at 70^0 F (21^0 C). Rotation of dehydrated foods within a four to five year period is best. Otherwise you'll want to at least check the quality of some of the more sensitive items—milk, butter, margarine and meats—on a regular basis.

Open Shelf Life

Upon opening, the food begins to oxidize and absorb moisture, increasing deterioration. You can minimize this by keeping open cans covered with airtight plastic lids except for brief periods when actually removing ingredients. About three dozen lids should be enough to cover all cans open at any one time. Dipping into a level can will expose the food less than pouring, and desiccants can be used to reduce moisture content. Store the open cans in a cool, dry area—not above stoves or next to dishwashers. Most importantly, rehydrated foods should be treated as fresh and used within a short period of time or refrigerated.

Covered properly, opened cans of air dried foods will keep from about three months to more than a year. High-fat foods have the shortest lives and fruits and vegetables the longest. Freeze dried foods, because of their open cell structure, tend to attract moisture much more readily and store for periods of only four to eight weeks to perhaps three months.

Air Dried versus Freeze Dried

Nutritional value. Freeze dried has slightly higher values when packed because of lower processing heats. However, air dried tends to loose nutrients more slowly because its shriveled form protects itself better than the porous structure of freeze dried. Within a year or so their value is approximately equal.

Shelf life. Air dried keeps a bit longer under the same conditions. The freeze drying leaves less moisture and is more effective at destroying microorganisms, but the resulting porous structure allows faster deterioration. This also explains why open shelf life for air dried is substantially longer. Foods using preservatives keep longer.

Appeal. Although some claim they can't tell the difference, subjective data is that freeze dried fruits and vegetables are plumper and appear more like fresh, but air dried have better flavor and texture. Except for pineapple, air dried fruits are particularly better.

Variety. Air dried offers a wider selection of fruits and vegetables, while more combinations are available freeze dried. Certain foods come in only one form. Milk and milk products, for example, are all air dried, but nearly all meats are only freeze dried.

Convenience. Freeze dried saves both time and fuel. Many are pre-cooked, and their porous nature allows many of them to be table-ready in five to fifteen minutes by simply pouring boiling water over them. Air dried often need hours of soaking in cold water or cooking in water for ten to twenty-five minutes before being ready. There are also many freeze dried casserole dishes, possibly reducing the number of cans open at any one time. This advantage is offset by their shorter open shelf lives, their being pre-seasoned to "normal" taste and the fact they cost about 20-25% more than the same individual foods not pre-mixed.

Cost. Freeze dried foods average about twice the cost of air dried, with the vegetables costing one and a half to three times and the fruits two and a half to more than three times their counterparts. This could mean an additional $500 or more per person for a year's supply compared with air dried.

Ease of Storage. Unlike freeze dried, air dried shrink to a fraction of their original size and, therefore, take up roughly one-third the space. Compressing can overcome this disadvantage for freeze dried but makes them even more expensive.

To Sum Up. Air dried costs half as much, takes one-third the space and lasts much longer after opening. Freeze dried are more convenient to prepare, require less fuel and offer the only dehydrated meat, fish and poultry similar to fresh. My personal choices would be air dried for most fruits and vegetables with freeze dried meats.

Dehydrated versus Canned

Claims are made that dehydrated foods weigh one-eighth as much as canned goods and take up only one-fifth the space. They are supposed to be more convenient with absolutely no waste. Their shelf lives are sometimes described as "more than fifteen years" or even "indefinite". They're even represented as costing half as much as canned goods because "you're not buying water at food prices". Often you are lead to believe that they taste like fresh-picked from the garden and that the original nutritional wholesomeness has been locked in. Together, these claims make dehydrated foods seem like improvements over fresh foods.

The fact is that many of these claims are greatly exaggerated, misleading, or simply false. Sales promotion pressure too easily distorts reality. Prejudiced words such as "ordinary", "mass-produced" and "penny-pinching chemical processing" are used to downgrade canned, while other words like "special", "exclusive" and "superior" are used to favorably impress. Selective positive information is played-up in simplistic charts while any negatives are ignored.

It's time to look at the facts:

Nutritional Values. All foods loose nutritional value in processing and during storage. Dehydrated foods are no exception, and research shows they loose considerable nutritional value during both stages.

All vegetables and some fruits are blanched prior to dehydrating to inactivate the enzymes and to fix colors. This blanching, along with washing, results in the leaching of water-soluble compounds such as vitamin C which can be reduced as much as 50%. The dehydration heat, along with the blanching heat, damages most of the major vitamins, the protein—particularly the lysine and methionine amino acids—and the essential fatty acids. Further losses come from the sulfites frequently added to reduce oxidation. Nearly all foods contain some fats and/or sugars, and that isn't changed by taking the water out. During storage the fats oxidize and the sugars brown, creating rancid tastes and undesirable colors. The lower moisture content actually increases the degradation of protein. With time, the food loses its ability to re-hydrate and becomes tough when reconstituted and cooked.

The tables of nutritional values put out by the dehydrated food companies won't tell you about the losses. With rare exceptions, they have little data on the losses and have simply calculated the table values using data for the fresh product as if no losses occur. However, there are some reliable research results from tests conducted by major universities and research laboratories for NASA and the military.

Research by the U.S. Army (published in the Journal of the American Dietetic Association, Vol. 39, No. 2, August 1961, pp. 105-116) showed high losses just from the dehydration process. Cabbage lost over half its vitamin C and more than 90% of its vitamin A. Corn lost about one-third of the vitamin A and upwards of two-thirds of the vitamin C. Both green beans and carrots lost more than two-thirds of their vitamin C. Freeze dried ground beef lost 90% of its thiamine, chicken lost over half its thiamine, riboflavin and niacin, and shrimp lost over half of its thiamine and over two-thirds of its niacin. And these figures ignore storage losses!

Indications of the loss during storage come from a study by NASA for the Skylab program (reported by Dr. Clayton S. Huber, one of the researchers, in Family Perspective, Vol. II, No. 3, Summer 1977, pp. 3-10, Brigham Young University Press). After sixteen months of storage, air dried pea soup lost over half its original after-processing amount of vitamin A, and potato soup lost about two-thirds of its. Air dried bacon wafers lost 25% of their thiamine in one year. In eighteen months freeze dried chicken and rice lost over one-third of its vitamin A, while scrambled eggs lost half of it within twelve months. Freeze dried strawberries, naturally high in vitamin C, lost over 60% of it after only fourteen months. They only retained 40% of the original vitamin C after dehydration, so after fourteen months of storage the freeze dried strawberries had less than one-sixth the vitamin C of fresh berries!

Other studies show that freeze dried beef stored for four years at room temperature lost 32% of the lysine, 40% of the tryptophan and 12% of the methionine and leucine amino acids. Freeze dried casseroles stored for forty-four months, although still acceptable for eating, suffered significant losses of thiamine and riboflavin as well as showing signs of rancidity and major changes in odor, texture, flavor and color.

Comparing dehydrated foods with canned foods shows that the vitamin A contents are roughly the same as is the vitamin C in corn. Canned carrots, on the other hand, only have about half as much vitamin C as the dehydrated version. Comparing meats, freeze dried ground beef has about 50% more thiamine but about the same riboflavin while the chicken is clearly superior in thiamine but inferior in riboflavin and niacin versus the canned.

Both dehydrated and canned foods suffer nutritional losses in processing and during storage. So do frozen foods. And a study of retort foods (MREs)—ham and chicken loaf, beef steak and beef stew—stored for four and a half years at room temperature showed losses after processing from one-third to more than half of the thiamine. No storage food will retain the nutritional values of its fresh original. You'll just have to choose which best suits you.

Taste and Appearance. Taste is very subjective, but many who have tried dehydrated foods do not like their taste as well as the equivalent canned products. Although some call them "delicious" and "fresh tasting", other descriptive terms used are "cardboardy", "inedible" and "artificial, chemical tasting". At the very least it shows how wide people's tastes vary! Certainly dehydrated foods do have their flavors and appearances changed during the processing and storage, and they are not "just like fresh" as some would have you believe. And, as was pointed out in the air versus freeze dried comparison, even appearances can be deceiving.

Shelf Life. Dehydrated food shelf life is often greatly exaggerated. Many dehydrated food companies base their "keeps forever without rotation" claim on the fact that dehydrated foods can be stored almost indefinitely without actual spoilage or decomposition. However, removal of the water not only drastically decreases the growth of microorganisms but also tends to concentrate the reactant compounds in the remaining water and leads to increased interactions during storage. And, as discussed in Chapter 5, the lack of actual spoilage doesn't guarantee the food will be nutritional nor edible.

Tests of freeze dried casseroles showed that after forty-five months they were definitely showing deterioration and some were nearing the end of their useful shelf life. Other tests, of differing validity, show dehydrated foods to remain viable during a four to ten year period. Generalizing is difficult but, at best, dehydrated foods may keep twice as long as the comparable canned. I recommend rotation within four to five years.

Cost Comparisons. Often dehydrated foods are touted to be inexpensive, particularly when compared with canned goods. They supposedly save you money and stretch your food budget. Don't you believe that nonsense. While dehydrated foods may well be less expensive than fresh, out-of-season produce, with extremely few exceptions they cost substantially more than regular canned goods.

As a general rule, air dried foods cost about two to three times as much and freeze dried are about four to six times the cost of canned foods. Obviously, some brands cost two to three times as much as others for the same amount of reconstituted product, retail outlets charge different prices and even canned goods don't all cost the same. It's easy to use Table 8-3, though, to make your own cost comparisons because it shows how many pounds of a particular dehydrated product it takes to provide an equivalent amount. Here is how you can calculate the cost comparisons:

EXAMPLE 1: A #10 can of dehydrated fruit cocktail costs $25 and contains 2½ pounds for a $10 per pound cost. Table 8-3 shows that you need 9.7 pounds for a serving per day for one year. Thus the cost would be $97. The local supermarket sells #303 cans of fruit cocktail for $.55 each and you need 91 of them for the equivalent amount, giving a cost of $50.05. Dividing the $97 by the $50.05 shows the dehydrated would cost 94% more than the canned, or about double.

EXAMPLE 2: Dehydrated green beans come in a one pound #10 can for $16. A serving per day for one year requires 5.3 pounds for a total cost of $84.80. Green beans at the supermarket are $.40 for a #303 can so 91 of them cost $36.40. Dividing the $84.80 by the $36.40 tells you the dehydrated cost 133% more than the canned (2⅓ times).

The above examples fairly represent the cost differences although your exact figures will vary. Always use Table 8-3 because comparison figures provided by the companies are often not accurate. Don't fall for the "but inflation will make dehydrated foods cost less" gambit, either. It just makes both cost more.

Space and Weight Savings. Although dehydrated foods may weigh only one-eighth as much as canned and, in the case of air dried, take up only one-fifth as much space, that certainly isn't the entire story.

Those great savings in weight and space are due to a drastic reduction in water content. But water is vital, second only to oxygen in importance to the human body, and dehydrated foods aren't much good without water to re-hydrate them. The fruits and vegetables need about a gallon per pound of dehydrated product, while the eggs and meats average one-third gallon. So while the dehydrated foods may be easier to store, conceal and transport, you should store lots of water for them. And water is heavy, takes up lots of space and is hard to move!

The space savings advantage also doesn't hold up in reality. Manufacturers tend to pack the cans lightly, using up additional space. This cuts the savings to where they take up about one-third the space of canned, but there is more to consider! Only a portion of any good storage plan is made up of fruits, vegetables and meats, the main dehydrated foods. The rest consists of grains, sugars, legumes, etc. that are the same regardless of the plan. When this is all considered, dehydrated food will only save one-fourth to one-fifth the total space. Actually, freeze dried uses more.

The same holds true for weight. Because dehydrated foods are only a portion of the total plan, they save only 40% or less of the total weight rather than the 90% claimed. No one is going to put a year's supply on their back and walk off with it! And it won't weigh any less than the basic plan outlined in Chapter 8.

Convenience. Dehydrated foods are suggested as more convenient and having "no waste, no pits and no peelings". What are they being compared with? If you've found pits or peelings in your canned, frozen or retort foods you had better switch brands fast! Other modes of food needn't be re-hydrated, and retort foods only need to be placed in boiling water for a few minutes. And what could be quicker or easier than simply opening and eating from a can as you can do with many canned foods?

To Sum Up. All modes of food have their advantages and disadvantages. You'll want at least some dehydrated foods in your plan but they are not the panacea some believe them to be. The dehydrated foods in my ideal plan would include powdered milk, buttermilk, potatoes, cheese, eggs, some fruits and vegetables, and a decent supply of freeze dried meats.

Buying Dehydrated Foods

Most dehydrated food is sold to people who don't take the time to thoroughly investigate what they are buying and, therefore, know very little about what they actually buy. Many salesmen also know nothing more about their product than the advertising literature tells them. If you don't want to be surprised, you must spend some time and effort making sure what you get is what you want.

There are many brands of dehydrated food available with more being added as others go out of business. This is because it's fairly easy to start offering dehydrated foods under your own brand name. Although nearly every company claims to sell only foods that are "clearly superior", the fact is nearly all of them merely purchase the already-dehydrated food in bulk from processors such as Beatrice Foods, General Foods and General Mills. Most use the same sources, and some even re-pack it by hand before placing their label on it and shipping to the customer or distributor.

Despite coming from the same basic suppliers, there is a wide variance in the quality of the product and packaging due to particular companies' buying standards and quality control. Often dehydrated foods are made from substandard pieces or over-ripe produce that can't be used for fresh, frozen or canned goods. Some companies are not above buying this inferior product and re-selling for abnormal profits. Some companies use better quality cans. There are also different methods of using inert gases and oxygen absorbers with widely varying results. Don't believe that an unique name for a process makes it anything special!

Follow these guidelines in buying:

1. Never buy in quantity without sampling. You should not only try each individual food (there are many differences among foods of the same brand) but also sample the competition. Compare the taste, texture and appearance of the re-hydrated as well as the dry. Test older product if at all possible to better approximate what the food will taste like after it is stored a while. Local dealers usually offer free samples, while mail order companies sell sample packs for a nominal fee. You can also buy the smaller packages used by backpackers and other outdoors men. Some brands also conduct tasting parties, but be aware that as a rule they like to offer samples of only the better-tasting items.

2. Buy by the weight of the product and not by the number of cans. It may seem obvious but some brands only put half as much in their cans as others do. Compare prices per pound of product. And realize that price is only one factor in a bargain.

3. Can labels should include a description of the food item and its ingredients, the method of dehydrating, product dry weight, complete directions for reconstituting, approximate fresh equivalent, amount of yield when reconstituted, date packed, nutritional information with calories and proper storage information. It is also helpful if some recipes are included. Check the can lip because some are too deep and difficult to open. Most companies also provide a plastic lid with each can to re-close after opening.

4. After buying, open all cartons, check to make sure you got what you expected and then reseal them. A few dealers prominently display the logotypes of well-known high-quality brands, but take out the more expensive items or substitute with cheaper brands. Most people never open the cartons to find out.

You can buy from local dealers or national mail order companies (see Chapter 32). Sales and specials are frequent, volume buying will often bring discounts and commercial and government contract overruns are sometimes available. Be aware that local supermarkets may also carry some dehydrated items, usually at much lower prices than a food storage dealer. These may include soups, onion and parsley flakes, powdered eggs, instant puddings, macaroni and cheese meals, instant potatoes, lemon crystals and freeze dried coffee. Sizes may even be more manageable for your family's needs. Most are packed in flimsy packaging and will need re-packing for long-term storage, but others will already be in suitable containers.

Dehydrating Your Own

When produce is harvested the food processors first take care of the needs for fresh produce and their large canning customers. What is left, often old and overripe, is then dehydrated at temperatures up to 400^0 F. The result is frequently a product inferior in quality and nutrition to what may be produced at home using a good dehydrator where you select quality produce and dry it at much lower heats—usually in the 110-145^0 F range. By purchasing fruits and vegetables in season or in bulk during specials or by growing your own, you can even save money. Proper dehydrating, packaging and storing will provide shelf lives of anywhere from six months to more than two years.

Frozen Foods

Although generally considered—along with retort foods—superior in nutritional value and appeal to canned or dehydrated foods, frozen foods still suffer considerable losses during processing and storage. After six to twelve months storage frozen fruits, for example, contain only 70% of the original vitamin C while vegetables retain only 50%. Frozen food is also costly to store, often tripling the initial price after one year. Shelf life is anywhere from about three months to somewhat beyond one year. But their biggest negative is their vulnerability.

Frozen food is totally dependent on refrigeration. Freezers can suffer mechanical breakdown at any time and need a continuing supply of electricity or gas. This makes them vulnerable in times of crisis.

One way around part of the vulnerability is to be independent of the utility company so that outages and shortages won't affect you as much. Refrigerators and freezers are available that run on propane or kerosene, which you can store (see Chapter 26). They could be used as a backup to your regular freezer.

What to Do When the Freezer Goes Off

If your freezer does go off, for whatever reason, there are some things you can do to salvage the food, but you'll have to act fast.

The first thing to realize is that even a non-working freezer will keep food frozen for some time. Just how long depends on how filled it is, the type of food, the size—bigger is better—and how cold the room is where the freezer is kept. A fully-stocked freezer can keep temperatures at satisfactory levels for two to three days or so providing it is kept closed. A partially-filled freezer may keep food only half as long. You can conserve cold by insulating the freezer with blankets and newspapers. Transfer foods that you will soon use to a good camping cooler to avoid opening the door any more than absolutely necessary.

Dry ice will extend the time. A twenty-five to fifty pound block will keep the temperature of a half-full freezer below freezing for two to three days. Put the food close together and then, using tongs or gloves, place the dry ice on a layer of heavy cardboard over the center of the food. A large block of ice will last longer than several small ones. Because dry ice evaporates and produces tremendous amounts of carbon dioxide, the area should be ventilated and the freezer door left slightly ajar to prevent a dangerous buildup of pressure.

If you have advance warning or are subject to frequent power failures, set the freezer to its lowest temperature setting. The colder it is at the start, the longer the food will keep. You may be interested in a power failure alarm to alert you whenever the power goes off.

Should your freezer be inoperable beyond these measures, you can do one of three things: (1) take the frozen food to a commercial locker—assuming the outage hasn't affected them, (2) immediately can, dry, smoke, or otherwise preserve the food, or (3) invite the neighborhood over for a feast!

When to Re-freeze

As a general rule, if a food is safe to eat it is safe to re-freeze. In practice, with most foods that means they have not thawed completely and are still under 40^0 F (5^0 C). How can you tell? Some ice crystals will still be present. Their existence means the food is between 32^0 and 40^0 F and can be re-frozen. Exceptions to this are variety meats, fish and other seafood that tends to spoil very quickly. Re-frozen foods will likely have a lower quality and won't keep as long. They should be used as soon as possible.

If foods have completely thawed, don't re-freeze. Use at once if still good or discard. Uncooked vegetables, meats and poultry can be cooked and then re-frozen while fruits can be canned or made into preserves. Fruit juice concentrates ferment when spoiled and can cause the cans to explode. Throw out any "off-flavor" fruits.

Fresh Foods

The only fresh foods you can consider for storage are those you can keep in root cellars and similar facilities (see Chapter 16). However, even these methods only provide storage lives from less than one month to a bit over six from the time of harvest into the spring. And they work best only in northern climates with generally cool or cold winters—an average of freezing or less is best. Apples, beets, carrots, onions, parsnips, pears, sweet and white potatoes, pumpkins and winter squash store fairly well with cabbage, rutabagas and turnips having shorter storage lives.

SUMMARY

1. Consider any budget limitations, desired convenience and personal preferences.
2. Know what you are getting. Sample all foods before buying in quantity and compare the competition for prices and quality.
3. The best plan will normally consist of a carefully planned, thoughtfully considered combination of modes appropriate to your needs.

8

YOUR FOOD STORAGE PLAN

Whether you are an old hand at food storage or just beginning, this chapter shows you how to design the best possible plan. By following a few simple steps you can determine exactly how much of what to store for your particular needs. If you already have some food storage you can compare this "ideal" plan with what you have stored. This will point out possible shortcomings, areas needing improvement or, perhaps, that your current plan is adequate. You can also use it to evaluate any commercial unit.

Planning Methods

A plan is vital to avoid indiscriminate stockpiling. Therefore, nearly every book on preparedness contains at least a method or two for your suggested use. The methods differ, however, and even a plan that looks good at first glance may turn out to be much less so in actual use. It is helpful to examine the various types of methods to see how well they fit your needs.

The List Method

Rare indeed is the preparedness book without a list of items you should store. Many even give multiple choices. The lists vary from extremely simple to quite complex but all share the same deficiencies.

First, the suggested amounts of the very same items often differ drastically. One list will recommend one hundred pounds of grains versus another's five hundred, twenty pounds of sugar or honey versus 180 or no peanut butter versus fifty pounds of it! Many ignore fats entirely. One list suggests milk "for those with children under three" while another recommends 150 pounds per person. Beans, if mentioned at all, range from fourteen to 150 pounds. A 150 pounds would mean more than two cups of cooked beans per person for every day of the year, winter and summer! Yet a shortage in any critical area can have very serious results. The obvious question is which list is best for you. Or do you just grab a list, any list, and hope it works?

A second concern is that most lists are made for the "average" adult woman and you are usually told to adapt it for children and men. But they almost never tell you how! The majority don't even tell you what they provide in total calories, protein and other nutrients to give you a place to start—and some that do are wrong.

In addition, lists invariably lack variety and often show ignorance of basic nutrition.

The result of simply following a list is that the storage often falls short. A family I know used such a list and felt they had a "good" storage plan. The time came, however, when they were forced to live from it for six months and the father found he was allergic to all that wheat they had stored. Many items ran out quickly, some had been overlooked entirely and others seemed like they'd never run out! Computer-analyzed surveys conducted by Utah State University of more than 5,000 storage plans showed the vast majority were considerably undersized and largely unbalanced. Most contained more than enough protein but were short on total calories, sugars, starches and milk. They usually were seriously low in fats and oils. Many contained foods the families didn't normally eat or even like. Sometimes only minor additions or changes could have greatly improved the plans.

At best, any list of specific items never quite fits your family's particular situation. At worst, the list will prove dangerously lacking but the discovery may be made too late to correct even if you know how. Frankly, a list is only as good as the knowledge and reliability of the person who developed it. With so little room for error, do you really want to trust any list without knowing for yourself?

What I Did Method

Found in a number of sources, this method is simply a specialized list of what one particular individual stored. The peculiar list given is probably far from your needs. They are more historical curiosities than anything else.

What You Normally Eat Method

This method mimics current eating habits and comes in two variations. The first is known as "copy-canning" and is simply buying two of everything you regularly use, putting one into storage while eating the other. The second is more accurate because a detailed record is kept of all food consumed during a particular time period, usually two weeks to a month. Then the total amount of food used during the period is multiplied out to find the amount necessary for an entire year. Both a summer and a winter period are usually recommended to account for seasonal variations. As is readily apparent, this requires a great deal of time and effort.

Although better than lists, this method has some major shortcomings.

First of all, you are not planning for normal times. This method is based on current nutritional needs and habits which not only change over time but will likely be very different during times of crisis due to extra work and stress. It won't always match those needs and it would take a large amount of additional effort to determine the nutritional content so it could be adapted.

Also, certain items eaten routinely now don't lend themselves to long-term storage. How do you go about making substitutions?

Perhaps the biggest problem for many is that storing the foods normally eaten can be very expensive and may be much more than their budget allows. Sure the steak you ate for dinner can be stored as freeze dried, but it may cost $25 a pound! Trying to duplicate the meat an average family of four eats in a year with freeze dried would cost in excess of $7,000 just for the meat!

Finally, are you sure a two-week "slice" from your diet will be all that well balanced? And have you included the food you eat away from home—over 30% of all meals? Any short-run imbalances now can easily be corrected, but that may not be true of your storage.

Basically, the end result gives a fair idea of your normal preferences and you will want to have similar information for the plans presented later. The method, however, is not ideal.

Rotating Menu Method

Here you pre-plan a number of meals and then use them on a rotating schedule to feed your family now. Once you know how often each will be used you calculate the total of all individual ingredients needed to last the appropriate period. Although it can be built around what the family likes and solves the "what shall I fix for dinner" syndrome, it shares the shortcomings of the "What You Normally Eat" method: 1) it won't match crisis needs, 2) you must substitute items, 3) it is expensive and 4) it may not be truly representative and balanced. It also takes a lot of time and effort to make work and results in an excessively rigid plan requiring constant updating as even minor changes occur. Again, somewhat useful in highlighting preferences, but again is not ideal.

Commercial Units

Some believe buying a pre-planned pre-packaged unit is the way to go. It seems an easy way of avoiding the time and thought required to put your own together. Nothing could be easier than just making out a check and enclosing it with the order. In reality, however, all you are doing is purchasing someone else's list, usually made up to provide as many calories and as much protein as cheaply as possible. In spite of lavish claims of furnishing well-balanced diets, many are poorly planned and have serious nutritional problems. Even the best are often not all they are cracked up to be. Designers and sellers with integrity admit units are not for the serious. Nearly all suffer from at least one of these weaknesses:

1. Low in calories. The average adult may not be alive in six months on the fewer than 1,000 calories per day offered in some "year's supplies"! At least 2,600 calories is recommended—and that compares with the average 3,576 consumed in the United States.
2. Low in amount or quality of protein. There should be a minimum of sixty grams protein per day with at least six grams from meat and eggs. Often gelatin and TVP are used instead, but they are inferior as well as cheaper sources.
3. Unbalanced in other areas. They may be low or entirely lacking in some nutrients while providing too much of others. Check carefully (using Table 9-1 if necessary):

Fats and oils:	40 to 100 grams per day
Calcium sources:	40 to 80 lbs dry milk or equivalent
Fruits & Vegetables:	two servings of each daily
Sugar sources:	50 to 80 lbs
Grains:	100+ lbs, four to eight times the amount of beans

4. Lack of variety. Fifty different foods or combinations may seem like a lot but comparing to the number stored in the average pantry quickly shows it could get monotonous fast. Seasonings and leavenings, ignored altogether by many plans, are necessities to enhance variety.
5. Not personalized. You shouldn't expect it to be because no company can know and plan around your individual needs and circumstances. All units are based on averages and will fit your personal preferences about as well as having the local supermarket clerk select your weekly groceries.

6. Very expensive. You can put together a better plan for one third the cost. They also don't save you money over "store-bought" foods. The claim of low-cost meals is only true for awfully small meals!

If you already have a commercial unit or still want one, you should at least compare it to the above guidelines. Never buy any unit without knowing what is in it. That means checking the quality by sampling each different food and knowing the total calories, protein and fat. Standards vary and companies do not prepare all items equally well.

The Perfect Plan

The perfect plan is one that fits your specific needs and circumstances perfectly. Because no two individuals or families are identical and needs and circumstances vary considerably, there can be no hard and fast rules, no set pattern for everyone to follow, and no easy "fill-in-the-blanks" method. But you know your situation better than anyone else, and the best plan for your needs is the one you come up with after careful, thoughtful planning. Your plan will be as unique as your family and only you can determine its size and makeup. This chapter shows you how, but you must do it.

Criteria for Adequate Plan

An extended crisis is not the time to discover that your food plan is unbalanced, insufficient or unacceptable to your family. To avoid that requires a "living" plan that is used and altered as needed. However, there are basic guidelines relevant to any plan:

1. Nutritionally adequate. Taking into account the individual ages, weights, sexes and dietary needs, it must provide sufficient calories, protein, fats, carbohydrates, vitamins and minerals in balance and moderation. This is best done by properly selecting from the various food groups.
2. Enough variety to avoid eating fatigue. This means different flavors, textures and colors to add interest to meals. A "one-theme" plan creates additional stress and can lead to loss of appetite and eventual malnutrition. Self-designed plans are commonly limited in variety, but following the steps outlined here easily avoids that. Some "treat" foods for special occasions can also help.

3. Allows individual and family preferences. It should resemble established eating habits as closely as practical. Accustomed tastes, likes, dislikes and desires should all be considered, especially for young children and the elderly. Any particularly favorite food should be included if possible, and the convenience or preparation and skills required should be taken into account.

4. Stores well. The methods of storage must match the climate. For example, the high heat and humidity of the tropics make food storage more difficult and may require greater dependence on a year-around "living" food supply—animals, garden or foraging.

5. Space and weight. The plan should fit available space and meet requirements for mobility and anticipated emergency portability.

6. Available. The items chosen should normally be readily available for easy replenishment.

7. Affordable. The plan should be of reasonable cost and within any budget limitations. Many luxury items may be omitted while still providing an adequate diet. For cost planning, there are three possible levels:

   Basic level. Exemplified by the 7-PLUS plan detailed later in this chapter, this is the minimal plan and can be done for about $300 per person by preparing your own bulk foods. Buying it already prepared in plastic buckets will about double it while #10 cans can triple the cost.

   Balanced level. This plan includes fruits, vegetables, eggs and canned meats and costs about $600 or so. Buying it pre-packaged in buckets will add 25% while #10 cans with dehydrated fruits and vegetables in place of canned will double the cost. This compares with the average $1,000-1,400 spent per person per year for food in the United States.

   Comfortable level. This means replacing some canned meat with freeze dried and adds $200-1,000⁺—depending on the number of servings—to the balanced plan. Using freeze dried fruits and vegetables would add another $500-800.

Designing Your Own Plan

You should have a good idea by now as to the plan level and modes of food your budget will allow. Unless you have the necessary means to immediately buy all other Priority I and II items along with a more advanced food plan, you should start with the basic plan. It can always be upgraded over time to an advanced plan as more money is available.

But regardless of the plan, keep these general points in mind:

1. You will probably want to include extra for additional mouths (new babies, unforeseen guest, sharing with friends and relatives), a longer than expected crisis and for barter.
2. Plan ahead. Needs change as babies mature and require different foods, and children grow up and eat more. I suggest planning two years ahead.
3. Review periodically. Re-evaluate your needs at least yearly and update your plan. Harvest time might be best because of abundant supplies.

At this point you are ready to start designing your own plan. You need some paper, pen or pencil, and a calculator will be very helpful. If your plans include any infants or young children, pregnant or nursing women or those with allergies or chronic health problems, turn now to the Special Dietary Needs section at the end of this chapter and read the appropriate parts. Write down any pertinent information and, as you return to this point and start through a plan, begin to make up your own list of included foods and amounts needed. Choose wisely.

NOTE: Don't worry about extreme accuracy in your calculations. Be careful and double-check all work but it's okay to round off. For metric conversion, 2.2 pounds equals one kilogram.

The 7-PLUS Basic Plan

Prior to detailing the 7-PLUS plan, it might be useful to look at a similar plan used and recommended by many. Often referred to as the Mormon Basic Four plan due to its origin, it consists of three hundred pounds of wheat, one hundred pounds of powdered milk, one hundred pounds of sugar or honey and five pounds of salt.

The plan provides adequate protein (ninety-four grams per day) and is absolutely the cheapest way of storing a year's supply. With the exception of milk it has a nearly unlimited shelf life, can be stored in less than twelve cubic feet using square cans and is the simplest, most trouble-free plan possible. Unfortunately, it also has some major drawbacks. Most importantly, it is essentially lacking in fat as well as the vitamins A, C and D. It offers an extremely limited variety of foods, requiring considerable skill and energy to prepare into palatable meals, for a very austere subsistence-level diet drastically different than most are accustomed to. Finally, it only contains 2,160 calories.

The 7-PLUS

Advantages of the 7-PLUS plan are its low cost, minimal need for rotation and its compactness and low weight. Compared to the Mormon Basic Four, it costs very little more and takes up a couple of extra cubic feet, but it contains 20% more calories. It also provides better nutritional balance and an improved, although still low, variety of foods. If it still doesn't look much like your usual fare, you'll definitely want some specialized cookbooks (see list in Chapter 31). The plan consists of:

1) Salt (½ table, ½ pickling & canning)	8 lbs
2) Milk, nonfat dry	60 lbs
3) Oil (2 gal liquid, 6 lbs shortening)	21 lbs
4) Sugar	65 lbs
5) Grains (wheat, rice, corn, etc.)	375 lbs
6) Legumes (beans, peas, lentils)	60 lbs
7) Multi-vitamins (with minerals)	365
+) Leavening agents (¾ lb yeast,1 lb baking powder) and seasonings (herbs, spices, flavorings, bouillon, etc.)	

Depending on the exact selection of grains and legumes, the amounts given provide about 2,600 calories, one hundred grams of protein and thirty-five grams of fat per day for one year. You can personalize it if desired by substituting any of the wide variety of foods discussed under the advanced plan in the proper ratios. This will, of course, increase the cost.

The plan is sufficient for the average person in a population (referred to as a population equivalent) and you can adapt it to your family using Table 8-1.

The final figure you get by using Table 8-1 is the number of times you need to multiply by the amounts listed for the 7-PLUS plan to meet your family's needs. Obviously it is a rough estimate; a much more exact method is used with the advanced plan, but you could choose to use it here, also. You probably should add 5% for waste.

To help you follow this and later calculations, an example family will be used to illustrate each. You will see exactly what they would do in each step to design their plan. I also have attempted to make the example selections representative of practical, economical choices. While being as close to average usage as possible, they are not suggested amounts appropriate for you. Only you can decide that.

TABLE 8-1. DETERMINING POPULATION EQUIVALENTS

	Ages	Percent of 2600 cal Required	Number in Category	Percent
Infants	0-1	35	X ___	= ___
Children	1-3	52	X ___	= ___
	4-8	81	X ___	= ___
Males	9-13	104	X ___	= ___
	14-18	125	X ___	= ___
	19-30	133	X ___	= ___
	31-50	123	X ___	= ___
	51+	115	X ___	= ___
Females	9-13	98	X ___	= ___
	14-18	94	X ___	= ___
	19-30	88	X ___	= ___
	31-50	85	X ___	= ___
	51+	83	X ___	= ___
	Pregnant	+12	X ___	= ___
	Nursing	+25	X ___	= ___
			Total	= ___

Total divided by 100 equals population equivalents.
           (move decimal 2 places to left)____ ÷ 100   = ___

EXAMPLE FAMILY: The family consists of four people, a middle age couple and two teenagers, a boy seventeen and a girl fourteen. Using the table and checking two years ahead:

			Current Year		Two Years Ahead	
Males	14-18	125	X _1_	= _125_	___	= ___
	19-30	133	X ___	= ___	1	= _133_
	31-50	123	X _1_	= _123_	1	= _123_
Females	14-18	94	X _1_	= _94_	1	= _94_
	19-30	88	X ___	= ___	___	= ___
	31-50	85	X _1_	= _85_	1	= _85_
			Total	= _427_	Total	= _435_

In this particular example it won't change much over two years. That will not always be the case. The example family thus chooses the higher figure, adds 5% for waste (+.22) and gets a 4.57 total. They then multiply the 4.57 by the amounts listed and get:

TABLE 8.2. RECOMMENDED DAILY DIETARY ALLOWANCES & REFERENCE INTAKES (RDIs)

Based on tables published by Food and Nutrition Board, National Academy of Sciences. Revised 1998.
Modified to reflect moderate activity level, stress and protein score of 70. Copyrighted © 2002 by Jack A. Spigarelli

	Age	Weight		Height		Energy Calories	Protein	Fat-Soluble Vitamins			Water-Soluble Vitamins							Minerals					
	years	kg	lb	cm	in	KCAL	Grams	Vitamin A R.E. µg	Vitamin D µg	Vitamin E mg	Vitamin C mg	Thiamin B1 mg	Riboflavin B2 mg	Niacin mg	Vitamin B6 mg	Folate µg	Vitamin B12 µg	Calcium mg	Phosphorus mg	Magnesium mg	Iron mg	Zinc mg	Iodine µg
INFANTS																							
	0-6 mo	6	13	60	24	lb x 54	lb x 1.1	420	5	3	35	0.2	0.3	2	0.1	65	0.4	210	100	30	10	3	40
	6-12 mo	9	20	71	28	lb x 49	lb x 1.0	400	5	4	35	0.3	0.4	4	0.3	80	0.5	270	275	75	15	5	50
CHILDREN																							
	1-3	13	29	90	35	1350	32	400	5	5	45	0.5	0.5	6	0.5	150	0.9	500	460	80	15	10	70
	4-8	24	53	122	48	2100	44	500	5	6	45	0.6	0.6	8	0.6	200	1.2	800	500	130	10	10	90
MALES																							
	9-13	38	84	147	58	2700	56	1000	5	8	50	0.9	0.9	12	1.0	300	1.8	1300	1250	240	18	15	150
	14-18	62	136	172	68	3250	74	1000	5	10	60	1.2	1.3	16	1.3	400	2.4	1300	1250	410	18	15	150
	19-30	70	154	177	70	3450	77	1000	5	10	60	1.2	1.3	16	1.3	400	2.4	1000	700	400	10	15	150
	31-50	70	154	178	70	3200	77	1000	5	10	60	1.2	1.3	16	1.3	400	2.4	1000	700	420	10	15	150
	51+	70	154	178	70	3000	77	1000	10	10	60	1.2	1.3	16	1.7	400	2.4	1200	700	420	10	15	150
FEMALES																							
	9-13	39	86	147	58	2550	57	800	5	8	50	0.9	0.9	12	1.0	300	1.8	1300	1250	240	18	15	150
	14-18	53	116	163	64	2450	63	800	5	8	60	1.0	1.0	14	1.2	400	2.4	1300	1250	360	18	15	150
	19-30	55	120	163	64	2300	60	800	5	8	60	1.1	1.1	14	1.3	400	2.4	1000	700	310	18	15	150
	31-50	55	120	163	64	2200	60	800	5	8	60	1.1	1.1	14	1.3	400	2.4	1000	700	320	18	15	150
	51+	55	120	163	64	2150	60	800	10	8	60	1.1	1.1	14	1.5	400	2.4	1200	700	320	10	15	150
Pregnant (last half)						+350	+41	+200	+0	+2	+20	+0.3	+0.3	+4	+0.4	+200	+0.2	+200	+100	+40	+60	+5	+25
Nursing						+650	+27	+400	+0	+3	+40	+0.4	+0.5	+3	+0.5	+100	+0.4	+200	+200	+30	+30	+10	+50

36 lbs salt (18 iodized table, 18 pickling and canning)
275 lbs milk, nonfat dry
96 lbs oil (9 gal liquid, 27 lbs shortening)
300 lbs sugar
1715 lbs grain (e.g. 1250 wheat, 275 rice, 50 corn, 100 oats,
       20 barley, 10 buckwheat, 10 rye)
275 lbs legumes (e.g. 70 pinto, 50 Navy, 30 red, 25 lima,
       30 Great Northern, 30 soy, 30 pea, 10 lentils)
1460 multi-vitamins (with minerals)
4 lbs yeast, 5 lbs baking powder, seasonings, etc.

The CUSTOM Advanced Plan

The great advantage of the CUSTOM plan is its flexibility. It literally will accommodate any storable food and allow as much variety as you may wish while maintaining nutritional balance—as long as the ten steps are carefully followed. Compared to the 7-PLUS plan, it will cost at least double, require more rotation, probably weigh more and take up more space. It will match the normal diet much more closely, however, and be satisfactory to all. The CUSTOM is more involved and takes some time and effort but it is fully illustrated with examples and not overly complicated.

STEP 1- Determining Energy Needs

Table 8-2 gives nutritional recommendations for various ages and sexes. Figures are based on listed weights and should be modified to reflect actual weights. For example, an adult male weighing 180 pounds would require 3,750 calories ($180 \div 154 = 1.17$ x $3,200 = 3,750$ rounded to the nearest fifty).

Use the table to estimate your energy needs. Obviously, it is based on average metabolism and yours may differ—many do. You can "fine-tune" for your needs by checking your current intake of calories and comparing with the table, realizing that it includes an average increase of 15% for additional crisis needs. If you anticipate even greater exertion you will want to increase the calories further (a large man doing hard labor or hunting on a cold day with snow on the ground can require in excess of 6,000 calories!) Plan for pregnant and nursing women and allow an additional 5% for waste (spillage, spoilage and food remaining on preparation and eating utensils).

EXAMPLE FAMILY: Assuming weights of 175 lbs, 136 lbs, 165 lbs and 95 lbs respectively, the calculations would be:

$$175 \div 154 = 1.14 \text{ x } 3,200 = \ 3,650$$
$$136 \div 120 = 1.13 \text{ x } 2,200 = \ 2,500$$
$$165 \div 154 = 1.07 \text{ x } 3,450 = \ 3,700$$
$$95 \div 116 = \ \ .82 \text{ x } 2,450 = \underline{\ 2,000}$$

$$\text{Subtotal} \qquad 11,850$$

$$\text{Add 5\% for waste} \qquad \underline{+ \ 600}$$

$$\text{Total calories per day} = \quad 12,450$$

STEP 2-Salt

Although current usage is probably excessive, the recommended amount is still eight grams per day. That amounts to 6½ pounds per year and is 25-50% less than normal average usage. Some occurs naturally in food, leaving about four pounds to store as salt. Because needs increase during illness and high environmental temperatures (such as in fallout shelters), it would be best to store five pounds of table salt per person. Another five pounds of pickling salt per person is recommended for canning, salting meat and fish, and other uses. Salt is cheap—store enough.

EXAMPLE FAMILY: They would store at least twenty pounds of iodized table salt and twenty pounds of pickling and canning salt.

NOTE: As you consider the various food items for inclusion in your plan, you will want to refer to the listings in Chapter 9 for detailed information on the individual foods. It would also be helpful to know your family's preferences for each, particularly in relation to similar foods. Whoever buys and cooks for the family most likely knows this already but, if you don't, simply keep track for a few weeks. For items used a bit at a time, you can mark the date you open it on the label and note when it's empty. Don't forget seasonal preferences.

STEP 3- Milk and Milk Products

Dairy products provide over 60% of the calcium in the average American diet. Milk contributes by far the greatest portion as well as supplying large quantities of high quality protein and some riboflavin. Fortified milk is also the major source of vitamin D. Therefore, you must either store substantial amounts of fortified milk or other sources and supplements for calcium and vitamin D.

Assuming the storage of milk and milk products, you must first determine your calcium requirement. Referring to table 8-2 shows calcium requirements from 500 to 1,300 mg (milligrams) per day. The survival diet normally is fairly high in wheat and other grains containing phytic acid, which binds and makes somewhat unavailable the calcium in the grains. Therefore, I recommend a minimum of 85% of total calcium needs comes from milk and milk products. Using nonfat powdered milk as the base, this means 5¼ pounds per year are needed for each 100 mg. Look at the table and calculate this number for your family. It is the minimum amount of milk and equivalent milk products you need to supply your calcium requirement. Some sources recommend an absolute minimum of 16 pounds per person, but that is very low and would not provide adequate calcium.

Now you need to know how much will be milk. This figure is based on your normal drinking pattern and will usually be a large proportion of the total milk and milk products. For some it may actually exceed that necessary to provide calcium and, in that case, the other milk products are just for enjoyment. Calculate the approximate number of glasses each person drinks per day and multiply the total by 18.25 to find the pounds of powdered milk per year. You'll probably want to add another 10% for use in cooking. If the total is less than the amount you found above to supply your calcium requirement, you will need additional milk products to at least equal the difference.

EXAMPLE FAMILY: The couple (she is neither pregnant nor nursing) needs 1,000 mg each while the teenagers require 1,300. The amount needed for calcium requirements is the equivalent of 240 lbs of powdered milk. Using two glasses per day for each adult and three for the teenagers totals ten glasses. Multiplying by 18.25 gives 182.5 and adding 10% for cooking totals two hundred pounds (rounded). They decide to store two hundred twenty-five pounds of powdered milk and enough other milk products to equal the calcium in twenty more pounds of powdered milk.

Buttermilk. Useful in cooking and baking, you may want one or two pounds per person. It can be substituted pound for pound for the powdered milk added for that purpose.

Evaporated milk. It takes six thirteen-fluid ounce cans to equal the calcium in one pound of powdered milk. If desired, six to twelve cans or more are suggested per person.

Cheese. The average American uses about twenty-two pounds of cheese while some Europeans use a lot more. You can store it in its various forms or even make it from powdered milk for less than the regular store price. The calcium in cheese will cost double or more that from milk, but the added enjoyment will most likely be worth it. Amounts you might consider for the various types are: one pound or so of Parmesan (one pound equals one pound of milk), one to two pounds of processed cheese spread (2⅓ pounds equal one pound of milk) and from one to ten pounds—depending on your budget and love for cheese—of dehydrated (two pounds of cheddar or one and a half pounds of Swiss equals one pound of milk). Freeze dried cottage cheese is reserved as a treat for the affluent!

EXAMPLE FAMILY: They choose six pounds of powdered buttermilk, twenty-four cans of evaporated milk, five pounds Parmesan and nine pounds dehydrated cheese (6 cheddar, 3 Swiss). This totals the equivalent of twenty pounds of powdered milk and, added to the two hundred twenty-five pounds of powdered milk, gives the calcium equivalent of 245 lbs of powdered milk (remember, they need 240 lbs minimum).

STEP 4- Fats and Oils

The American diet is high in fat, averaging 40% of all calories consumed. Recommendations are that it be reduced (pun not intended) to about 30% for better health. At the opposite extreme are survival diets containing none or minimal fats. That too is unhealthy. A fat content below 10% is actually dangerous. I recommend 10-12½% of total calories come from the fats and oils group (additional fats come from other foods as well). Decide on your percentage and find the calories that should be from the fats and oils group. Dividing this number by eleven gives you the amount of fats and oils in pounds for a year.

Vegetable oils. Liquid oils and shortening should comprise about 8% of total calories with probably at least some in shortening due to its long shelf life. Some people may choose to store less shortening because of the hydrogenated oils, but they will have to rotate other oils more frequently. Calculate for your plan. Since both are 100% fat, they will be used as the base for the remaining items in the group. It takes 1.4 pounds of powdered shortening to equal one pound of fat.

Butter and margarine. Normally making up 25% of the added diet fat, you may want to consider less if using dehydrated because of the substantial expense. It takes one and a quarter pounds of regular butter or margarine to equal one pound of fat and approximately the same for dehydrated. You can also consider the butter-flavored shortening to give butter flavoring to baked and fried foods.

Mayonnaise. Mayonnaise and similar dressings have a high fat content and are, therefore, included with this group. You may want two to four quarts per person (1 quart mayonnaise equals 1.6 pounds of fat while one quart Miracle Whip equals one pound of fat).

Bacon. Nice to flavor eggs and other dishes, you might consider one to three pounds per person. It takes 1.4 pounds to equal one pound of fat.

Peanut butter. Although not normally thought of as fats, nuts and nut butters are unusually high in it. A suggested amount is ten pounds of regular or six pounds of dehydrated—more if you have children who crave it, or less if you can't stand it. It takes two pounds of regular or three pounds of dehydrated to equal one pound of fat.

Nuts and seeds. You will want to consider storing cans of peanuts, mixed nuts, almonds or cashews and unshelled nuts such as almonds, and walnuts. It takes one and a half pounds of shelled nuts (two pounds of peanuts, cashews and seeds) or three pounds of unshelled nuts (eight pounds of black walnuts) to equal one pound of fat.

EXAMPLE FAMILY: Assuming approximately 10% of their total calories from the fats and oils group gives 113 total pounds of fat (12,450 x 10% ÷ 11 = 113) with 90 pounds of liquid oil and shortening (12,450 x 8% ÷ 11 = 90). They divide the latter up between 45 pounds of shortening and six gallons liquid oil (approximately forty-six pounds). The remaining twenty-three pounds of fat (113-90=23) comes from four pounds of canned bacon, fifteen pounds of peanut butter, four quarts of mayonnaise and eight pounds of dehydrated margarine.

STEP 5-Fruits and Vegetables

Fruits and vegetables are the primary source for vitamins A and C in the regular diet. Although they can be largely replaced by a good multi-vitamin, most would prefer the appeal of their flavor, texture and color variety if at all possible. Some may wish to replace up to one serving with ten to twelve pounds of sprouting seeds to add crispness to salads, sandwiches, etc. (see Chapter 12). Table 8-3 lists the amount of fruits and vegetables needed to provide one serving per day for one year. Serving sizes are generally based on a half cup serving, and are not necessarily directly equal to other commonly accepted serving sizes.

Fruits. The malnutrition in war-ravaged Europe after World War II was probably due more to the lack of fruit than any other one thing. Two servings of fruit per person per day are recommended. If you expect to get much vitamin C, you'll need a half serving from either oranges or grapefruit (canned segments, juice or dehydrated). Tang would work and tomatoes contribute as well. Calculate the dried and dehydrated servings first, then the canned. Splurge foods could include blueberries and freeze dried strawberries.

EXAMPLE FAMILY: They need eight total servings of fruit, including two for vitamin C. Because of the expense of dehydrated orange or grapefruit juice, they decide on twenty-two pounds of Tang (equals two four-ounce servings daily) for the vitamin C requirement. They also choose sixteen pounds of dried prunes (.89 serving), twenty pounds of dried raisins (1.43 servings), four pounds dehydrated apple slices (.38 servings) and four pounds of dehydrated banana flakes (.32 servings). This totals approximately five servings, leaving three more, which they fill with #303 cans: seventy-two unsweetened applesauce, sixty peaches in heavy syrup, sixty fruit cocktail in juice pack, forty-eight pears in heavy syrup and twenty-seven #2 cans of pineapple in heavy syrup.

Vegetables. I recommended three and a half servings per person per day. As most of your vitamin A will come from vegetables, you should have either a one-third serving of carrots or a one-quarter serving of carrots together with a one-quarter serving of spinach and sweet potatoes combined. Further, you should consider a three-quarter serving of tomatoes and one serving of white potatoes (perhaps half that for a young child, more for a male teenager). The potato servings are almost double the size of the others used. Remaining servings should be divided up among a good selection of other vegetables.

EXAMPLE FAMILY: They need fourteen total daily servings. Potatoes will make up four servings (eighty-eight pounds of dehydrated powder and sliced) and tomatoes will be another three servings (96

TABLE 8-3.
AMOUNT OF FRUITS AND VEGETABLES FOR
1 SERVING PER DAY FOR 1 YEAR

FOOD	FRESH	DEHYDRATED
FRUITS		
Apples	68 lbs	10.6 lbs
Applesauce, unsweetened		10.6 lbs
Apricots		10.4 lbs
Bananas, flakes		12.4 lbs
Cherries, sweet		12.6 lbs
sour		11.3 lbs
Fruit cocktail, blend or mix		9.7 lbs
Grapefruit juice, crystals		10.5 lbs
Orange juice, crystals		12.0 lbs
Peaches		8.3 lbs
Pears		8.3 lbs
Pineapple		9.1 lbs
Plums or prunes	18 lbs (dried)	11.5 lbs
Raisins	14 lbs (dried)	12.7 lbs
Strawberries		6.0 lbs
VEGETABLES		
Beans, green		5.3 lbs
Beets		9.3 lbs
Cabbage	76 lbs	5.4 lbs
Carrots	74 lbs	7.5 lbs
Corn, sweet		15.8 lbs
Peas, garden		15.3 lbs
Potatoes	121 lbs	22.0 lbs
Spinach		6.2 lbs
Sweet potatoes	46 lbs	11.2 lbs
Tomatoes, powder		6.3 lbs

CANNED: 91 #303, 73 #2, 56 #2½, 31¾ #3, or 14 #10 cans
HOME CANNED: 91 pints or 46 quarts

#303 cans whole, ninety-six eight-ounce cans sauce, thirty-two six-ounce cans paste and sixteen #3 cans juice). They add the remainder in #303 cans: ninety-six carrots, forty-eight spinach, forty sweet potatoes, 144 corn (half whole, half creamed), 120 green beans, ninety-six peas and forty- eight sauerkraut.

STEP 6- Sugars

Sugars are an important energy source and greatly increase palatability. The normal American diet gets 24% of its total calories from sugars. Approximately 6% is naturally occurring sugars in fruits, vegetables and dairy products with the remaining 18% added in the form of refined and processed sugars. It is recommended this 18% be lowered to 10% for a more healthful diet, a reduction of one-third in total sugars. Use this 10% as a base, adding 1-2% if including children to help them meet their relatively high energy needs. Add an additional ten pounds per person if most of the fruits are either dehydrated or canned in water or juice pack. Divide by 4.75 to find pounds.

EXAMPLE FAMILY: The family includes children so they decide on 11% sugar. This equals 288 pounds of sugars (12,450 x 11% ÷ 4.75 = 288). They plan on mostly canned fruit in regular sugar syrups so do not add additional sugar. (However, they may want to add ten pounds of sugar per person for canning fruit later).

Sugar is used as the base with all other substitutions calculated by how many pounds of sugar they will replace. The amounts needed to replace one pound of sugar are: 1¼ pounds of honey, 1¾ pounds of molasses, one pint table syrup, jam, jelly, preserves, marmalade, or apple and fruit butters, one pound of Jello or similar gelatin dessert, sweetened drink mix (e.g. TANG), tapioca and hard candy, and 1⅓ pounds of pudding mix.

EXAMPLE FAMILY: Because they already included twenty-two pounds of Tang, they only need 266 pounds more of sugars. They decide on twenty pounds of honey, twenty pints jams and jellies, twenty-four pounds of Jello, twelve pounds of pudding mixes and four pounds tapioca. That totals seventy-three pounds of sugars, leaving 193 pounds for twenty pounds of brown, eighteen pounds of confectioner's (powdered) and 155 pounds white granulated sugar.

STEP 7- Animal Protein

Approximately 60% of the total protein in a normal American diet comes from meat and eggs. Because of its expense and difficulty in storing, however, your plan will most likely include much less. The recommendations given here provide from 10-30% and, with the milk products, supply sufficient animal protein for a high-quality diet.

Eggs. The survival diet is not the place to worry over the cholesterol controversy and eggs are the absolute best protein available. You'll want them for scrambling, omelets and use in baking. My recommendation is for a minimum of three eggs per week (five pounds of whole egg powder) with seven the best (eleven pounds of whole egg powder). You'll need almost double that if you use scrambling egg mix—or you could get some of each. Custards also fit into this category.

EXAMPLE FAMILY: They decide on five eggs each per week for a total of twenty eggs per week. They can get that from 33 pounds of whole egg powder or about sixty pounds of scrambling egg mix. They want both and settle on twenty-one pounds of whole egg powder and twenty-one pounds of scrambling egg mix.

Meat, fish and poultry. The average American eats two to three servings of meat daily, but the survival diet can make do with substantially less. Even adding just 5% meat to a bean dish gives approximately the same quality of protein as all meat—at much less cost. I recommend a minimum of a hundred up to 365 servings per person for one year. Decide the number of servings you want per person and then get the total. Now, using table 8-4, you can apportion the total number of servings among the various meats you want to store. The "serving" used in the table has been standardized so that, no matter what the meat, the same number of servings contains the same total amount of protein. Any meat not listed may be included by simply determining its protein content—usually stated on the container. It takes three hundred grams of protein to equal seventeen of the table servings.

Canned meats—commercial or home canned—provide the most for the money and will probably be the bulk of your storage. Dried, smoked, retort (MRE) and freeze dried meats can also be considered. Although costing four to eight times the protein of canned, you may want to store small amounts of freeze dried beef patties, steak, etc. as "splurge" foods if your budget allows.

Combinations (i.e. beef stew, chili con carne, tamales, etc.) can also be used but, since only a portion of their protein comes from meat, you will have to use your judgement. If meat is listed among the first few ingredients on the label and appears to make up a substantial portion, you may want to count half the total listed protein. If listed lower or not a large portion, you can still include it in your plan but I wouldn't count its protein in your servings. Another item, soups, are included here because they don't fit better elsewhere. However, they are low or contain no animal protein, and I wouldn't count them in your servings, either. If you want to use them, protein concentrates and TVP would be included in this group.

EXAMPLE FAMILY: They decide on a serving of meat every other day. That totals 730 servings for the four of them. Using table 8-4, they choose one hundred 6-ounce cans of tuna, twenty-four 12-ounce cans of corned beef, twenty-four 12-ounces cans of roast beef, twenty-four 6¾-ounce cans of chicken, twenty-four 6¾-ounce cans of turkey, twenty-four 6¾-ounce cans of ham, forty-eight 5-ounce cans of Vienna sausage and six 15½-ounce cans of salmon. This actually gives approximately 742 servings. They also include 288 cans (seventy-two each) of condensed soups (10½-11 oz): ninety-six tomato, ninety-six mushroom, twenty-four chicken noodle, twenty-four cream of chicken, twenty-four vegetable beef, twelve beef noodle and twelve clam chowder.

STEP 8- Calculating Remainder

Before continuing, it is necessary to calculate the total calories (on a per day basis) included in the plan to this point. This tells how many calories remain to be provided by the last major group, the vegetable proteins. Using the list of items included so far in your plan and table 9-1 at the end of Chapter 9, calculate the calories for each item and then total. For items not in the table, you can find the calories from the label and divide by 365 to prorate over one year. The "total calories"figure is then subtracted from the "total calories" found in STEP 1 to find the remainder.

EXAMPLE FAMILY: They have two hundred twenty-five pounds of powdered milk in their plan. Table 9-1 shows that fifty pounds of milk prorated over one year gives 266 calories per day. So they have 960 calories per day (4.25 x 226 = 960). Their next item is six pounds of

TABLE 8-4. ANIMAL PROTEIN SERVING EQUIVALENTS

The calculations are based on the approximate amount of protein contained in each particular meat item compared to the protein contained in a three-ounce serving of fresh lean ground beef. This allows for standardization.

Food and Amount	Servings	Amount for 100 servings
CANNED MEAT, POULTRY AND FISH		
Tuna, 48 6-oz cans	122	15.4 lbs
Potted meat, 48 3¼-oz cans	44	22.2 lbs
Roast beef, 24 12-oz cans	116	15.6 lbs
Corned beef, 24 12-oz cans	117	15.3 lbs
Chicken, 24 6¾-oz cans	57	17.9 lbs
Turkey, 24 6¾-oz cans	55	18.6 lbs
Vienna sausage, 48 5-oz cans	54	27.7 lbs
Ham, 24 6¾-oz cans	48	21.2 lbs
Salmon, 24 15½-oz cans	122	19.0 lbs
Treet, 24 12-oz cans	60	30.0 lbs
Spam, 24 12-oz cans	70	25.9 lbs
Prem, 24 12-oz cans	54	33.4 lbs
	Servings Per lb	100 servings
FREEZE DRIED MEAT, POULTRY AND FISH		
Beef, ground patties, raw	12	8.3 lbs
Beef, diced, pre-cooked	18	5.6 lbs
Beef, ribeye steak, raw	20	5.0 lbs
Fish, cod fillets	23	4.4 lbs
Chicken, diced, pre-cooked	17	5.9 lbs
Ham, diced, pre-cooked	11	9.3 lbs
Pork, sausage patties, pre-cooked	11	9.0 lbs
Pork, chops or slices, raw	15	6.9 lbs
Shrimp, raw	22	4.6 lbs
Tuna, pre-cooked	24	4.1 lbs
Turkey, diced, pre-cooked	19	5.3 lbs
DRIED MEAT		
Beef jerky	11	8.8 lbs

Individual items are listed within each group roughly in order of their cost per protein unit with the least expensive at the top and the most expensive at the bottom. The actual cost depends greatly on where and when the item is purchased and, in practice, you will have to compare the prices you pay for each. You can make exact cost comparisons at any time by simply multiplying the current cost per pound for an item by the amount listed for 100 servings and comparing this total with the total for any other item.

powdered buttermilk. Table 9-1 gives forty-eight calories for ten pounds so they have twenty-nine calories from buttermilk (six pounds is 60% of ten pounds and .6 x 48 = 29). This procedure is continued until the entire list of stored items is completed, showing a total of 5,850 calories. Subtracting this from the 12,450 calories needed gives 6600 remaining.

STEP 9- Vegetable Proteins

The vegetable proteins make up the balance of your plan's calories and consist of the grains and legumes.

First, you must decide upon a ratio between the grains and legumes. Ideally, to provide the highest protein quality, this ratio should be 1.8 pounds of grains per pound of legumes (1.8:1). However, this is usually more beans than desired and not necessary. A ratio of 4 to 1 works well for everyone while even an 8 to 1 ratio is sufficient for healthy adults. If you have provided the recommended servings of milk, eggs and meat, this ratio is not critical and most would then choose an 8:1 ratio. Otherwise, you're better off choosing 4 to 1.

After choosing your ratio, take the number of calories remaining and divide by 4.25 to find the total pounds of vegetable proteins needed. Now add the two sides of your chosen ratio together (4 to 1 = 5, 8 to 1 = 9) and divide this into the number of pounds you just calculated to find the pounds of legumes. Subtracting that figure from the total pounds of vegetable proteins gives you the pounds of grains. Then apportion the amounts between the various items of each type.

Grains. This includes the whole grains, flours, pastas, breakfast cereals, crackers and mixes.. Current grain consumption is 150 pounds per person but in 1910 it was double that. Regardless of what else you have in your plan, you should have at least two hundred fifty pounds of grains and the majority should be whole grains with the rest processed (flour). Unless rice is your basic, you'll probably want 60-80% of the total in wheat and wheat products. Don't store more than fifty pounds per person as flour. Suggestions are: ten to twenty-five pounds of pasta, ten to fifteen pounds of cornmeal, ten to fifteen pounds of oatmeal, fifteen to twenty-five pounds of rice, one to two pounds of popcorn and two to five pounds each of barley, buckwheat, millet and rye. Combinations such as macaroni and cheese can be included here as well as the various cereals, crackers and mixes. Just subtract their total pounds from that needed for grains.

Legumes. Get a good selection for a variety of uses. Soybeans are very versatile if you know how to use them.

EXAMPLE FAMILY: They choose an 8:1 ratio. The 6,600 calories remaining divided by 4.25 gives 1,553 pounds of vegetable proteins. Dividing now by nine (from their ratio) shows 173 pounds should be legumes. Subtracting the 173 from the 1,553 tells them 1,380 pounds should be grains. They plan on making their own cereals, crackers, etc., but do want to include two dozen cake mixes for convenience. The mixes equal about twenty-eight pounds so they need an additional 1,352 pounds of grains. They select: eighty pounds of pasta, one hundred pounds of rice, fifty pounds of corn, twelve pounds of popcorn, fifty pounds of oatmeal, fifteen pounds of rye, fifteen pounds of buckwheat, twenty pounds of barley, ten pounds of millet and fifty pounds of triticale.

This leaves 950 pounds for 750 pounds of wheat and two hundred pounds of all-purpose flour. The 173 pounds of legumes are divided up: fifty pounds of pinto, forty pounds of red kidney, twenty pounds of white Navy, ten pounds of Great Northern, ten pounds of lima, fifteen pounds of soybeans, twenty-five pounds of dried peas and five pounds of lentils.

STEP 10- Adjuncts

Adjuncts complete your plan. Go through the list of adjuncts in Chapter 9 and decide the amounts you want of each. Your normal usage—see what you use in a month—can be your guide. Whatever you decide, don't skimp on herbs, spices and other seasonings. They are relatively cheap and a little goes a long way towards enlivening otherwise dull meals. Again, variety is important. This is where a few cans of this and a can of that will really enhance your plan with added flavor, color and texture. Finally, include any desired vitamin and mineral supplements.

Since tastes and desires differ so widely, there can be no "recommended" amounts but, as a possible help, here are suggestions for some items: two to six pounds of bouillon (half or more beef, rest chicken); one to two pounds each of cornstarch, baking powder, baking soda, dehydrated onions and dehydrated sweet and sour cream; one half to one pound of yeast and dehydrated celery; one quarter to one half pound of dehydrated green bell peppers; one to two gallons of vinegar. You also might want relishes, pickles and a selection of beverage mixes.

Some "treat" foods would be nice (olives, mushrooms, coconut, mandarin oranges, etc.) and a few specials for the holidays (cranberry sauce, mincemeat, maraschino cherries, pumpkin). And chocolate chips for cookies!

How and Where to Buy

Assuming you have followed the guidelines fairly closely and accurately, you have now designed a plan adequate for your needs. Before rushing out and accumulating your list of items, however, there are a few additional considerations.

Choose the Right Sizes

As you know, foods don't keep forever once their container is opened, especially without refrigeration. Some foods, such as canned meats, may have to be used within hours after opening and the sizes must be chosen accordingly. Others, such as the dehydrated foods, can be used over a period of months if cared for properly. For these, the appropriate container size is one where the contents will be used up before the open shelf life is exceeded. For example, if an item has an open shelf life of three months (see Chapter 9 for shelf lives) and you need twenty pounds for one year, then the maximum amount per container would be five pounds (twenty pounds divided by the four three-month periods in the year). Check your list of food items and determine the appropriate container sizes for each.

EXAMPLE FAMILY: In checking their list, they find that dehydrated cheese has an open shelf life of four-plus months. Their plan includes 6 pounds of cheddar and 3 pounds of Swiss. Dividing both amounts by three (for the three four-month periods in a year) gives 2 pounds and 1 pound as the maximum amount of each per container. Referring to price lists, they find the average #10 can of dehydrated cheese contains 3½ pounds while a #2½ can has about one pound. Thus, they would store both the cheddar and the Swiss in #2½ cans. If they had double the amount of cheddar they could have stored it in #10 cans. They then continue checking the rest of their list.

Use a System

Unless you've procrastinated too long, there is no need to buy it all overnight. Hurrying can cause costly mistakes while adding even relatively small amounts on a regular basis can soon complete the plan. Use your Master Shopping List of Chapter 3. Try to keep your buying in balance as much as practical, getting a month's supply of everything before increasing the amount of any one individual item. And, guided by shelf lives in determining desired rotation, make out your replenishment schedule.

Shop For Quality and Price

Seldom will you find a single source that offers a complete selection of the highest quality items at the best price. It pays to shop around.

Local sources can be located by looking in your "Yellow Pages" under bakers, feed dealers, flour, food brokers, foods-dehydrated, food products, grain brokers or dealers, grocery wholesalers and millers. Don't hesitate to ask for quantity prices. Then compare the sources. Don't overlook freight costs because they can substantially increase the total price. You can save 20-50% of normal prices by becoming a dealer or distributor for a nominal fee with some dehydrated food companies and a few allow "wholesale" purchasing. Restaurant supply, warehouse clubs and similar outlets often offer "institutional" sizes of dehydrated and other foods that are the same as sold by the dehydrated companies but under an original label at lower prices.

For additional savings, use the tips under Budget Basics in Chapter 2. Often the most economical time to buy food is at harvest time when supply is at its peak, but you must always be aware of close outs offering old goods.

Using Your Food Storage

Working from your replenishment schedule, start to work storage foods into your regular menu. As mentioned earlier, do this gradually. There is no need to create resistance, particularly from children, by attempting to alter cooking and eating habits drastically at once. Introduce the more normal items first so the changes don't draw attention. Embellishing some foods with "extras" can help their acceptance (e.g. bacon and green pepper with powdered scrambled eggs or slivers of almonds or walnuts when using powdered butter on green beans). Develop a good stock of recipes for the items, especially for those you're not familiar with One of the biggest challenges in using storage food is to present interesting meals with eye-appeal and you may need to work at that. Buy any specialized cookbooks as you buy the items.

If called upon to depend entirely on your storage, you may discover another problem. Because a plan doesn't always match normal usage, there is a tendency to use some items at a different rate than projected. This is especially true of "treat" items or others stored in less than normal quantities. For example, if you've chosen to store only one-quarter the butter you normally use—yet your family uses it at the normal rate—it will be entirely gone after just three months! You can solve this problem by apportioning the food carefully and accurately over the time period. Divide the total amounts of each food into weekly "allowances" and then plan your menu from that allotment. You will find it easiest if you transfer the weekly inventory on a regular basis to a different location than the rest of your storage. During actual sustained use you will also want to take a physical inventory much more frequently to assure your control is adequate.

Test Your Plan

Okay, now you've got a plan adequate for your needs. At least you think it is. Obviously, the only way to really know is by surviving whatever crisis happens to appear but, short of that, you can put it to a trial test. Have amounts of each storage item on hand to last for at least a week—enough time to see results—and go to it. This means living solely off the storage items—sack lunches rather than restaurants and cafeterias, please! And buon appetito!

SPECIAL DIETARY NEEDS

Some individuals, because of their age or condition, have special dietary needs that must be taken into account when designing a suitable plan. The basic and advanced plans outlined in this chapter can still be used simply by making the necessary modifications. For example, a diabetic may want to cut back even further on the sugar sources, perhaps learn to make bread with malt in place of sugar and preserve with fruit juices in canning. Individual concerns covered here include: infants and young children, pregnant or nursing women and those allergic to any of the basic storage foods.

Infants and Young Children

Babies are seldom surprise visitors, usually giving nearly nine months warning. My recommendation is that you prepare for their arrival as soon as you know you are expecting. Buy whatever they will need to make it through their first year and don't count it in your regular program.

The best and most practical food for new babies is nature's own —mother's milk. Unless special problems prevent it, you should plan on breast feeding to assure the baby an adequate diet as well as to pass on natural immunities. The nutrients in breast milk most closely match the infants needs and tend to be digested and absorbed more easily than from other sources. With vitamin supplements, breast milk is sufficient for the first four to six months by itself. (Women nursing infants have increased nutritional requirements covered in a later section you should also read.)

If you can't or don't want to breast feed, you must either store formula or make your own from storage foods. You'll also want a supply of baby bottles and nipples. To estimate your needs, it might be helpful to know that the average infant is fed milk-based formula for five-plus months and consumes around 170 quarts of ready-to-feed or fifty-two quarts of concentrate. Coinciding figures for soy-based formulas are eight months and 192 quarts ready-to-feed or sixty quarts concentrate. Similar amounts of homemade would require approximately 180 cans of evaporated milk—or thirty-two pounds of powdered milk and 1½ gallons of vegetable oil—combined with eleven pounds of sugar.

With adequate breast milk or formula, solid foods can be delayed until about six months of age. Then you can feed foods made from common storage items, such as rice and corn, or from a stock of commercially-packed food. Again, as a guide, the average baby in its first year will go through six pounds of dry baby cereal and 720 jars of baby food. Much of this could readily be made from normal storage foods less expensively by including a baby food grinder. I'd store more dry cereal than the average and applesauce, banana flakes, custards and mashed potatoes are particularly useful.

By the time an infant is one year old, he should be eating nearly the same foods as the other family members. Young children, however, have high energy and protein requirements for their size. They need a diet with at least 10-20% fat and sufficient complete protein to meet their needs for proper growth and development. They also continue to need vitamins A, C, and D as well as calcium, fluoride and iron.

Vitamins

Breast fed infants need a vitamin D supplement and also one for vitamin A if the mother's diet lacks it. Commercial formulas are nearly all fortified but, if fed homemade formulas, infants require a supplement containing vitamin C plus vitamins A and D if made from unfortified powdered milk. As they get older—three to six months—they also need an iron supplement unless supplied by properly fortified foods. You may want to store a fluoride supplement for all children if the water isn't naturally fluoridated.

A standard daily vitamin pill providing approximately 5000 IU (1500 RE) of vitamin A, 400 IU (10 μg) of vitamin D and 50-100 mg of vitamin C can be used. Other vitamins in normal doses are harmless. The infant should receive one-quarter to one-half pill each day, crushed to a fine powder between two spoons and dissolved in a small amount of fluid that he can easily swallow. Emergency sources would be sprouted grains or legumes for vitamin C and cod liver oil for A and D. Exposing the infant's skin to sunlight for a few hours daily will produce some vitamin D. Initial exposure should be short, no more than ten minutes.

Pregnant and Nursing Women

If you are pregnant or nursing, your diet should reflect your increased nutritional needs. To retain your health and raise normal, healthy infants requires increased energy, protein, iron, calcium and vitamins. Increased nutritional needs are the most critical during the third trimester of pregnancy. Additional requirements for both conditions are listed in table 8-2 and, as soon as you know you are expecting, you should include the increased needs in your plan.

Allergies

If any are allergic to wheat, corn, milk, eggs, peanut butter, or other particular foods, the plan can be developed using substitutes. Gluten-free baking can be done, for example, with rice, soya, oats and cornstarch flour. The calcium from milk can be replaced by supplements or other sources such as canned fish with edible bones, soybean cake, sesame seeds, brewer's yeast, carob flour, egg yolk, nuts, or fresh dark green vegetables. You could also simply store a special supplement preparation containing the enzyme lactase that would allow the use of milk. If you have any problems in this area you might want a specialized cookbook :

Allergy Cooking with Ease: The No Wheat, Milk, Eggs, Corn, Soy, Yeast, Sugar, Grain & Gluten Cookbook by Dumke and Crook
The Allergy Baker by Carol Rudoff (out of print, buy used)

HOUSEHOLD ANIMALS

If you expect to use guard dogs for security or keep other pets, you must plan ahead for their food and other needs.

For dogs, you can store a year's supply of their regular food. Both the wet and dry will keep two to more than five years, and you can rotate within that period. Sacks can be protected from moisture and insects by coating with paraffin or the food can be packed in plastic buckets with dry ice. If you want to save storage space and weight as well as have a lower stool volume, you might want to consider a specially-formulated brand like Science Diet. Although costing more per pound, it contains all needed vitamins and the total cost is about the same.

You could make your own dog food from common storage foods in an emergency. It'll cost a bit less than ready-made but the bother might not be worth it.

9

INDIVIDUAL STORAGE FOODS

This chapter presents specific information on the individual food items, in generally the same order as the prior chapter. Table 9-1 at the end of the chapter lists basic nutritional data for the major foods when a specified amount is prorated over a one year period. Frozen foods are not included because of their vulnerability. AD and FD are used for air-dried and freeze-dried dehydrated foods respectively.

Salt

Besides being essential for body processes, salt is used for many other purposes. It is a flavor enhancer, controls fermentation in baking and cheeses, preserves food by retarding bacteria growth and is used in making butter and in tanning. It can also be used as a gargle and dentifrice for brushing teeth.

Table salt is used for normal cooking and eating, and contains an anti-caking agent to improve its pouring qualities in high humidity. Iodized salt is required wherever produce is grown in iodine deficient soil. Aging may cause the iodine to separate and produce a yellow discoloring, but the salt is still good. Pickling and canning salt does not contain an anti-caking agent and will not cloud water as table salt may if used in pickling and canning. Rock salt comes in blocks, large pieces or coarsely-crushed, and is used to feed domestic animals, to attract wild animals or to preserve meats, make ice cream or tan hides.

Salt is not affected by air, light or heat, and will store indefinitely if protected from moisture in a tightly-covered container. In low-humidity areas it can be left in the original cardboard, cloth or paper container, but in high-humidity areas it should be transferred to a plastic or glass container. It corrodes most metals.

Milk

Milk is used for drinking, pouring over fruits and cereal, in baking and in making white sauces, ice cream and puddings. Milk can be made into custards and cheeses with rennet tablets, and yogurt and butter-milk can be made with the proper bacteria cultures.

Powdered Milk

Some people object to the "chalky" taste of powdered milk and think they don't like it, when their objection is really to the taste of skim milk. Powdered nonfat milk that has been mixed and then allowed to cool for a few hours—overnight is best—is impossible to tell from regular skim milk. It all depends on what you're used to. You can gradually become accustomed to powdered milk by combining it with whole fluid milk in increasing ratios. A 1:1 ratio approximates 2% milk, and our family uses a 2:1 ratio (two parts powdered to one part regular fluid). Either will save you one-fourth to one-third of your normal milk bill while also rotating your storage in one and a half to two years. Attempts to "improve" the taste by adding coconut oil, saccharin, sugar, evaporated milk, powdered cream, fruit juice or vanilla flavoring seem troublesome compared with just getting used to it.

Moisture is powdered milk's worst enemy, causing caking, darkening, stale flavors and rapid deterioration of nutritional values. Temperature is the next priority concern because of its substantial effects. Ultraviolet and fluorescent light turn the fat content rancid and destroy some vitamins. If you plan on re-packing the milk, do it as soon after buying as practical. Fill containers as full as possible and vibrate to compact. Be sure to clean the container lip of any milk powder before placing the lid on to insure a good seal. Fumigation is unnecessary, but store away from strong odors.

A pound of powdered milk makes five quarts (1¼ gallons) when reconstituted. Milk that has developed off-flavors can often still be used in cooking. Because you will probably be using the same containers over and over to reconstitute the milk in, you should be extra careful to keep them clean. Wash them after each use, being sure no milk residue builds up. At least monthly clean them with detergent, rinse with a chlorine bleach and let air dry to avoid bacteria problems.

Regular Non-fat Dry Milk. The preferred form for storage, it is available from bakery supply stores, wholesale outlets and sometimes grocery stores in twenty-five, fifty and hundred pound bags. Left in the plastic-lined laminated paper in a cool, dry location without rodent problems, it will keep three-plus years. Re-packing in metal, glass or plastic containers or buying it in #10 cans may increase the shelf life to five to seven-plus years. In fifty-pound bags, it costs about half the price of regular liquid milk. Commercially packed in plastic buckets nearly doubles its cost, while #10 cans almost triples the price. Buy the spray-dried Extra grade because it has a lower moisture content and fewer bacteria than the Standard grade. It should also be fortified with vitamins A and D.

If you re-pack it, you'll find it pours and splashes similarly to water and creates dust, so it's best to do it outside on a windless day. Open shelf life is about three to four months if you take care to keep tightly covered except when quickly removing some for use. Long-term storage containers should be appropriately sized so that open shelf life will not be exceeded. To minimize exposure to atmospheric moisture you'll probably want to transfer a two to four-week supply to a smaller container (about one half to one gallon per person) for everyday use. Normal strength is ¾ cup powder per quart, but some like it stronger. Mixing is easiest by far with a blender, but a wire whisk, egg beater or shaker can be used when electricity is unavailable. You can also make a paste with a small amount of very warm—not hot—water, and then add additional water as you would in making gravy.

Instant Non-fat Dry Milk. The "instantizing" process results in a larger, more porous particle that mixes more readily than regular. However, it costs about 25% more, requires one-third more space, is more prone to flavor changes and doesn't have quite the same shelf life. Also, because the process requires heating twice, it has slightly lower nutritional values. It requires 1⅓ cup powder per quart. With few exceptions, it is fortified with vitamins A and D, and comes in metal cans, small boxes and twenty-five pound bags. Open shelf life is about two to three months.

Regular Whole Dry Milk. Because of its high butterfat content, it keeps only about one to two years. Packing in an inert atmosphere in metal cans may prolong this up to three years. Its flavor compares with fresh fluid milk, it costs about 25-50% more than regular non-fat dry milk and is used chiefly for infant formulas. Open shelf life is only about three to six weeks or so. It is available from some health food stores and warehouse outlets.

Buttermilk Powder. Saco Foods makes a powder from real sweet-cream cultured buttermilk. While not recommended for drinking, it is great in batters for biscuits, cakes, muffins and pancakes. It comes in a one-pound cardboard can that makes five quarts and keeps for over a year. In better containers its shelf life would approximate that of regular non-fat dry milk. Because of settling, it takes only ⅔ cup per quart. Other sources also have buttermilk powder in metal cans at about twice the price per pound.

Canned Milk

With time the fats and other solids in canned milk tend to separate and settle out. This can be prevented by turning or agitating the cans every few months. Shaking cans vigorously before opening also helps. If lumps do form the milk is still usable. Also, the darkening and strong stale taste it may develop with age is not harmful.

Whole Milk. Shelf life is one-plus year, and it costs seven to ten times the cost of bulk powdered milk and about three times that of powdered milk in #10 cans.

Evaporated Milk. Available in skim or whole, it can be used for whipped toppings, as a cream substitute in sauces, soups and chowders or mixed with equal amounts of water to replace regular milk. Shelf life is two to three years, but a yearly rotation is recommended. Cost is about double that of bulk powdered milk but only two-thirds that in #10 cans.

Condensed Milk. Similar to evaporated but sweetened with approximately 40% sugar. Used almost exclusively for making candy, cookies and desserts. Shelf life is about the same as evaporated.

SAP Milk

Sterilized Aseptically Packaged (SAP) milk stores for eight-plus months without refrigeration. Some say it tastes "cooked" and "chalky", while others feel it is undistinguishable from regular fluid milk.

Cheese

Cheese can be stored fresh, canned or dehydrated.

Fresh. Hard brick cheese will keep several years if tightly wrapped in heavy plastic or foil to exclude air. It will also keep six to eight months by wrapping in a cloth which is first soaked in vinegar and then allowed to dry. After that period of time has elapsed, it can be re-wrapped. The storage life can be extended further by placing the wrapped cheese in a plastic bag with a twist tie. Also, a paraffin coating will keep the cheese from drying out. Mold gives cheese a musty taste but is not harmful to eat and can be cut off.

Parmesan cheese may be purchased grated in half-pound, pound and two and a half pound containers. It is especially good with pasta, soups and vegetables, and will keep more than a year in the original container if kept cool and dry. Open shelf life is two to three months if kept closed when not being used.

Canned. Pasteurized cheese spreads—such as Cheez Whiz—come in jars and cans. The glass jars will keep about one to three years if kept cool, while the canned cheese may keep as long as six to seven years. Open shelf life is about two months.

Dehydrated. Air-dried cheese comes in cheddar, Swiss and American, and can be reconstituted with either water or oil. It can be used directly with macaroni and casseroles, reconstituted as a cheese spread or formed into a block resembling processed cheese. A pound makes about one and a half to two pounds reconstituted. However, although tasty, it is not like fresh cheese. Shelf life is five-plus years, and it keeps about four-plus months after opening. Most use BHA or BHT as preservatives.

Freeze-dried cottage cheese. FD cottage cheese can be used for salads, in cheese cake, Jello, lasagna and stroganoff. It is very expensive with the calcium costing over fifty times as much as that from bulk powdered milk. Shelf life is three to five years; open shelf life is two-plus weeks. It makes about five times the original weight when reconstituted.

Making Your Own Cheese

You can make fresh soft, hard and cottage cheese from bulk powdered milk for about one-third the price of dehydrated. You'll need to store rennet, Junket tablets, buttermilk powder or freeze-dried yogurt or cheese culture. Lemon juice or vinegar will also start the curd-making process. One pound of powdered milk makes about one pound of cheese. The same culture that makes cheeses can be used to make buttermilk or sour cream, too. A different culture is used for yogurt. Both cultures keep for a couple of years, and are available from health food stores and mail order sources (see Chapter 32).

Fats and Oils

Necessary for baking, frying and cooking, fats and oils should be kept as cool as possible, preferably below 60^0 F (16^0 C). Containers must be airtight and exclude light. Dark brown or green glass is better than clear, but neither is as good as opaque.

Liquid Vegetable Oils. Used for pan and deep-fat frying, greasing pans for cooking and in making mayonnaise and salad dressings, nothing contains more calories in less weight or space. Oil is one of the most over-looked but most valuable items in food storage plans. Unopened opaque plastic containers will keep two to three-plus years at 70^0 F (21^0 C) or lower. Open shelf life is four to six months. In metal containers kept cooler, oil will keep ten-plus years. However, metal containers increase the price often four to five times and they are quite prone to leaking.

Shortening. Shortening is used extensively in baking and frying. Regular shortening comes in three or six-pound #5 cans with a fifteen-plus year shelf life. Open shelf life is about six to nine months. You can tell when shortening is no longer good by its color and taste; it should be bland tasting and not pink, light brown or yellow in color, unless it's the butter-flavored shortening. Powdered shortening is available and can be used in recipes not requiring creaming, but why would you want to store it. The powdered shortening's oil content costs five to eight times as much as regular oil or shortening, and you can't fry or grease with it even if reconstituted with oil rather than water because it leaves a residue that curdles. Shelf life is about five-plus years. Shortening is a hydrogenated oil as is margarine.

Margarine. Canned regular margarine will store for three to four years. A spray-dried margarine powder, containing dry milk, whey solids and sodium caseinate, is also available. Its shelf life is three-plus years, and its costs about three to seven times the price of regular margarine. Like the powdered shortening, it will not melt and can't be used for greasing or frying. Reconstituting with water gives a creamy, whipped texture lacking the characteristic oily taste. Using oil rather than water makes a grainy product. The best proportion seems to be one part oil and one part water to five parts powder. Color is light yellow, and the flavor, although not exactly like margarine, is good.

Butter. Again, available canned or as a spray-dried powder that doesn't melt and contains milk solids. The powder reconstitutes similarly to margarine powder, and can't be used for frying or greasing even if made with oil. Shelf life is about three-plus years, and open shelf life is four to six months. Costs are about two to five times regular butter and 75% more than powdered margarine. There are dehydrated butter flavor granules that can make a liquid butter sauce or be used directly on eggs and vegetables. A half-ounce packet equals the flavor in a quarter-pound of butter. Costs are slightly more than regular margarine, but one-third the cost of regular butter and only one-eighth that of dehydrated margarine. It keeps for years although it must be refrigerated after reconstitution. It also does not melt and curdles and browns when subjected to high heat due to its carbohydrate contents. A packet can be mixed with four teaspoons of water and eight teaspoons of shortening to get about two and a quarter ounces of a "butter" with good taste and color. However, that doubles the cost (but its still about half the cost of dehydrated margarine).

Mayonnaise and Miracle Whip

Both have a high fat content, a shelf life of one-plus years, and keep two to three months after opening if refrigerated.

Bacon

Excellent as a flavoring with eggs and in casseroles. Canned bacon will keep five to seven-plus years.

Nuts and Seeds

Nuts, seeds and nut butters are high in fat and also contain large amounts of protein.

Peanut Butter. A versatile high-energy protein food with wide acceptance, it comes in jars or cans. The creamy homogenized types have a three-plus years shelf life, and keep two to four months after opening. The crunchy types keep about half that long, and the old-fashioned, containing no anti-oxidants, keep only six to nine-plus months. The oil may separate out, and age may affect texture somewhat, but it is still edible. A dehydrated peanut butter powder is available, but many find it too grainy and not very edible. Try it before buying. It keeps about five-plus years, can be used directly in baking and costs two to six times the price of regular peanut butter. It can be reconstituted with water, but most people prefer it with oil and a small amount of salt and sugar or honey for added flavor.

Nuts and Seeds. Nuts and seeds need protection from oxygen and high temperatures to prevent rancidity because they are over 50% fat. Excess moisture results in mold. Hard shelled nuts—almonds, Brazil, filberts, pecans and walnuts—are somewhat protected by their shells, and can be stored unshelled in metal or plastic containers for a number of years. Raw, unshelled peanuts can be kept five-plus years. Unshelled almonds don't keep as well. Shelled nuts can be dried in the oven on low heat—below 110^0 F (43^0 C) for an hour or so, fumigated with dry ice and stored in suitable containers for one to two years. Hermetically-sealed vacuum packed cans keep somewhat longer. Sunflower and sesame seeds can be stored the same way as shelled nuts.

Fruits

Canned fruits come in a great variety and keep best at 35-40^0 F (2-5^0 C). Shelf life is two to four-plus years with fruit juices and highly-colored fruits such as berries, cherries and plums on the lower end. Some people suggest inverting the cans regularly to redistribute the contents.

Dehydrated fruits keep three to five-plus years. Open shelf life for AD is about six months to one-plus years, but FD absorb air moisture quickly and only keep two to four weeks after opening. Shelf life for home dehydrated is more variable. Many dehydrated fruits can be eaten "as is" for a snack or reconstituted with cold or hot water for use as cooked fruit in side dishes, salads, baking or cooking. Freeze dried have a tendency to over-re-hydrate and become mushy.

Apples. Store fresh up to six-plus months, canned slices or applesauce for three years, or as dehydrated diced, sliced or applesauce. Good for snack, apple pie, salads, cakes, muffins and breads. Some AD granules are flavored for desserts, and applesauce is often half sugar. The dehydrated slices are described by many as "cardboardy" when reconstituted.

Bananas. The most popular fresh fruit, you probably won't be storing any that way! Dehydrated flakes or powder can be used as puree and in cakes and pies. The slices or chips coated with coconut oil and sugar or honey are difficult to re-hydrated, but are delicious as a snack.

Fruit Mix. Consisting of many different fruit combinations, it comes canned, AD and FD as fruit blend, cocktail, galaxy, mix or salad. With a bit of sugar and some cold water, the dehydrated varieties are suitable for filling a pie or cobbler, but don't expect them to match fruit cocktail from a can. They often are cardboardy and quite flavorless. Also, some brands may consist mainly of apples, even though other items may be listed first on the label.

Citrus Juices. Grapefruit, lemon, lime and orange juices are sometimes available as dehydrated crystals, but you may have to hunt a bit for a source. They are also available canned or in bottles.

Pineapple. Pineapple comes sliced, crushed or as a juice in cans, and as dehydrated chunks and juice. The FD is like fresh in that the enzymes remain active and won't allow Jello to set.

Raisins. Regular raisins will keep two to three-plus years. They are also available as AD with lower moisture than regular and as FD in cereals and snacks.

Vegetables

Canned vegetables have a three to five-plus year shelf life. Inverting the cans on a regular basis may help.

Dehydrated vegetables last three to eight-plus years (home dehydrated keep anywhere from one year up). Open shelf life is one-plus year for AD but only four to eight-plus weeks for FD. Some are pre-seasoned to average taste, and others may need some seasonings to make them palatable.

Potatoes. This South American native is fourth in world production behind wheat, corn and rice, and yields more food more quickly on less land than the other major crops. It is 99.9% fat free, and is so nutritious—vitamin C, many B vitamins, iron—that a Scandinavian man lived healthily for three hundred days on them plus some margarine. Annual consumption in the United States is currently 116 pounds per person, but was 198 pounds in 1910 and the people of Boliva average 310 pounds.

Sweet Potatoes. Unrelated to the white potatoes, they are also all-star performers in nutrition. The canned keep four to five-plus years.

Tomatoes. Technically a fruit, tomatoes are used as a vegetable, and are a good source of vitamins A and C. Necessary in many Italian and Mexican dishes and for meat dishes, stews, casseroles and in ketchup. Tomatoes keep two to four-plus years in specially-enameled cans. Dehydrated tomato powder doesn't make great tomato juice, but it can be mixed to almost any consistency for sauce or paste.

Sugars

Sugars are simple carbohydrates and come in more than a hundred forms with at least twenty-one kinds occurring naturally in foods. The most commonly used as sweeteners are sucrose, glucose and fructose. Sucrose, the most abundant, is known to us as ordinary white table sugar that is refined from sugar cane or beets. It is also found naturally in fruits, vegetables and grains. Glucose, also called dextrose, is the blood sugar that fuels the body. It is the least sweet of the sugars and is often called corn sugar because it is found in corn and other vegetables. Fructose, or levulose, is the sweetest sugar of all when used in cold beverages, but is much less sweet when used in hot beverages and for baking. It is found naturally in fruits and honey. Sucrose is a double sugar composed of half fructose and half glucose.

Unfortunately, many myths and half-truths surround sugar and its use. It is frequently referred to as an "empty calorie" because it contributes nothing beyond taste and calories while requiring additional nutritive factors for digestion. This viewpoint may have some validity for the average diet, where nearly one-fourth of all calories come from sugar, but the argument is suspect for the survival diet with a much lower probable intake. Also children have high caloric needs for their weight and may be unable to obtain sufficient energy if restricted from concentrated sources. Sugars are a partial substitute for fats in that regard.

Contrary to popular opinion that a high intake of sugar causes diabetes, hypoglycemia, cardiovascular diseases, etc., the predominance of scientific evidence provides no proven cause and effect relationships. In fact, considerable evidence indicates that diets high in carbohydrates, whether from starches or sugars, result in improved glucose tolerance for diabetics. Obesity is certainly a factor in diabetes, but obesity is a result of excess calories regardless of the source. Claims of health problems from sugar are often based on erroneously interpreted, selective data. For example, Cuba, Colombia, Costa Rica and Venezuela all have high sugar consumption, but are usually ignored by "scientific" studies because they also have a low incidence of coronary heart disease. Finland and Sweden have similar sugar consumption, but Finland has much more heart disease. Recent scientific pronouncements have tended to absolve sugar for diabetes and similar diseases.

It is true that sugars feed the mouth bacteria, forming an acid that eats tooth enamel and causes cavities. However, this is true of all fermentable carbohydrates, including fruits, and depends not as much on the amount eaten as how often and how long they stay in contact with the teeth. Sticky substances—like honey and molasses—tend to cling to the teeth, staying longer in the mouth, and are therefore more likely to cause cavities than white sugar.

White Sugar. White sugar is the juice squeezed from cane or sugar beets that has been physically cleaned of impurities—dirt and insect fragments—had the molasses removed and then been concentrated. It is not chemically altered in any way and is as natural as any other sugar. It is a basic food and not the "deadly poison" claimed by health food faddists. The fact is the body handles all sugars the same way.

It comes as granulated table sugar and confectioner's or powdered sugar. It is a very stable food and will keep indefinitely if protected from moisture and contamination. High heat turns it yellow but doesn't harm it—that's what appears as browning during baking! The original bags are sufficient in low-humidity areas, but plastic or metal buckets and cans are best otherwise. Hard lumped sugar can be pulverized with a hammer or placed in water and made into a syrup.

Turbinado Sugar. Often erroneously called raw sugar—the FDA prohibits raw sugar sales unless impurities are removed—it undergoes the same refining as white sugar, but not all of the molasses is removed. It has a slight molasses taste and a higher tendency to harden.

Brown Sugar. Approximately 95% sucrose, brown sugar is normally made from white sugar by simply mixing in a small amount of molasses. The more molasses, the darker and stronger the flavor. You can make your own by adding four tablespoons of molasses per cup of white sugar. Brown sugar's higher moisture content needs to be retained or it will harden. It can be softened by placing a slice of apple, fresh bread, lemon or potato in the container for a period of time, or by sprinkling water over it and placing in an oven at 250^0 F for a few minutes. It keeps indefinitely if protected from too much moisture.

Honey. Honey is a sugar formed by an enzyme from the dilute sucrose found in nectar. Its exact composition depends on the particular nectar sources, but its chief sugars are fructose, glucose and sucrose.

Despite exaggerated claims by enthusiasts, it is not nutritionally superior to white sugar in any meaningful way. Both are easily and quickly digested and absorbed into the blood. Even the minute quantities of additional nutrients found in honey are insignificant when eaten in normal amounts. For example, it would require a cup of honey per day to get just 10% of the RDA for iron, four to five cups for 10% of the phosphorus and calcium, and ten cups for 10% of the thiamine! There is some inconclusive evidence that it may be slightly safer for diabetes or hypoglycemia. On the other hand, some people may be allergic to the pollen in honey.

Honey is not recommended for infants under one year of age because it is a possible source of infant botulism. Improper handling may contaminate honey with botulism spores which, although it resists bacterial growth, it does not kill. The belief is that the spores remain dormant in the honey. Adults and children regularly ingest the spores, and they are customarily harmless. However, infants may not have developed the antibacterial activity in their digestive tracts to prevent the spores from germinating and producing the toxin. Most susceptible are those between one and eight months of age.

Honey is somewhat sweeter than sugar and has 367 fewer calories per pound. However, because it is denser, a tablespoon of honey has one-third more calories than one of sugar. It is also much more expensive, usually costing roughly three times as much per pound. In many cases it can be substituted for sugar if desired. It gives baked goods a distinctive flavor and aroma, and may improve the texture and browning in some. Honey also attracts water, and baked goods made from it tend to remain moist and stay fresh longer.

The nectar source determines the flavor, aroma and color, and there is a wide variety. Usually the lighter the color, the milder the flavor. Most honey comes from clover in the northeastern United States, from alfalfa in the western United States and from heather in Europe. Other sources—stronger flavored—include citrus blossoms, tupelo and tulip trees, wild sage, horsemint, basswood, sourwood and cultivated buckwheat. Sometimes blends are offered but, whatever you choose, make sure you like it before stocking up.

Water content is critical for long-term storage. Honey may legally contain up to 20% added water to prevent crystallization, but this allows fermentation and mold within a short time unless kept refrigerated. Pure undiluted honey, still containing 15-18% water, tends to crystallize with time and cold, but will keep indefinitely. It attracts moisture and must be kept tightly closed. Re-packing is messy, so buy it in the containers you want for storage. Honey stored in the large five-gallon metal cans that has crystallized can easily be re-liquified by placing the can in the sun for a few days or on a rack in a water-filled pan over a burner on low heat. The metal can will cause a slight black discoloration around the edge after many years, but it is harmless. Glass jars let light in and that also causes color and flavor changes. If re-packing, remember to leave space for expansion as the honey crystallizes.

Honey naturally becomes darker and stronger flavored with age, but it isn't harmed in any way, and the process is reversed by re-liquefying. Use temperatures of 160^0 F (70^0 C) or less to avoid changing the color and flavor. Small amounts can be placed in a pan of hot water, and larger containers may be placed near—not on—a heater or set on a low rack in the oven (a gas pilot light may be enough).

Fructose. Pure fructose—96-100% fructose—comes in tablet, liquid, granular crystal and powder forms. It is manufactured commercially from regular sugar because extracting it from fruit or honey is impractical for mass production and would be prohibitively expensive. Still, it costs three to more than ten times as much as regular white sugar. It also attracts moisture more readily and has a strong tendency to lump and cake, even in a low-humidity environment. Its perceived sweetness is considered to be up to twice that of white sugar when used in high acid, cool or cold foods and beverages, but about the same sweetness in room temperature, hot or baked products. Some believe that pure fructose may be slightly better for diabetics because it uses less insulin and is more slowly absorbed, reducing blood sugar fluctuations. It also may reduce dental decay 25%, and it has a "cleaner, fresher" taste, allowing the distinctive tastes of fruit flavors to come through more in drinks and jams.

Pure fructose should not be confused with the High Fructose Corn Syrups, which are derived from corn and are used commercially to sweeten everything from mayonnaise and baked products to soft drinks, ice cream and frozen yogurt. This liquid syrup is actually a mix of glucose and fructose, and costs less than regular white sugar, which is exactly why it is so prevalent.

Syrups. Corn syrup consists mainly of dextrose and is produced from corn. It is a major ingredient of most table syrups, and keeps two-plus years in an air-tight container. Maple syrup comes from the sugar maple tree sap, is primarily sucrose, is expensive and will keep from five to ten-plus years in it pure, undiluted form. Sorghum syrup comes from the sorghum grain, a large coarse grass, and looks much like molasses.

Molasses. Most molasses is a by-product of making white sugar. It is largely sucrose and keeps four to ten-plus years. Blackstrap molasses, the third extraction or final by-product, is the most concentrated source of vitamins and minerals, but still with insignificant amounts. Even a tablespoon per day would barely provide 10% of the RDA for calcium and iron. Four tablespoons per day would provide only 10% of the RDA for vitamin B_2, five tablespoons would be needed for 10% of the RDA for niacin, and seven and a half tablespoons for 10% of the RDA for vitamin B_1. Molasses is useful to add flavor and variety to baking.

Jams and Jellies. Jams, jellies, marmalades and preserves are high in sugar content. Keep them cool and dark to preserve their flavors and colors. Mold that may form on top can be scraped off if you make sure and get it all. They keep two to three-plus years.

Gelatin Desserts. Often referred to by the brand name Jello, they are almost straight sugar. If kept dry and dark they will keep five to ten-plus years before losing their color, flavor and "setting" ability.

Pre-sweetened Drink Mixes. Under brand names like Tang, Kool-Aid, Wylers, and Hawaiian Punch, they come in many flavors and are nearly all sugar. Although convenient, they cost roughly 25% more than the unsweetened packages sweetened with your own bulk sugar. Breakfast drinks like Tang usually provide 100% of the RDA for vitamin C in each four-ounce serving, but other drinks often have only one-tenth as much. Hot cocoa and chocolate drink mixes also contain lots of sugar.

Tapioca. Prepared from the cassava plant, it has a high sugar content. It is used to make puddings and to thicken soups.

Puddings. Puddings are also high in sugars and are, therefore, considered in this grouping.

Animal Proteins

Animal proteins include milk, cheese and other dairy products listed previously. Costs per gram of meat protein are easily compared using table 8-4.

Eggs

Eggs are commonly regarded as the best quality protein available. They are the basis for many dishes and perform vital functions in many recipes.

Powdered Eggs. Although fresh eggs can be stored for some time using waterglass, paraffin and varnish solutions, by far the predominant method is by dehydrating them. AD powdered eggs come in four forms: whole, whites, yolks and a scrambling mix containing powdered milk and oil. Whole egg powder has the equivalent of 32-33 eggs per pound and, while costing two to three times as much as fresh eggs, is fairly inexpensive compared to other storable animal proteins. The mix seems cheaper, but only because it has about half the egg protein with the rest from milk. Shelf life is two to four-plus years and three to four months after opening. Treat as fresh egg after reconstituting. Unpasteurized egg mixes should only be used for thoroughly-cooked or baked dishes. Egg powder readily absorbs moisture, making it lumpy and stronger flavored as well as decreasing vitamins B1 and C. Heat damages its flavor, solubility and thickening ability.

FD Eggs. Available in a number of variations, they are approximately the same to as much as double the cost of AD egg. Shelf life is about the same, but they keep only four weeks or so after opening. Some are ready to eat with the addition of boiling water.

Meats, Poultry and Fish

Some consider meat a definite luxury items in a storage plan, while others look on it as a necessity. Without a doubt, unless you are a confirmed vegetarian, it can definitely add to a plan's palatability and make it seem much more like "normal" eating. Even the addition of small amounts of animal protein to vegetable proteins raises the protein quality substantially for little cost.

Dried. Dried and smoked meat and fish can be kept up to several years in appropriate containers. Some of the more common dried meats are chipped beef, jerky and pemmican. Commercial jerky is usually highly spiced, but if you eat much jerky you'll prefer little or no seasonings added.

Canned. Canned meats, poultry and fish have shelf lives of three to five-plus years if kept at 70^0 F $(21^0$ C) or cooler. The protein content of water-packed tuna is higher than that of oil-packed according to Table 8-4, but that is simply because of the differences in the analyses results used. Figures given in the table are based on averages and, in reality, the protein content of both types of tuna would be the same. Obviously, the oil-packed would contain more calories due to the oil. Whole chicken—with the bone—is available, as well as just the meat. Combinations with meat vary widely in meat protein content and cost more for what you get.

MREs (Meals Ready to Eat) / Retort. MREs are mostly combination meals with only a few all-meat such as chicken patties. They can be eaten directly from the retort pouch or heated five minutes in boiling water. Some are self-heating. Shelf lives are five-plus years.

Freeze Dried. Beef, chicken, pork, and turkey are available. Some are already cooked and ready to eat after adding boiling water, and others are raw and must be cooked after reconstituting. Both types should be treated as fresh meat after the water is added. There are also many combination meals. Shelf lives are five-plus years but, due to moisture attraction, open shelf life is only four to eight weeks with prudent precautions. The meat is quite expensive, averaging about five to eight times the cost of comparable canned meat. In most storage plans FD meats are "splurge" foods, but they would be nice on occasion.

Beef comes as pre-cooked diced at about $12-15 per reconstituted pound in #10 cans, as pre-cooked or raw ground beef patties at about the same cost, or as raw ribeye steaks. The diced and ground can be used in many ways to enhance meals. You can fry or barbecue the steaks, but they are too expensive to be considered anything other than the occasional treat.

Chicken, turkey and pork all come as pre-cooked diced meat. Their taste can be improved by lightly heating in a frying pan for a minute or two after re-hydrating. The pork is good added to egg and other dishes.

There used to be a wider selection of FD meats and, who knows, maybe public demand will make a larger selection available again in the future.

A large selection of combination entrees that include FD meat is available. Although combinations save you from opening half a dozen cans to prepare a single dish, they cost about the same per gram of protein as all meat, which they aren't. After some time in storage, foods that are canned together tend to also blend their flavors until they pretty much taste the same. Combination FD foods also have shorter shelf lives. Separate ingredients do take a bit more effort, but cost substantially less and look and taste better. Be aware that stated serving sizes are often rather small, and you could need two or three per person!

Meat Substitutes

Certain food items are offered as substitutes for meat protein and should be considered here.

Protein Concentrates

Powdered protein concentrates are normally made from milk or soy proteins—or a combination—with lesser amounts of other ingredients and sweeteners. They come in a variety of flavors, can be dissolved in milk or fruit juice, or mixed directly with other foods to supplement the protein content. Price varies considerably. Shelf life is three to seven years, and open shelf life is one-plus year.

Some have quite poor protein quality and others are fairly good, but even the best don't claim to be equal or superior to egg protein. The better quality concentrates cost about the same per gram of protein as powdered egg and one and a half to two times the cost of many canned meats. Personally, I prefer the powdered egg and canned meats. Protein concentrates would save one-third the space and about half the weight if concealment and portability are major concerns, but they're pretty hard to eat straight from a can! If you decide to store some protein concentrate as a supplement, be sure to get a high quality one that dissolves readily—even the best coat drinking glasses—and tastes good to you.

TVP

Textured vegetable protein (TVP)—also known as TSP and some other names—is made from soybean protein that has been spun into fibers and then fashioned into various forms to imitate different meats. These "pseudo-meats" are claimed to duplicate the look, texture and taste of the real thing at reduced prices. They come plain and flavored and, except for the bacon bits, are reconstituted and then cooked as real meat would be. Shelf life is three to five-plus years.

Cost is its major selling point, but palatability is its biggest problem. Few who have tried it straight would put it in the same class with real meat. Its protein quality, even though made from soybeans and normally fortified with extra methionine, is still inferior to nearly all animal sources. Some people are also concerned with the effect the large quantities of additives may have on the digestive tract. It can be used as an extender with some success— many cafeterias, schools and some fast food outlets use it—but studies have shown that levels of 20-30% TVP significantly decrease the flavor, juiciness and palatability of the meat as well as leave an aftertaste. Try before buying it.

Gluten

Like TVP, gluten is a vegetable protein that—because of its very low cost—is suggested by some as a replacement for meat protein. It is a stretchy, elastic substance contained in all cereal grains except rice and corn, but found in its most complete form in wheat. It can be made to look and taste something like various meats with flavorings, or sweetened for desserts. Gluten is made from wheat by washing out the starch granules from developed dough. The wheat germ, most of the water-soluble vitamins and minerals, and a small percentage of the protein ends up in the wash water. The water can be used in breads and soups, and the starch can be dried for baby powder or thickening in place of cornstarch. The whole wheat kernel isn't a high quality protein to begin with and the resulting gluten is much inferior to meat, being only half as good at sustaining growing children. Gluten can add variety to your diet, but I don't recommend that you use it to replace animal protein.

Gelatin

Unsweetened gelatin is an almost tasteless, odorless powder obtained by boiling bones, hides, hoofs and other animal tissues. A gluey substance, it is 100% protein, but lacks essential amino acids and is very low quality and incomplete. It is used in the preparation of many foods because of its "setting" qualities. Because it is readily available, stores well and is very cheap, it is used extensively in some low-quality commercial units. Use it only as an adjunct in your plan.

Soups

Vegetable soups, sometimes with added meat, have a shelf life of two to three-plus years. They are convenient and add variety. A few—mushroom, chicken, onion and tomato—are often used as seasoning in other dishes.

Vegetable Proteins

Bulk vegetable proteins provide more nutrition for the money than any other food. Processing, such as milling, rolling or being formed into pasta, raises the price, and mixes, casseroles and breakfast cereals are even more expensive. Although they are partial proteins, grains and legumes can be combined to greatly increase their quality, and both are improved when added to small quantities of animal proteins. Try before buying in quantity for storage. Moisture is by far their main storage enemy.

Cereal Grains

Cereal grains are excellent sources of protein, the vitamin B complex and E, essential fatty acids, minerals and fiber. Each kernel consists of three parts: 1) the germ that sprouts and contains nearly all the oils and many other important nutrients, 2) the starch which is the food supply for the germ as it grows after sprouting and is the largest part of the kernel, and 3) the hull or bran layer that surrounds, seals and protects the kernel. Whole grains are much more nutritive and keep much longer without going rancid than milled grains. The bran and germ are normally removed during milling to give flour its lighter color and to prevent rapid rancidity.

Amaranth. A staple food in ancient America, it is making a comeback. Its tiny white seeds are nearly 15% protein with a high lysine content unusual for grains. It makes a complete protein when mixed with wheat. The toasted seeds can be boiled for gruel or porridge, or milled into flour for flat breads and mixing with other flours. It can also be popped and stuck together with honey or molasses for a Mexican version of popcorn balls. Amaranth is easily grown from seed and is heat and drought resistant

Barley. One of the oldest known cereal grains, it is a short, stubby kernel with a hard outer shell. Low in gluten, it can be mixed with flour containing gluten to get sweet, cake-like breads with nutty flavors. The hulled has a brown appearance, and the pearled has been polished to remove the bran for a white, translucent look. It is used for breakfast cereal, in soups and casseroles and to make hot drinks. Shelf life is ten-plus years.

Buckwheat. Not a true cereal grain, buckwheat is nevertheless a superior protein because of its high lysine content, and it was a favorite flour in pilgrim times. It has a strong, distinctive taste mellowed by other flours and is commonly used for pancakes. Those allergic to certain grains may find they can eat buckwheat. Whole roasted buckwheat mush—"kasha"—is a staple for East Europeans and Ukrainians, and in the Far East it is made into the "soba" noodle dish.

Corn. Corn was first grown by the American Indian and called "maize" by them. It was eaten by nearly everyone in some form for breakfast and dinner almost every day during the earlier "pioneer" period. Dried field corn can be made into hominy and corn grits, or ground into meal and flour for flat cakes, mush and quick breads. The flour can be mixed with other flours to give a crunchy, crumbly texture and sweet taste to yeast breads. All commercial cornmeal is required to be enriched because it is de-germed during milling, but you can grind your own and have better flavor with higher nutrition. Whole dried field corn keeps five to ten-plus years, while cornmeal keeps three-plus years. Fumigation is normally not necessary. Moisture should be 12% or less.

Popcorn is a special strain of corn with a very hard hull. It will keep five to ten-plus years, but it must be kept tightly covered to retain its moisture content so it will pop when heated. It makes a very inexpensive and nourishing treat that could add variety, lift spirits and ease hard times. You can also use it to decorate Christmas trees, feeding it to the birds after use. Get a hot air popper if you plan on doing the popping over a fire.

Millet. The primary grain in China before rice, it is one of the most ancient and still a staple in Ethiopia, India and North China. The kernels look like very tiny, round pale golden seeds. They have a sweet, nutty flavor when lightly toasted before milling, and swell greatly when cooked, providing more servings per pound than other grains. It cooks fast with a tender yet chewy texture, and its rather bland, egg-like taste readily takes a variety of seasonings. It is ideal baby food because of its low acid content, making it easy to digest. Millet can be used as a breakfast cereal, in soups, stews, casseroles and desserts, and as a main dish. It gives a crunchier texture to wheat bread. It is high in iron and essential amino acids, and is less allergic than some grains.

Oats. Native to Central Asia, oats are a favorite breakfast cereal throughout northern Europe and the British Isles. The kernel is a long, light brown grain with a bland, sweet taste. They can't be readily processed at home, so buy them already in the form you want. Whole oat groats are the whole grain after removing the hull. Steel-cut groats have been cut into several pieces (sometimes called Scotch oats) which can then be rolled into flakes. They are steamed (pre-cooked) lightly, and the thinness of the flake determines whether they are regular or quick-cooking oats. Shelf life is four to five-plus years. Soaking oatmeal overnight in a warm place will help reduce the phytic acid when cooked that would otherwise inhibit calcium absorption from the oats.

Rice. Half the world considers rice the "staff of life" rather than wheat, and it is the most widely consumed cereal grain. It comes as long, medium or short kernels covered with a green-brown husk. Brown rice has the husk removed, while white rice has been polished to also remove the germ and several bran layers. White rice is preferred for storage because of its ten-plus years shelf life. Brown rice has a much higher fat content, goes rancid more quickly and only keeps two-plus years. Almost all white rice is enriched and the nutritional differences are minimal. Long grains cook up fluffy and separate, medium grains are tender, moist and clingy, and short grains are very clingy and cook to a creamier texture. Rice is one of the first infant foods and is helpful for people suffering from diarrhea. It can be used in a gluten-free diet. White rice should have less than 14% moisture, while brown rice should contain less than 12%.

Rye. An important bread grain in Scandinavia and Russia, it is a wholesome, high-stamina favorite with a sweet, nutty flavor. Gluten content is low, and it is best mixed with wheat for breads. A good source of potassium, phosphorus and iron. It stores five-plus years.

Sorghum. The major cereal grain in Africa, sorghum has roundish brown seeds with yellow and red mixed in. The lighter varieties taste best and can be boiled, ground into meal or milled into flour. It has a strong flavor and is best mixed with other flours. Moisture content should be 12% or less.

Triticale. Pronounced trit-uh-CAY-lee, it is a relatively new hybrid with the amino acids and sweet, nutty taste of rye combined with the general baking qualities of wheat. It is higher in protein than either and is especially high in lysine. The kernels are larger than wheat and plumper than rye. It has a low gluten content and should be mixed with wheat for bread. Many commercial mills refuse to grind it because it gums up their mills.

Wheat. Known as the "staff of life", wheat is a nutritious, versatile grain without peer for storage. It is the least expensive food per calorie, and will easily store twenty-plus years if properly protected from moisture. It is rich in B vitamins, vitamin E and the essential fatty acids, iron and fiber.

Get hard #1 winter or #2 or better spring wheat. Many varieties grown in different areas are suitable, and actual protein content and other characteristics depend not only on the variety, but also to a large extent on the environmental and soil conditions that particular growing year. Spring wheat tends to be larger and plumper with a higher protein and moisture content. Protein content should be at least 12%, but extremely high protein content can be undesirable. Kernels shriveled by frost or drought may have abnormally high protein, but they are also low in starch and make poor bread due to low gluten content.

Moisture content should be 10% or less. Freshly-threshed "field grade" wheat contains 14-16% and must be dried. You can get an idea of the moisture content just by looking at the kernel; a shiny kernel contains low moisture while a quite plump one has high moisture. Exact moisture content can be determined by carefully weighing out twenty ounces of grain from the middle of the container and placing it in a pan or tray to a depth of a half inch or so. Place it in an oven for two hours at 180^0 F (80^0 C), and then re-weigh. Each ounce lost shows approximately 5% moisture content. For 10% or less moisture it should have lost two ounces or less.

It should be clean and insect-free—dockage below ½%—cereal grade for human consumption. Normally it is cleaned at least twice in "air washes" and also screened two or three times, but it will still contain some contaminants you'll want to cull prior to milling. Don't buy any grain that has been washed with water or pre-treated for use as seed. You might save one-third to one-half by buying directly from the farmer and cleaning your own, but you'll probably have to dry it, too. Drop the wheat slowly through the air from a fan into a high-sided clean container. Fan it several times. Then run it through a screen—like on screen doors. You may also want to pick through by hand after sieving.

The wheat should be relatively free of cracked kernels and should be of uniform size and shape, not too plump nor shriveled. There shouldn't be a large percentage of yellow berry—chalky, yellow kernels or portions in a normally flinty wheat—because they lower protein content. A small amount isn't too objectionable.

Wheat can be purchased in bulk from flour mills and grain dealers. Preparing your own for storage is easy and inexpensive, while buying it already packed in plastic buckets will cost 50-100% more. Getting it in #10 cans will cost three to four times as much and isn't worth the extra expense. Turning or aeration, as some recommend, is not necessary as long as the moisture content is kept below 10%. Wheat stored in sacks without a moisture barrier will draw moisture from humid air. Germination slowly declines over time, but 50% of some wheat kept for twenty years in a garage at 12^0 to 117^0 F sprouted.

Finally, don't forget to store a grain mill (see Chapter 10). There are expedient methods to grind whole grains without a mill, but you won't want to use them unless absolutely necessary.

Flour

Flour costs one-fourth to one-third more than whole grains, doesn't store anywhere near as long and is more sensitive to heat. It is convenient, but don't store more than you normally use in a year's time. Moisture can drastically reduce its shelf life, so store it in sacks in very dry areas or in airtight plastic or metal containers. Fumigation is useless because of its density.

Enriched all-purpose white flour contains less protein, fiber, vitamin E and essential fatty acids and calcium than the whole wheat it came from. It is convenient and desirable for some uses. It is milled at about 13½% moisture and keeps two to three years at 70^0 F (21^0 C) with a 12-13% moisture content but only one to two years at 14½%. Even lower moisture can prolong shelf life to five to seven years.

Real whole wheat flour has a high fat content, tends to become rancid and keeps for much less time than white. Much of the "whole wheat flour" sold commercially is simply white flour that has had some bran and a little wheat germ added. Just make your own from whole wheat as needed. Breads made from whole wheat flour tend to be heavier and crumblier, but with good recipes and practice they needn't be that way at all. They also don't need to be sweet like those made with all that honey some cooks seem so fond of. Properly done, whole wheat bread will make most commercial bread loose its appeal forever.

Pasta

Pasta comes in a wide variety of shapes and sizes, and is made from semolina, the starch portion of the durum wheat—the hardest wheat grown. The quality of the pasta changes with the quality of the durum wheat available each particular year. Low-quality pasta is often made from blends or even other wheats. The best pastas give the best results, and you're better off finding a brand you like and staying with it. Low-quality ones are starchier, cook up gluey and are less tasty. Pasta doesn't deserve the "empty calorie" label, but contains the basic wholesomeness of wheat and provides essential carbohydrates as well as useful amounts of B vitamins, iron and calcium. It is easy to store, quick to prepare in a wide variety of dishes, high in protein, low in fat and readily digestible. Italians eat sixty pounds yearly per person, and the average American about ten pounds.

Pasta is very inexpensive in large ten or twenty-pound boxes that store three to five-plus years if kept sealed in a dry place at 70^0 F or less. It can be fumigated like grain and will keep even longer in better containers. Pasta sluffs off layers and becomes stale with age.

Mixes

There are many mixes that are both convenient and less costly than the individual ingredients. Most can be kept in the original containers in a dry area for a short period of time, but should be re-packed in better containers for long-term storage in humid areas. Shelf life is at least a year or two in most all cases.

Baby Foods

You can make simple cereals from home-milled whole grains, particularly rice and rolled oats, or store ready-made baby cereals. They come in half and one-pound boxes, and normally keep about two years before becoming rancid. Canned baby food in various combinations also keep one to two-plus years. Powdered formula keeps longer than the ready-mixed.

Beans, Peas and Lentils

Dried legumes are the richest source of vegetable protein and are important as supplements to the grains. They are high in vitamin B_1, iron, calcium, phosphorus, potassium and fiber and, with the exception of soybeans, are low in fat. They are not usually fumigated and will store five-plus years in airtight containers.

Dry beans should be cooked before eating to destroy the growth-inhibiting substances which prevent much of the bean protein from being digested and absorbed. This is also true after sprouting. Beans cause flatulence in most people due to the presence of certain indigestible carbohydrates that ferment in the colon, producing gas. The best way to reduce this problem is to pre-soak the beans, discarding the water a number of times. Sprouting also reduces the tendency.

Packers use many brand names but the quality of the beans depends on their selection from that year's crop, good or bad. Select beans with as few defects as possible, uniform in size for uniform cooking and a bright, even color. A dull or low-color bean is usually old. Even the best seed cleaner occasionally passes bean-size rocks and dirt clods, so you should always hand-sort before using. Don't buy beans treated for planting.

The proper storage of beans begins with moisture control. Too much moisture rots the beans and too little causes "hard shell" where the beans become very tough with a papery skin. They don't absorb water during soaking and become nearly uncookable. This condition can be overcome somewhat by blanching with steam or boiling for one to two minutes prior to soaking, but it is better prevented by storing beans in an airtight, moisture-proof container. Properly stored, they will keep five to ten-plus years but, allowed to dry out, they may develop hard shell in two to three years. Moisture content is best in the 8-10% range.

Canned beans are substantially more expensive than dry, but may be convenient enough to have a small supply on hand.

There are hundreds of varieties of beans depending on the locale and local preferences. Some of the more widely available ones are:

Black. Related to turtle beans, they look like small, dark ovals and are a major food source in Mexico, the Caribbean and the American Southwest. Used in casseroles, salads, soups and stews.

Blackeye. Also known as blackeye peas or cowpeas, they originated in Asia and are small, oval-shaped creamy white with a distinctive black spot or "eye" on one side. Used mostly in Southern cooking, they combine particularly well with pork and chicken.

Garbanzo. Also called chickpea or ceci, this bean is popular along the Mediterranean and throughout the Middle East to India. A pale round nut-shaped and flavored bean, excellent over tossed salads, in soups, stews and casseroles and for sprouting. Can be roasted and ground for a hot beverage.

Fava. Sometimes called broad beans, they are large and flat, resemble lima beans and often substitute for lima or garbanzo beans.

Great Northern. A large white, kidney-shaped bean with distinctive flavor. An outstanding baked bean also good in soups, salads and casseroles.

Kidney. Named for its shape, it comes in light and dark red varieties and is the favorite of Latin America. The dark red are sold almost exclusively canned. An all-purpose bean, both are great in chili and many Mexican dishes as well as in salads, casseroles, soups and meat dishes.

Lima. A pale, broad flat bean commonly available as large—butter beans—or baby beans. The unique, delicate flavor goes well with many dishes.

Mung. Mung beans are small, round pale drab green to black beans normally used as sprouts in oriental and other dishes. Also good in salads, on sandwiches or lightly stir-fried. More expensive than most other beans.

Navy. Also known as small white beans, this classic is a must for Boston Baked Beans and with ham. Holds shape well if cooked slowly.

Pea. A small, oval white bean excellent baked.

Pink. Much like the pinto, it has a milder flavor than the red bean and is often featured in Mexican-American dishes.

Pinto. Also called red Mexican or calico bean because of distinctive speckled brown and white coloring, they become all brown during cooking. A staple of Mexican cooking, their succulent flavor is found in chili, burritos, tostadas, and as refried beans. Can be substituted for red and kidney in most recipes. Less tiresome over long periods of time than many other beans. Especially good as a meat extender.

Red. A small bright red pea bean popular in chili and bean salads.

Soy. A round bean of various color, it contains the most complete and highest percentage of protein of any vegetable. Its mild taste readily takes on other flavorings. Many oriental dishes are made from it as well as a soy milk and ice cream. Soybeans must be cooked first to destroy the trypsin-inhibiting substances that prevent full utilization of the protein. This destruction is best accomplished when wet. The phytic acid in the beans also decreases the absorption of zinc. Other beans are 50-60% starch, but soybeans contain no starch, are higher in fat and don't cook the same. They don't become soft nearly as quickly. Orientals consider fermented soybeans and products more readily digested and more palatable. A good soybean cookbook is recommended if you store them in quantity.

Store clean, whole dry beans with a moisture content of 11% or less. Because of high fat content, they do not keep as well as some others but will still keep four to five-plus years.

Peas. Dried yellow peas have mild flavor while green are more distinctive. Whole peas can be sprouted, used whole, or ground up for soup and other dishes. Split usually cost more, are less nutritious due to oxidation and won't keep as long. Both are rich in vitamins A and B, iron, calcium, potassium and phosphorus. They are made from field peas.

Lentils. The most nutritious legume next to soybeans, they are small, flat and disc-shaped with a mild flavor that blends well with other foods.

Adjuncts

Beverages. Unsweetened soft drink mixes, usually making two quarts per package, suffer some flavor loss after two-plus years. Electrolytically balanced drinks such as Gatorade are excellent for shelter storage and for persons suffering from burns and diarrhea. Cocoa and chocolate drink mixes keep three to four-plus years if kept dry. Coffee and tea store two to five years with airtight containers best. Pero (made in Germany from cereal grains), Postum (from bran, wheat and molasses) and Ovaltine are other possibilities. Root beer extract could be nice for special occasions.

Bouillon. Comes in beef, chicken and other flavors in cube and granular form. Keeps two to five-plus years with granular keeping the longest. Probably want one to two pounds minimum up to ten to twelve pounds per person if used heavily for gluten and other meatless dishes. Good seasonings for soup broths, rice and other dishes.

Chocolate, Cocoa, Carob and Butterscotch Chips What's life without chocolate?! Perhaps two to ten pounds per person for making treats. Keep the chips dry and cool. Heat causes a white-grey film on chocolate called "bloom", but it doesn't affect flavor. All store two to three-plus years if protected. Carob is a low fat, no caffeine, chocolate substitute that is sweeter than chocolate, has a high calcium content and contains no oxalic acid like chocolate does, making the calcium more absorbable. Other candy, particularly hard candy, could be stored.

Cornstarch. One to four pounds per person for thickening gravies, sauces, soups, stews, pie fillings and puddings. Stores five to ten-plus years.

Corn syrup. Karo is used for numerous purposes, including most candy making.

Crackers. If you didn't include them under grains, consider some now. Graham, saltine and soda crackers keep two to five-plus years if protected from moisture.

Cream. Powdered sweet and sour cream could add a lot to a survival diet. Store one to two pounds of each per person. They keep two to four years and have open shelf lives of four to six months. Powdered sour cream makes about four cups per pound and can be used for cream cheese as well. Powdered sweet cream makes about nine cups per pound and makes top or whipping cream. Non-dairy creamers are also available and keep two-plus years. Dream Whip powdered whipped topping keeps similarly.

Flavorings and Extracts. Most store two-plus years and one year after opening but, because of alcohol bases, they need to be kept tightly closed to avoid evaporation and additional concentration. Almond, lemon, maple, peppermint, rum and vanilla should be considered. Lemon and lime juice keep well until opened, then need refrigeration. Lemon and orange peel granules are also available.

Food Colorings. Store a variety of colors to add appeal to food.

Frostings and Toppings. Dry and canned frosting mixes, marsh-mallows and toppings—butterscotch, caramel, chocolate and straw berry—could help add variety and interest. Cake and cookie decorations can also be stored. Most keep one year or more.

Fruits and Fillings. You might store a couple pounds of coconut, a few cans of mandarin oranges, cranberry sauce, and pie and fruit filling for special occasions. Others include maraschino cherries, blackberries, blueberries, dates, figs and mincemeat. All keep a year or longer.

Gelatin. Unflavored gelatin (Knox) keeps for years if kept dry.

Gum. Chewing gum could be a nice treat for children. It will keep for years, but may become quite hard and stale.

Herbs and Spices. Herbs and spices are essential to avoid monotony. They should be stored in a cool, dark and dry place in airtight containers to prevent evaporation of oils and aromas. Most will keep for two-plus years with whole keeping better than ground. Herbs keep less well. Buy fresh—bright, not faded, colors and strong characteristic aromas—and not in too large quantities that will loose potency prior to use. Use this list so you won't overlook any you feel necessary:

☐ Allspice: ground
☐ Anise seed
☐ Basil: sweet dried leaf,
    flakes
☐ Bay leaves
☐ Borage: leaf, seed
☐ Caraway seed

☐ Mace: ground
☐ Marjoram: sweet dried leaf,
    ground
☐ Ming: dried chopped
☐ Mustard: dry powder, seed
☐ Nutmeg: ground
☐ Onion salt

☐ Cardamon seed
☐ Celery salt
☐ Chili pepper and powder
☐ Chives
☐ Cinnamon: sticks, ground
☐ Cloves: ground, whole
☐ Coriander: ground
☐ Cumin: ground, seed
☐ Curry powder
☐ Dill: dried weed, seed
☐ Fennel seed
☐ Garlic: minced, powder, salt
☐ Ginger: ground
☐ Italian seasoning
☐ Horseradish
☐ Hot pepper sauce
☐ Lemon balm
☐ Oregano: dried leaf, ground
☐ Paprika
☐ Parsley flakes
☐ Pepper: black and white, whole and ground
☐ Pickling, poultry and pumpkin pie
☐ Red (cayenne) pepper
☐ Rosemary: whole, ground
☐ Saffron
☐ Sage: ground rubbed
☐ Savory: ground
☐ Sesame seed
☐ Tarragon: dried whole leaf
☐ Thyme: dried leaf, ground
☐ Turmeric: ground

Ice Cream. Freeze-dried ice cream doesn't resemble regular frozen ice cream, but it does make an interesting and tasty snack. There are even ice cream sandwiches available. Talk about "roughing it"!

Mushrooms. Some cans of mushrooms could spice up salads, meats and pizza. Also available freeze-dried; one pound FD equals 10 pounds of fresh.

Leavenings. Powdered dry yeast in unopened cans will keep two to three-plus years if kept cool. You may want one-half to one and a half pounds per person. It turns brown, slimy and develops a strong odor with age. Yeast should bubble within twenty minutes or it's probably dead. You can also make your own everlasting yeast sponge at home or store freeze-dried sourdough starter. Have two starts in case you accidentally lose one. If they ever turn orange, throw them out. Baking powder stores in the original cans for four to five-plus years. You can test a small amount by adding water to see if it still fizzes. About one to three pounds per person of baking powder is needed. You can make your own baking powder from baking soda and cream of tartar or calcium phosphate. Baking soda keeps many years and is useful for many things—with salt as a toothpaste, deodorant, cleaner, first aid, fire extinguisher—and you may want to store two to five pounds per person. Re-pack in glass or metal, or wrap box in plastic.

Pectin. For jams and jellies, the liquid in brown bottles should be kept in the dark. The powder must be kept dry and protected from insects. Both will keep two-plus years if kept cool.

Relishes. Most keep two-plus years. Green and ripe black olives, dill, sweet, bread and butter pickles, and relishes are the basic choices.

Rennet. Rennet is used to curdle milk for cheese and desserts. Twelve Hansen's tablets will make about ten pounds of cheese. Junket tablets come with directions for making cheeses, custards and ice cream, and are sold in the pudding and gelatin section of many supermarkets.

Sauces, Gravies and Dressings. Beef and chicken gravy mixes, canned sauces and gravies, salad dressing mixes, etc. can be considered. Other items are Soy, Tabasco, Worcestershire, A-1, cocktail, salsa, hot, barbecue and meat sauces.

Seafood. Anchovies, clams, crab, kipper snacks, oysters, sardines and shrimp can certainly add variety.

Seasoning Mixes. Beef stew, chili, enchilada, meatloaf, sloppy joe, spaghetti, taco seasoning and other mixes would be helpful at times. Like all spices they loose their potency over time.

Spreads. Ketchup keeps three to four years if kept cool and dark. Prepared yellow mustard keeps two-plus years. Sandwich spreads are also options.

Vegetables. You may want to store a quarter to a half pound of dehydrated green bell peppers, one to two pounds of onions of dehydrated (powder, chopped and sliced) and a quarter to a half pound of dehydrated celery. Other vegetables that can be stored include pimento, water chestnuts, pumpkin, asparagus, bamboo shoots and green chilis.

Vinegar. Store one to two gallons per person. Distilled keeps longer than cider, but both keep two-plus years or longer. Vinegar can evaporate if left open, and a slight cloudy appearance doesn't affect quality at all.

Vitamin and Mineral Supplements

Vitamin shelf life depends on ingredients and form. Hard-pressed tablets and soft gelatin capsules keep the longest, while chewable tablets don't keep as long because they readily absorb moisture (shows as speckled appearance). Some brands store longer than others—ask your pharmacist which keeps best—and many include expiration dates, usually conservative. Kept cool, dark, dry and in airtight containers, most store one and a half to five-plus years. Moisture destroys potency, particularly of vitamin C. Dark brown bottles help keep out light, or you can store in the original cartons. Foil seals under caps help keep air out. All supplements with iron should be kept out of the reach of children.

Concentrated Food

A number of food powders, tablets and bars are sold as compact, light-weight survival foods. Most are made from soy protein with basically the same quality protein. Some are sold as high energy sources low in calories—a contradiction of claims. Whatever their true values, remember this: no matter how concentrated or light-weight, no truly balanced food can contain more than 2600 calories per pound, and that's an average day's need. Buyer beware.

Miracle Foods

Some foods are advertised as the "perfect storage food", so let's look at the facts.

Vegetable Protein Combinations. This product is a blend of vegetable proteins—most notably beans and grains—and is normally formed into pasta and other shapes. The manufacturer of one brand claims that his "discovery" of the age-old principle of combining grains with legumes to improve protein quality is revolutionary! As balanced as their amino acid profile may be, their protein quality does not exceed that obtained by simply eating the combinations of grains and beans in the same meal. And, no matter how cheap the price, the mixing and forming of the ingredients makes them cost more than the grains and beans they are made from. On top of that, they are often sold through multi-level distribution programs, which substantially increases the cost further.

Spirulina. Dried spirulina plankton is touted by some as the "wonder food of the future" and the "ultimate survival food". It is a variety of blue-green algae similar to the familiar slimy green seaweed at the beach, and is sold to be mixed with water or juice—to disguise the taste—to make a drink that is a "complete" food with "balanced nutrients". One ad claims it is "far superior to soy beans, cheese, fish, meat, eggs or milk". The raw truth flatly refutes that claim.

While very high in protein content, the quality of the protein is less than that of either soy or peanut protein and no where near the quality of meat or milk, let alone eggs. It is the highest known source of vitamin B_{12} but is low in B_1 and B_6. It is also low in bulk, and not having enough bulk causes the body to loose muscle tone to where the digestive tract won't move food through normally. And it is very low in calories, and calories are what ultimately keep us alive. It is definitely not the "high energy" food often claimed. There is also some evidence that in substantial quantities it greatly increased the amount of uric acid in the blood, which may lead to arthritic and kidney problems.

Then there is its high cost. It retails for about twice the cost of freeze-dried steak and about ten times the cost of soy meal. Both are better quality protein. A year's supply—anywhere from five to twenty-plus pounds depending on the advertising source—will only supply 1-4% of the average calorie needs. You'd still need lots of other food to survive. Spirulina is not recommended at all as a storage food.

TABLE 9-1.A

Proximate Value of Food When Prorated Over 1 Year on a Daily Basis					
Food Cheese	Amount pro- rated	Energ kcal/ day	Protei gm/ day	Fat gm/ day	Carbo- hydrate gm/day
Milk Products					
Milk, regular nonfat, dry	50 lbs	226	22.3	0.5	32.5
Milk, instant nonfat, dry	50 lbs	223	22.2	0.4	32.1
Milk, evaporated					
13-fl oz., #1 tall can	48 cans	73	3.7	4.2	5.2
Buttermilk, dry	10 lbs	48	4.3	0.7	6.2
Cheese, cheddar, dehydrated	10 lbs	77	3.4	6.4	1.2
Cheese, Swiss, dehydrated	10 lbs	71	3.7	5.5	1.0
Cheese, cottage, freeze dried	10 lbs	82	9.5	3.4	2.7
Cheese, Parmesan	10 lbs	49	4.5	3.2	0.4
Cheez Whiz	10 lbs	36	2.0	2.7	1.0
Fats					
Oil, 3 gallons	23 lbs	253	0	28.6	0
Shortening, 6 3-lb cans	18 lbs	198	0	22.4	0
Shortening, dehydrated	10 lbs	94	1.2	8.8	1.8
Butter, dehydrated	10 lbs	92	1.2	9.1	1.6
Margarine, canned	10 lbs	89	0.1	10.1	trace
Margarine, dehydrated	10 lbs	92	1.2	9.1	1.6
Mayonnaise, 5 quarts	10 lbs	89	0.1	9.9	0.3
Miracle Whip, 4 quarts	9 lbs	49	0.1	4.7	1.6
Bacon, canned	10 lbs	85	1.1	8.9	0.1
Nuts and Seeds					
Almonds, unshelled	50 lbs	189	5.9	17.2	6.2
shelled	50 lbs	372	11.6	33.7	12.1
Brazil, unshelled	50 lbs	195	4.3	19.9	3.2
Filberts, unshelled	50 lbs	181	3.6	17.8	4.8
shelled	50 lbs	394	7.8	38.8	10.4
Pecans, unshelled	50 lbs	226	3.0	23.5	4.8
shelled	50 lbs	427	5.7	44.2	9.1
Walnuts, English, unshelled	50 lbs	182	4.1	17.9	4.4
shelled	50 lbs	405	9.2	39.8	9.8
Walnuts, black, unshelled	50 lbs	86	2.8	8.1	2.0
Peanuts, unshelled raw	50 lbs	256	11.8	21.5	8.4
shelled raw	50 lbs	350	16.2	29.5	11.6
Peanut butter, regular	10 lbs	73	3.1	6.3	2.3
Peanut butter, dehydrated	10 lbs	65	5.5	4.0	1.9
Sesame seeds	10 lbs	70	2.3	6.1	2.7
Sunflower seeds, hulled	10 lbs	70	3.0	6.9	2.5
Fruits, fresh					
Apples	50 lbs	34	0.1	0.4	8.5

TABLE 9-1.B

Proximate Value of Food When Prorated Over 1 Year on a Daily Basis					
Food	Amount pro-rated	Energ kcal/ day	Protei gm/ day	Fat gm/ day	Carbo-hydrate gm/day
Fruits, home canned					
Applesauce, sweetened	10 qts	23	trace	trace	5.9
unsweetened	10 qts	10	trace	trace	2.7
Apricots, heavy syrup	10 qts	21	0.1	trace	5.5
light syrup	10 qts	16	0.2	trace	4.2
Cherries, sweet with pits					
heavy syrup	10 qts	19	0.2	trace	4.8
light syrup	10 qts	15	0.2	trace	3.9
Peaches, heavy syrup	10 qts	19	0.1	trace	5.0
light syrup	10 qts	14	0.1	trace	3.8
Pears, heavy syrup	10 qts	19	trace	trace	4.9
light syrup	10 qts	15	trace	trace	3.9
Plums, purple, heavy syrup	10 qts	20	0.1	trace	5.2
light syrup	10 qts	15	0.1	trace	4.0
Fruits, canned					
Applesauce					
sweetened, 16-oz #303	24 cans	27	0.1	trace	7.1
unsweetened, 16-oz #303	24 cans	12	0.1	trace	3.2
Apricots					
heavy syrup, 16-oz #303	24 cans	26	0.2	trace	6.6
juice pack, 16-oz #303	24 cans	16	0.3	0.1	4.1
Cherries, sweet with pits					
heavy syrup, 16-oz #303	24 cans	23	0.3	0.1	5.8
Fruit cocktail					
heavy syrup, 16-oz #303	24 cans	23	0.1	trace	5.9
juice pack, 16-oz #303	24 cans	14	0.1	trace	4.4
Grapefruit, juice					
unsweetened, 46-oz #3	12 cans	19	0.2	0.1	4.6
Grapefruit, segments					
light syrup, 16-oz #303	24 cans	21	0.2	trace	5.3
Orange juice					
sweetened, 46-oz #3	12 cans	25	0.3	0.1	5.8
unsweetened, 46-oz #3	12 cans	22	0.4	0.1	5.2
Peaches					
heavy syrup, 16-oz #303	24 cans	23	0.1	trace	6.0
juice pack, 16-oz #303	24 cans	13	0.2	trace	3.5
Pears					
heavy syrup, 16-oz #303	24 cans	23	0.1	0.1	5.9
juice pack, 16-oz #303	24 cans	14	0.1	0.1	3.5

TABLE 9-1.C

Proximate Value of Food When Prorated Over 1 Year on a Daily Basis					
Food	Amount pro-rated	Energ kcal/ day	Protei gm/ day	Fat gm/ day	Carbo-hydrate gm/day
Pineapple					
heavy syrup, 20-oz #2	24 cans	28	0.1	trace	7.2
juice pack, 20-oz #2	24 cans	22	0.1	trace	5.6
Fruits, dried					
Apples, 24% water	10 lbs	34	0.1	0.2	8.9
Apricots, 25% water	10 lbs	32	0.6	0.1	8.3
Figs, 23% water	10 lbs	34	0.5	0.2	8.6
Peaches, 25% water	10 lbs	33	0.4	0.1	8.4
Pears, 26% water	10 lbs	33	0.4	0.2	9.8
Prunes, 28% water	10 lbs	27	0.2	0.1	7.1
Raisins, 18% water	10 lbs	36	0.3	trace	9.6
Fruits, dehydrated					
Apples, 2½% water	10 lbs	44	0.2	0.2	11.4
Applesauce, unsweetened	10 lbs	44	0.2	0.1	11.4
Apricots, 3½% water	10 lbs	41	0.7	0.1	10.5
Banana flakes, 3% water	10 lbs	42	0.5	0.1	11.0
chips (with honey and oil)	10 lbs	68	0.4	4.2	7.9
Fruit blend or mix	10 lbs	45	0.6	0.1	10.6
Grapefruit juice					
crystals, 1% water	10 lbs	47	0.6	0.1	11.2
Orange juice					
crystals, 1% water	10 lbs	47	0.6	0.2	11.0
Peaches, 3% water	10 lbs	42	0.6	0.1	10.9
Pears	10 lbs	44	0.5	0.2	9.8
Pineapple, freeze dried	10 lbs	49	0.4	0.2	12.1
Plums, freeze dried	10 lbs	44	0.4	0.1	11.5
Prunes, 2½% water	10 lbs	43	0.4	0.1	11.3
Raisins, low moisture	10 lbs	42	0.4	trace	11.4
Strawberries, freeze dried	10 lbs	42	0.7	0.2	10.7
Vegetables, fresh					
Beets, without tops	25 lbs	9	0.3	trace	2.2
Cabbage, trimmed	25 lbs	7	0.4	0.1	1.5
Carrots, without tops	25 lbs	11	0.3	trace	2.5
Onions	25 lbs	11	0.4	trace	2.5
Potatoes, white	100 lbs	76	2.1	0.1	17.2
Pumpkin	100 lbs	23	0.9	0.1	5.6
Squash, winter					
Acorn	100 lbs	42	1.4	0.1	10.6
Butternut	100 lbs	47	1.2	0.1	12.2
Hubbard	100 lbs	32	1.2	0.2	7.7

TABLE 9-1.D

Food	Amount pro-rated	Energ kcal/day	Protei gm/day	Fat gm/day	Carbo-hydrate gm/day
Proximate Value of Food When Prorated Over 1 Year on a Daily Basis					
Sweet potatoes	100 lbs	115	1.7	0.4	26.5
Taros, raw					
corms and tubers	100 lbs	102	2.0	0.2	24.7
leaves and stems	100 lbs	50	3.7	1.0	9.2
Vegetables, home canned					
Green beans	20 pts	4	0.2	trace	1.0
Beets	20 pts	8	0.2	trace	2.0
Corn, whole	20 pts	17	0.5	0.2	4.1
Peas	20 pts	15	0.9	0.1	2.7
Tomatoes, whole or juice	10 qts	5	0.2	trace	1.0
Sauerkraut	10 qts	4	0.2	trace	1.0
Vegetables, canned					
Green beans, 16-oz #303	24 cans	5	0.3	trace	1.3
Beets, 16-oz #303	24 cans	10	0.3	trace	2.4
Carrots, 16-oz #303	24 cans	8	0.2	0.1	1.9
Corn, whole wet, 17-oz #303	24 cans	21	0.6	0.2	5.0
whole vacuum, 17-oz #303	24 cans	26	0.8	0.2	6.5
cream style, 17-oz #303	24 cans	26	0.7	0.2	6.3
Peas, Alaska (Early or					
June), 16-oz #303	24 cans	20	1.0	0.1	3.7
Sweet (Sugar), 16-oz #303	24 cans	17	1.0	0.1	3.1
Potatoes, white, whole					
15-oz #303	24 cans	12	0.3	0.1	2.7
Pumpkin, 16-oz #303	24 cans	10	0.3	0.1	2.4
Sauerkraut, 16-oz #303	24 cans	5	0.3	0.1	1.2
Spinach, 15-oz #303	24 cans	5	0.6	0.1	0.8
Sweet Potatoes					
syrup pack, 16-oz #303	24 cans	34	0.3	0.1	8.2
vacuum (solid), 16-oz #303	24 cans	32	0.6	0.1	7.4
Tomatoes					
whole, 15-oz #303	24 cans	6	0.3	0.1	1.2
sauce, 8-oz can	24 cans	6	0.3	trace	1.3
paste, 6-oz can	24 cans	9	0.4	trace	2.1
juice, 46-oz #3	12 cans	8	0.4	trace	1.9
Vegetables, dehydrated					
Green beans	10 lbs	38	2.3	0.1	7.1
Beets	10 lbs	41	1.5	0.1	8.8
Cabbage, 4% water	10 lbs	38	1.5	0.2	9.2
Carrots, 4% water	10 lbs	42	0.8	0.2	10.1
Celery	10 lbs	39	1.6	0.1	7.8

TABLE 9-1.E

Food	Amount pro-rated	Energ kcal/day	Protei gm/day	Fat gm/day	Carbo-hydrate gm/day
Proximate Value of Food When Prorated Over 1 Year on a Daily Basis					
Corn, whole sweet	10 lbs	47	1.5	0.4	9.5
Mushrooms, freeze dried	10 lbs	37	3.2	0.2	5.8
Onions, 4% water	10 lbs	44	1.1	0.2	10.2
Peas	10 lbs	42	3.2	0.2	7.0
Potatoes					
granules with milk	10 lbs	44	1.4	0.1	9.7
granules without milk	10 lbs	44	1.0	0.1	10.0
flakes without milk	10 lbs	45	0.9	0.1	10.4
diced	10 lbs	44	0.9	0.1	10.1
hashed browns	10 lbs	46	0.5	0.1	10.2
sliced	10 lbs	44	1.0	0.1	9.9
Peppers, green bell	10 lbs	29	1.4	0	7.7
Spinach	10 lbs	37	3.9	0.2	4.8
Squash, freeze dried	10 lbs	44	1.1	0.1	11.0
Sweet potatoes, 2.8% water	10 lbs	47	0.5	0.1	11.2
Tomato, crystals, 1% water	10 lbs	38	1.4	0.3	8.5
Sugars					
Sugar, white granulated or powder	50 lbs	239	0	0	61.8
brown	50 lbs	232	0	0	59.9
Honey	50 lbs	189	0.2	0	51.1
Jams and preserves, 7 pts	10 lbs	34	0.1	trace	8.7
Jellies, 7 pts	10 lbs	34	trace	trace	8.8
Gelatin dessert	9 lbs	41	1.1	0	9.8
Cane syrup	10 lbs	33	0	0	8.4
Corn syrup, light or dark	10 lbs	36	0	0	9.3
Maple syrup	10 lbs	31	0	0	8.1
Sorghum syrup	10 lbs	32	0	0	8.4
Molasses, blackstrap, 2 gal	23 lbs	61	0	0	15.7
Powdered drink mix	11 lbs	53	0	0	13.4
Tang, 2 #10 cans	11 lbs	53	0	0	13.4
Pudding mixes (average)	10 lbs	46	0.1	0.1	11.8
Tapioca	10 lbs	44	0.1	trace	10.7
Egg custard mix, bake	10 lbs	53	2.6	0.9	8.3
no-bake	10 lbs	52	0.9	0	11.3
Eggs, dehydrated					
Whole	10 lbs	74	5.8	5.1	0.5
Scrambling mix, with milk and oil	10 lbs	70	3.3	4.9	38.4
Whites, powder	10 lbs	46	10.0	trace	0.7

Sardines

TABLE 9-1.F

Proximate Value of Food When Prorated Over 1 Year on a Daily Basis					
Food	Amount pro-rated	Energ kcal/ day	Protei gm/ day	Fat gm/ day	Carbo-hydrate gm/day
Yolks	10 lbs	83	4.1	7.0	0.3
Scrambled, with butter freeze dried	10 lbs	63	4.8	3.2	3.2
Scrambled, pre-cooked freeze dried	10 lbs	81	5.8	4.6	1.2
Meat, poultry and fish, canned					
Chicken, 6¾-oz can	24 cans	25	2.7	1.5	0
Corn beef, 12-oz can	24 cans	48	5.7	2.7	0
Ham, cured	10 lbs	24	2.3	1.5	0.1
deviled, 6¾-oz can	24 cans	44	1.8	4.1	0
Potted meat, beef, chicken or turkey, 3¼-oz can	24 cans	15	1.1	1.2	0
Prem, 12-oz can	24 cans	79	2.6	7.1	0.8
Salmon, pink, 16-oz can	24 cans	42	6.1	1.8	0
red, 16-oz can	24 cans	51	6.1	2.8	0
Roast beef, 12-oz can	24 cans	50	5.6	2.9	0
Spam, 12-oz can	24 cans	66	3.4	5.6	0.3
Treet, 12-oz can	24 cans	82	2.9	7.1	1.1
Tuna, oil pack, 6-oz can undrained	48 cans	64	5.5	4.6	0
drained solids	48 cans	37	5.5	1.5	0
water pack, 6-oz can	48 cans	29	6.2	0.2	0
Turkey, 6¾-oz can	24 cans	25	2.6	1.6	0
Vienna sausage, 5-oz can	48 cans	45	2.6	3.7	0.1
Meat, poultry and fish, freeze dried					
Beef, diced, pre-cooked	10 lbs	67	8.8	2.8	0
Beef, patties, raw	10 lbs	78	5.8	5.8	0
Beef, ribeye steak, raw	10 lbs	71	9.6	2.5	0
Chicken, diced, pre-cooked	10 lbs	64	8.2	3.0	0
Cod, fillet steaks	10 lbs	58	11.1	0	0
Ham, diced, pre-cooked	10 lbs	87	5.2	7.0	0
Pork chops, raw	10 lbs	64	7.1	3.5	0
Sausage, patties, raw	10 lbs	73	5.4	4.9	0.5
Shrimp, Pacific	10 lbs	55	10.4	0	0
Tuna, pre-cooked	10 lbs	83	11.7	5.8	0
Turkey, diced, pre-cooked	10 lbs	66	9.1	2.2	0
Meat, dry					
Beef jerky	10 lbs	46	5.5	1.8	0

TABLE 9-1.G

Food	Amount pro-rated	Energ kcal/day	Protei gm/day	Fat gm/day	Carbo-hydrate gm/day
Proximate Value of Food When Prorated Over 1 Year on a Daily Basis					
Meat Substitutes					
Textured soy protein unflavored	50 lbs	218	34.2	trace	19.9
T.V.P. chunks					
beef flavored	50 lbs	263	47.6	0.9	28.6
chicken flavored	50 lbs	211	32.3	1.8	16.5
ham flavored	50 lbs	281	24.0	15.5	11.7
bacon flavored bits	10 lbs	49	5.5	2.6	3.0
Grains, dry					
Barley, pearled	100 lbs	434	10.2	1.2	97.9
Buckwheat	100 lbs	416	14.5	3.0	90.6
Corn, field	100 lbs	433	11.1	4.8	89.7
Corn grits	100 lbs	450	10.8	1.0	97.1
Cornmeal	100 lbs	441	11.4	4.8	91.6
Flour, all-purpose	100 lbs	452	13.0	1.2	94.6
Millet	100 lbs	406	12.3	3.6	90.6
Oatmeal, rolled oats	100 lbs	485	17.6	9.2	84.8
Popcorn	100 lbs	450	14.8	5.8	89.6
Rice, brown	100 lbs	447	9.3	2.4	96.2
white	100 lbs	451	8.3	0.5	99.9
Rye	100 lbs	415	15.0	2.1	91.2
Sorghum	100 lbs	413	13.7	4.1	90.7
Triticale	100 lbs	410	21.4	1.3	71.2
Wheat, whole-grain, hard					
red winter, 12.3% protein	100 lbs	410	15.3	2.2	89.1
red spring, 14% protein	100 lbs	410	17.4	2.7	85.9
Wheat, rolled	100 lbs	422	12.3	2.5	94.7
flakes	100 lbs	440	12.7	2.0	99.9
Pastas					
Macaroni	10 lbs	46	1.6	0.1	9.3
Noodles, egg	10 lbs	48	1.6	0.6	8.9
Spaghetti	10 lbs	46	1.6	0.1	9.3
Legumes, dry					
Beans, white (Navy, Great Northern)	50 lbs	211	13.9	1.0	38.1
Beans, red (Kidney)	50 lbs	213	14.0	0.9	38.5
Beans, pinto	50 lbs	217	14.2	0.7	39.6
Beans, black and brown	50 lbs	211	13.9	0.9	38.0
Beans, lima	50 lbs	214	12.7	1.0	39.8

TABLE 9-1.H

Proximate Value of Food When Prorated Over 1 Year on a Daily Basis					
Food	Amount pro-rated	Energ kcal/day	Protei gm/day	Fat gm/day	Carbo-hydrate gm/day
Beans, garbanzo (chickpea)	50 lbs	224	12.7	3.0	37.9
Lentils, whole	50 lbs	211	15.3	0.7	37.3
Peas, blackeye (cowpea)	50 lbs	213	14.2	0.9	38.3
Peas, green or yellow					
split	50 lbs	216	15.0	0,6	39.0
whole	50 lbs	211	15.0	0.8	37.5
Soybeans	50 lbs	250	21.2	11.0	20.8
Soups, condensed					
Beef noodle, 10¾-oz can	48 cans	23	1.3	0.9	2.3
Chicken, cream, 10¾-oz can	48 cans	32	1.0	1.9	2.7
Chicken gumbo, 10¾-oz can	48 cans	18	1.0	0.5	2.4
Chicken noodle, 10¾-oz can	48 cans	21	1.1	0.6	2.6
Clam chowder, 10¾-oz can	48 cans	35	1.6	1.1	4.6
Minestrone, 10½-oz can	48 cans	34	1.6	1.1	4.5
Mushroom, cream, 10¾-oz	48 cans	44	0.8	3.2	3.4
Tomato, 10¾-oz can	48 cans	29	0.6	0.8	5.1
Vegetable beef, 10½-oz can	48 cans	25	1.6	0.7	3.1
Soups, dehydrated					
Beef noodle	10 lbs	48	1.7	0.9	8.1
Chicken noodle	10 lbs	48	1.8	1.2	7.2
Chicken rice	10 lbs	44	1.1	0.8	7.8
Onion	10 lbs	43	1.7	1.3	6.7
Pea, green	10 lbs	45	2.8	0.5	7.7
Tomato vegetable					
with noodles	10 lbs	43	1.1	1.0	7.8
Miscellaneous					
Beef and vegetable stew					
15-oz #303 can	24 cans	22	1.6	0.9	2.0
Spaghetti in tomato and					
cheese, 14¾-oz can	24 cans	21	0.6	0.2	4.2
Spaghetti with meatballs					
14¾-oz can	24 cans	28	1.3	1.1	3.1
Bouillon	10 lbs	15	2.5	0.4	0.6
Carbo flour	10 lbs	22	0.6	0.2	10.0
Crackers, graham	10 lbs	48	1.0	1.2	9.1
saltine	10 lbs	54	1.1	1.5	8.9
soda	10 lbs	55	1.1	1.6	8.8
Cream, sour, powder	10 lbs	83	1.9	7.0	2.9
sweet, powder	10 lbs	93	1.7	9.0	1.2

TABLE 9-1.I

Food	Amount pro-rated	Energ kcal/day	Protei gm/day	Fat gm/day	Carbo-hydrate gm/day
Proximate Value of Food When Prorated Over 1 Year on a Daily Basis					
Chocolate, baking	10 lbs	63	1.3	6.6	3.6
milk	10 lbs	65	1.0	4.0	7.1
semisweet	10 lbs	63	0.5	4.4	7.1
Cocoa	10 lbs	37	2.1	2.9	6.0
Hot chocolate mix	10 lbs	49	1.2	1.3	9.2
Geletin, dry	10 lbs	42	10.6	trace	0
Marshmallow	10 lbs	40	0.2	trace	10.0

10

FOOD PREPARATION EQUIPMENT AND SUPPLIES

Equipment and supplies are needed to properly prepare storage food. Some may differ from those normally used, and their selection criteria should be appropriately modified to meet crisis situations.

Electric power may be nonexistent or only available on an intermittent basis during crises. You won't want to depend exclusively on the electric appliances found in most kitchens. For those you consider indispensable, you should have a non-electric alternative. Small twelve-volt power converters are also available that allow most appliances to be powered by a car's alternator—assuming the car has gas! Secondly, most electric appliances are more difficult to maintain and repair without the right spare parts, and replacement may be impossible. Many of the "finer things in life" are also breakable. So plan head now by selecting equipment based on durability, simplicity and ease of repair.

Processing Tools

Using storage foods often means doing your own processing and can require an assortment of tools. Some you may already have, while others you'll need to buy after carefully considering your requirements.

Grain Mills

A grain mill is the single most important tool for those using whole grains and should be bought carefully. Whatever type or brand you choose, be sure it is a quality mill. A poor one will be inconvenient, give poor results and probably never be used until absolutely necessary.

When looking at the alternatives you need to have first made some basic decisions and understand your particular needs. Do you want it to grind fine flour for baking, crack wheat for cereals, or both? Are you going to need it for hard, dry grains like wheat or will you also be using it for soybeans and making peanut butter? Will you use it regularly and will it be convenient where it will be stored? Now you can examine each mill. Does it perform as advertised? Does it adjust to the variety of settings you need and produce flour texture suitable to you? Is it quick enough, not messy during use, and easy to clean? Is the general design efficient and safe? Is it built to last or wear a long time, and is it simple and easy to repair? Now, consider the alternatives.

Basically mills come in electric or manual models and grind with a stone, a metal burr plate or some combination of the two.

Metal plates are more versatile, being able to handle many oily or wet substances without clogging or absorbing the oil. They usually will do soybeans, some will take peanuts, and a few will even grind dry bones into bonemeal. If they do gum up, they can be washed and they can be sharpened when they become dull. Get quality, however, since the cheaper plated metals often flake off into the product.

Stones are more temperamental. Grinding grains or legumes containing more than 10-12% moisture creates a gluey substance that glazes the stone—reducing the grinding action—and can clog the machine. It may burn on fast-turning stones in electric mills, ruining the stone. Oily legumes like soybeans and peanuts will gum up the stone and make it useless. And although you can clean it somewhat by running a handful of popcorn through on a coarse setting, you should never wash the stone. Stones also produce more powder when cracking grain or splitting peas. They do have their advantages, though. Generally they make finer flour, wear considerably longer, and create less heat at finer settings. The grind also improves with age as the stones grind themselves to a perfect fit.

Electric Mills

For effortless convenience you can't beat an electric mill. They run all the way from coffee mills with special pulverising blades for coarse flour for under $50 to those $275 and up that often produce fine cake and pastry flour. Housings may be metal, plastic, formica or wood. Be aware that wood is harder to clean and weevil can burrow into it and make themselves at home eating the leftover flour. Untreated wood also absorbs moisture that helps attract weevil.

Grinding high-moisture grain in an electric stone mill can crack the stone. The heat turns the moisture into steam with the expansion causing the cracking. If you see steam coming from the mill during use, turn it off and dry the grain before trying it again. Faster grinds with either type create hotter temperatures, but both run considerably cooler than commercial milling and neither affects the nutritional value appreciably because of the short time involved.

Among the best is the K-Tec Kitchen Mill ($250). Also check out the mills offered through the major preparedness suppliers (see Chapter 32). Lehman's has mills from $275 all the way to $1500 for a commercial size! You might consider Retsel's Mill Rite at $420. Often used mills can be found at a fraction of their original cost, and many will perform satisfactorily.

K-Tec Kitchen mill

Lehman electric mill

Converting Electric Mills

Many electrics had conversion kits for hand or bicycle operation at additional cost; maybe some still do. Supposedly if the electricity is out you simply power the mill with one of the conversions. In reality it is usually not advisable. Electrics mills are made to turn at 1500-2000 RPM and being turned by hand at sixty RPM gives a minimal to non-existent output. One individual reported less than a cup of flour after twenty minutes of arduous hand cranking. And arduous it is. The motor may spin the stone effortlessly but turning it by hand is quite difficult.

An even more serious problem rarely mentioned is that, with the exception of the Retsel—the best for hand conversion, when you turn the stone by hand you also turn the motor. That not only takes additional effort but, because you can't turn the shaft as smoothly as the motor, you'll probably wear out the bearings and ruin the motor altogether. Bicycle conversions are a bit easier on the muscle power requirement and won't ruin the bearings as quickly. However, they still require a bicycle, take up a lot of space and cost more. Often the price of a conversion kit would pay for a hand mill and then some.

Hand Mills

Hand mills are generally much cheaper than electric mills, and some can be adapted for bicycles and motors. They are usually slower grinding—taking from four to more than twenty minutes for a pound of fine flour—and require effort. Most will demand heavy work that will be hot, tiring, and really strain the biceps. And don't be fooled by tests with soft grains such as buckwheat, millet, or oats—try the harder wheat! Some hand mills require re-grinding wheat before it's fine enough for flour, and they often wobble on coarse settings, producing flour with uneven texture. Check the quality of the flour, the amount produced for the effort, and the ease and comfort of the grinding operation before deciding.

Most preparedness dealers sell a selection of hand mills, both with stone and metal burrs. Lehman's has a hand mill ($159) and a roller mill for cereal that has an attachment for flour ($134 for both). Retsel offers the Little Ark ($111) and the Uni-Ark ($121). The Corona grain mill is $50 from Atlan Formularies. It would be good to actually try before you buy to see how easy it is to turn and what kind of flour it produces. Avoid cheap pot-metal mills of any kind.

Lehman grain mill

Best of Both Worlds

So buy an electric mill for normal use and a manual one for when the power is out. Or buy a hand mill that just about combines the best of both. There are two mills that fit that description:

The Country Living Grain Mill is made in the USA, costs $366 or so (depending on source), is an almond color and is available from Walton, Yellowstone Trading and Homestead Products among others.

Country Living mill

The Diamant Mill from Denmark is made from cast iron (making it very heavy), has a green finish and costs $599 from Lehman's.

Both use iron/steel burrs and will quickly mill everything from very fine pastry flour to beans, nuts, and cracking grain for cereal and even animal feed. Either would be a good choice. Both could be converted to motorized operation if desired—all you need is a v-belt, pulley and motor.

Ideally, get an electric mill and one of the

above mills. If you can't afford both, I recommend an electric with a less expensive hand mill, or the Country Living or Diamant by itself.

Bread Mixers

If you plan on making much bread you'll want a good mixer capable of handling dough. Again, you may want a manual dough mixer for "no power" situations and an electric for the rest.

There are any number of good mixers on the market, but be sure to get one with enough power to regularly mix bread. KitchenAid and the heavier Sunbeam Mixmasters are adequate with the K-Tec Champ ($330), Bosch and the Magic Mill DLX 2000 Assistent among the best.

Magic Mill mixer

Other Tools

You should consider a good ball-bearing rotary egg beater, a meat grinder, a potato masher, and a manual heavy-duty can opener. Have a good set of kitchen knives—Forschner, Gerber, Henckel, and Wusthof- Trident are all good brands—with a French chef's, slicer, paring, boning, and serrated bread knives at a minimum. Fillet and chopping knives would also be handy as would butchering knives—Dexter-Russell are good—and skinning knives. Get a butchering set of four, six, eight, and ten-inch drop point blades of high carbon steel with the tang and blade forged from a single piece of stock. A six-inch full-curved blade makes the best skinner. Kyocera makes some very good and sharp knives of ceramic zirconia you might consider, also. Expensive but nice and sharp.

Whatever knives you have, it is important for safe and easy use to keep them sharp. That means a sharpening steel or ceramic rod to straighten the blade edges each time used and a whetstone, diamond-impregnated rod, or other abrasive for occasional sharpening.

A blender would be good for mixing powdered milk, but wire whisks can be use. Also you may want to have:

☐ food and meat slicer	☐ manual pasta maker	☐ flour sifter
☐ hand ice cream freezer	☐ food grater	☐ juicers
☐ kitchen shears	☐ poultry shears	☐ wire whisks

☐ potato peeler   ☐ chopping block   ☐ bread board
☐ bottle opener

Cooking Equipment

If you plan on cooking on wood stoves, in fireplaces or over camp-fires, you'd better have a set of pots and pans equal to the task. The light-weight, sophisticated steel or aluminum ones with the non-stick coatings will develop hot spots and quickly burn through if used directly on or over a fire. You'd be wise to get a good set of heavy cast iron pots, kettles, skillets, griddles and dutch ovens. Cast iron works best for long, slow cooking over all heats, is easy to clean and lasts forever if properly seasoned. It also can be buried under coals and conserves heat. Fireplaces must also have an iron rod or swinging arm crane if you expect to suspend kettles in them.

A pressure cooker will cut the cooking time for beans and dehydrated foods. Whatever you cook in, never cook in galvanized items because they can give you zinc poisoning. And remember that many kitchen wares are glass or otherwise breakable, and you should have some more durable alternatives.

Also:

☐ fireplace corn   ☐ reflector oven   ☐ bread pans
    popper
☐ measuring cups   ☐ wooden utensils   ☐ shredders
☐ candy   ☐ meat   ☐ strainers
    thermometer   thermometer
☐ cookie sheets   ☐ muffin tins   ☐ waffle iron
☐ hand toaster   ☐ colander   ☐ grills
☐ roasting pans   ☐ rolling pin   ☐ spoons
☐ spatulas   ☐ scales   ☐ ladles
☐ dipper   ☐ baker's scraper   ☐ hot pads
☐ meat mallets   ☐ ice crusher   ☐ measuring spoons
☐ timer   ☐ cake/pie pans

Cookbooks

Although you may need to make some substitutions, many of your regular recipes will be usable. However, you may want some specialized cookbooks for recipes covering particular foods you plan on storing such as whole grains, legumes, powdered milk and dehydrated foods. Also, because they are so different from what most people are used to, a book or two on wood stove and fireplace cooking may be real helps if you plan on using either as an alternative cooking method. Some books are listed in Chapter 31.

Eating, Cleaning and Kitchen Supplies

Stainless steel utensils and dishes could solve the breakage problem. Also consider disposable utensils and paper napkins, plates, and cups for use when water is in low supply. Store all paper products in a dry and somewhat cool area and protect from rodents.

Also:

☐ dish drain & rack	☐ dish pan	☐ steel wool
☐ dish detergent	☐ scouring pads	☐ cheesecloth
☐ wax paper	☐ plastic bags	☐ aluminum foil
☐ garbage bags	☐ grocery bags	☐ paper towels
☐ plastic wrap	☐ mouse traps	☐ rat poison

☐ extra lids to re-close dehydrated food cans (both #2½ and #10)

Special Needs

Butter-making. A hand or electric butter churn. A plain glass jar can do the same thing, but it's slower. Butter molds would be nice.

Cheese-making. Instructions, cheesecloth, dairy thermometer and a large enamel or stainless steel double boiler. A cheese press would be good, but you can make your own from various materials.

Yogurt-making. A yogurt maker—or make your own, again.

11

EMERGENCY WATER SUPPLY

Without water a person will soon suffer exhaustion, dehydration, cramps, heat stroke and illness. Death will occur within four to ten days. Water is also necessary for food preparation and minimal sanitation needs. And you never know when your normal sources of supply might become polluted with disease, contaminated with chemicals, or poisoned by terrorists. Further, your supply may be shut off completely due to drought, power outages, labor disputes, floods, landslides, earthquakes or nuclear war. The only viable solution is to have your own water reserves and be able to purify additional water if required.

Water Storage

The average person in the United States uses about 6,500 gallons of water a year. Obviously much less would be needed under crisis conditions. But, because it is bulky, heavy and hard to contain, it is impractical for most people to store even an emergency supply for an entire year. However, assuming only temporary disruptions of an ongoing source of supply, you should store at least a two or three week supply (the latter allows a week to repair waterlines, etc. after a two-week disruption). The amount needed for that period will vary depending on a person's age, physical condition and activity level, the type of food consumed, the environment, the climate and the season.

Minimum needs, for drinking and cooking only, are a half gallon (two liters) per person per day. Hot environments—weather, climates, or hot and humid fallout shelters—can double that amount. Infants, children, nursing mothers, the ill (particularly those with diarrhea) and those doing heavy physical labor may require more. I recommend storing twenty to thirty gallons per person for the two to three-week period. That amount allows a half gallon per day for drinking, a half gallon per day for hygiene (brushing teeth, bathing, cleaning dishes and clothing), two gallons per week for cooking and a gallon per week reserve. If you store much dehydrated food, store an additional two to five gallons per person.

How to store

Water can be stored in both portable and permanent containers made from plastic, glass, fiberglass, or enamel-lined metal. Never use any container that has previously contained fuel, poisons, or other toxic chemicals or materials because minute amounts may remain in the pores of the container material. All containers of water should be clearly labeled and dated.

Used milk cartons, bleach jugs and empty canning jars can be used. Be sure to wash them thoroughly prior to use. Or you can purchase food-grade plastic buckets, drums, or barrels up to 55-gallon size. Some of the best storage containers are the heavy-duty five-gallon polypropylene buckets with very tight-fitting gasketed lids, handles and pop-up pouring spouts. They are also stackable. Water beds shouldn't be used because their materials contain pesticidal chemicals, and they also often use inorganic chemical compounds as conditioners that leave unsafe residues in the water that can't be entirely removed by many purifiers.

Larger amounts of water can be stored in swimming pools, large underground tanks, cistern/reservoirs, or by connecting a tank directly into the main water main to ensure always-fresh water. The tank should have a secondary outlet with a hand pump and anti-syphon valves on its main outlet and inlet.

Large containers are more usable with a hand pump; a larger rotary pump would be better for larger tanks, fire fighting, etc. and a high volume high pressure pump might also be considered. Store spare parts, particularly pump cylinder leathers and rope gaskets.

Water stored in containers for any appreciable length of time should be "conditioned", using either of the following methods, to prevent the growth of organisms in it:

Bleach: use eight drops per gallon of clear water or half teaspoon per five gallon container and let stand about twenty minutes. Then if you can still smell chlorine it can be stored; if not, retreat. Bleach loses potency with age and should be rotated yearly and kept tightly-capped in a cool location.

Heat: can the water by filling clean jars or cans to within a half to one inch of the top and then placing them in a pressure cooker for five minutes at ten psi or boiling in a water bath (twenty minutes for quart, twenty-five minutes for a half gallon). The water will keep for years.

Water must be stored where it will not freeze and break the container nor be accidentally contaminated. It should be sampled on a regular basis, perhaps every three to six months. If the water smells or looks dark, cloudy, or tastes bad, it should be changed. Water that has lost the air normally trapped in it tastes flat, but that can be reversed by shaking the container vigorously or by pouring the water back and forth between containers. A kitchen blender will also work.

Purification

Contaminated water can carry bacteria, viruses and amoebae causing diseases such as dysentery, cholera, typhoid and infectious hepatitis. It can also contain harmful parasites, chemicals, pesticides, heavy metals and radioactivity as well as be filled with algae, sediment and silt particles, and have a bad odor and taste. Since many of these pollutants can't be readily detected, all water from unknown sources or of uncertain purity should be purified prior to using for drinking, cooking, preparing food and drinks, or brushing teeth.

Although there are many methods of "purifying" water, they work with varying degrees of effectiveness on possible pollutants and none is absolutely perfect. Examine the methods carefully and choose those that will best fit the expected problems. Perhaps some combination of methods would be best. My recommendation would be to store iodine crystals or tablets along with one of the better filters.

Prior to purifying any water containing suspended particles it is always best to remove the particles by allowing them to settle to the bottom or by straining through several layers of a paper towel or clean cloth. Use ground water if at all possible but if you are forced to use surface water avoid sources containing floating material or with a dark color or odor.

The methods of purifying water are:

Boiling

Vigorously boiling water for one full minute will kill all bacteria, but other harmful microorganisms may require up to three minutes. The time should be doubled for each 5,000 feet of altitude and if the water is dirty. Complete sterility may take boiling up to twenty minutes at fifteen pounds in a pressure cooker. Boiling also removes some volatile chemicals but doesn't get rid of other chemicals or particulate contaminants. The flat taste of boiled water can be improved with the same methods used for stored water.

Chemical Disinfection

Iodine and chlorine are the principle chemicals used for disinfection of water. Either, with care, will make water safe from most harmful bacteria and other organisms, but neither kills sheep liver flukes nor removes sediment, radioactivity, or any possible chemical contaminants. They give the water a chemical odor and taste which can be concealed by punch powder or removed with a carbon filter.

The exact amount of either required for complete disinfection depends on the temperature of the water, its alkalinity, amount of suspended solids, and the quantity and type of dissolved organic compounds. This "guessing game" can largely be solved by adding obviously excessive amounts, necessary only with highly polluted water, which are then removed with an activated carbon filter. A chlorine comparator test kit can be purchased from a swimming pool supply or discount store to test for chlorine residual. If water contains too much chlorine to taste good, it can be made more palatable by letting it stand exposed to the air for a few hours or by aerating several times.

Iodine is the most dependable of the two because it is less affected by heavy organic pollution and alkalinity and is effective over a wider temperature range. However, a few people are sensitive to it, particularly those being treated for hyperthyroidism. It is also not recommended for pregnant women, and may lead to goiter problems in some if used for long periods of time.

Chlorine, on the other hand, is not very effective in cold, alkaline water and may be useless against bacteria in water with high organic pollution. It also combines with the organic matter to form THMs (trihalomethanes), suspected of causing cancer.

The following suggested doses should be doubled if the water is cold (below 47^0 F or 8^0 C) or cloudy, colored or muddy.

Iodine
1. Iodine Crystals: USP grade resublimed iodine. It kills the hardiest organisms including algae, bacteria and their spores, viruses, amoebae and their infective cysts. The crystals have an unlimited shelf life and are not affected by temperature; they must however be kept tightly sealed to prevent vaporization. They are available from chemical supply stores and some pharmacies.

   For treating small quantities of water, place four to eight grams in a one-ounce wide-mouth clear glass bottle with a leak-proof hard plastic bakelite cap. The bottle can be pre-marked in ten milliliter segments for easier measuring; the cap holds about 2½ ml. This bottle can be repeatedly used by filling it with water, shaking vigorously for thirty to sixty seconds, letting the crystals settle out and then pouring the saturated solution into the water to be treated. Use 12½ ml per quart (liter) at 77^0 F (25^0 C) for fifteen minutes. At 40^0 F (4^0 C) use twenty ml. Use half the dose for twice the time for a milder taste.

POLAR PURE is a brand name of iodine crystals in a bottle with a built-in thermometer; you simply fill the bottle with water, wait the prescribed time (colder water takes longer) and then use the solution to disinfect the water. One bottle will treat up to 2,000 quarts of water.

Don't swallow any crystals because they are poisonous and can make you severally ill. They can also create toxic fumes if exposed to the air in a small enclosed space.

2. Iodine Tablets: tetraglycine hydroperiodide, sold under the brand names Potable Aqua, Globaline and Coghlan's. Some contain a buffer to increase effectiveness in alkaline water. Shelf life may be up to four years in an amber wax-sealed bottle at room temperatures. A temperature of 120^0 F (49^0 C) reduces shelf life to only six months, and exposure to air for four days reduces effectiveness by one third. Tablets change from gray to yellow as they lose potency. Use one tablet per quart for thirty minutes.

3. 2% Tincture of Iodine: household iodine commonly found in medicine cabinets and first aid kits. Has a short shelf life and should be stored in dark glass bottles. Palatability is not the best. Use five drops per quart for thirty minutes.

Chlorine

1. Bleach: ordinary household bleach, liquid or powder, containing sodium hypochlorite (be sure it's the only active ingredient). Some have blueing chemical added that may give a bad taste. Chlorine evaporates from open bottles and even into the air space within bottles as the liquid level drops. Expect a two-year shelf life at best and double the dose if over a year old. Use eight drops per gallon (one scant teaspoon per ten gallons), stir or agitate and then wait thirty minutes. If there isn't a slight chlorine odor, repeat and wait an additional fifteen minutes.

2. High-test granular calcium hypochlorite: roughly 70% available chlorine. Dissolve heaping teaspoon (about one-quarter ounce) per two gallons water to make a stock solution. One pint of this stock solution will treat 12½ gallons of water.

3. Halazone Tablets. May be useless in water containing heavy organic pollution and against resistant forms of viruses and amoebic cysts. Shelf life is two years at room temperatures if sealed. Exposure to air for forty-eight hours decreases potency 75% and shelf life is only five months at 89^0 F (32^0 C). One tablet per quart for thirty minutes.

Mechanical Filtering

Columns of sand, clay, or other porous material can physically strain some impurities from water. Commercial filters, available in sizes from small portable units to large central systems, generally use two methods, sometimes combined: activated carbon and microfiltration. Both types remove most suspended particles and, therefore, clog easily in water containing lots of sediment or algae. Although slow, pre-filtering the water through a basket-type paper coffee filter will greatly reduce this problem.

Activated carbon has a honey-combed internal structure that is highly adsorptive. It improves the taste and odor of water and removes any chlorine, chloroform, hydrogen sulfide, THMs and other hydrocarbons. It also removes or reduces the concentration of many organic chemicals, including pesticides and herbicides, industrial chemicals and compounds like PCB, PBB and TCE, dissolved organics, heavy metals and some trace minerals. Bacteria and viruses are only partially removed and fluoride, nitrates, salts and asbestos fibers are unaffected. Minute pieces of carbon sometimes break off into the water. Carbon filters are more effective the fresher they are and the more carbon they contain.

Microfilters are basically of two types: ceramic and fiber. Ceramic filters with a 250-350 micron pore size are used as permanent in-line sediment filters cleaned periodically by backflushing. Other ceramic filters, often with submicron pore size, are used to filter out cysts, bacteria and even viruses. Recommended effective pore sizes are two microns or less for amoebic cysts, .2 micron for bacteria and .01 micron for viruses. They remove parasites, fungi, radioactive solids, asbestos and fiberglass fibers. Dissolved minerals, many toxic chemicals and salts are not affected nor will the filters purify brackish or salt water.

Fiber filters have five to sixty micron pore sizes and are not as effective as ceramic. They are used mainly for removing sediment and, depending on the water quality, may require frequent replacement.

Silver in trace amounts is often infused in the filter material. This supposedly inhibits bacteria trapped by the filter from multiplying on its surface, resulting in a "bacteriostatic" filter. Its effectiveness is debatable and its use allows minute amounts of silver to enter the filtered water.

An ion-exchange resin bed is sometimes used in combination with a filter. Because most bacterial and collodial contaminants are charged, the oppositely-charged resin materials help remove them. The resins also remove fluoride, calcium, magnesium, soluble iron, nitrates, silica and silicates, sodium, sulfate, dissolved solids, copper, arsenic, heavy metals and selenium. They do not remove organic chemicals nor all microorganisms.

NOTE ON EPA REGISTRATION: Many filters are sold under the mistaken notion that an EPA registration number proves their effectiveness as a water purifier. Not so. The EPA classifies water treatment units into one of three categories:

1. Units that simply filter with no other claims need not be registered with the EPA.
2. Filters that use silver, because it is considered a pesticide, must be registered with the EPA. A registration number is given if it is proven indeed bacteriostatic, if it does not allow more than fifty ppb (parts per billion) of silver into the water and if all other claims are proved.
3. A unit is considered a purification device and receives an establishment number if it removes a specified minimum of the cysts, bacteria and viruses from reasonable clear, microbiologically suspect water.

With that understanding, there are a number of filters and purifiers that will meet your needs. The following filters and purifiers are available at most sporting goods stores and major preparedness dealers are currently recommended (and where not generally available an address is given in Chapter 32):

Katadyn water filters

Katadyn Pocket Filter ($200, replacement filter $165): Small portable twenty ounce unit with a .2 micron clay candle that can be cleaned periodically with a nylon brush supplied. A built-in hydraulic

Katadyn Pocket

pump produces the **Katadyn Siphon filter**
necessary fifty psi   **Katadyn Expedition**
pressure and delivers a quart (liter) per
minute. Infinite shelf life. Also available are the Mini ($90), the Combi,
the TRK Drip, a much slower (quart per hour) Siphon Filter and the
large Expedition that delivers one gallon (four liters) per minute.

First-Need (General Ecology) Deluxe ($86, $39 replacement
canister), Trav-L-Pure ($144) and Base Camp ($507) chemical-free

purifiers. They also have the Microlite water
filter ($35). General Ecology makes the First-
Need and Seagull purifiers using the same
basic filter technology.

Seagull (General Ecology) IV X-1P ($465,
$68 replacement cartridge) "structured matrix"
chemical-free purifier with a manual pump.
One of the best, filters to .1 micron nominal
and .4 micron absolute. Removes pesticides,
herbicides and some chemicals.

Seagull IV X-IP LTF

PUR Voyageur ($75, $40 .3 micron replacement cartridge, up to 100
gallons per cartridge, quart per minute, 11 ounces), Scout ($90, 14
ounces) and Explorer ($130, 1.5 quarts per minute) purifiers, and the
Guide ($80) and Hiker ($60, quart per minute) microfilters.

MSR Miniworks filter ($70, .6 quart minute, 14 ounces).

Other Methods

Reverse osmosis filters are actually mechanical filters using a
porous membrane. They require relatively high water pressure (fifty
pounds) to force the water through the membrane and most use
electricity. These filters remove most possible contaminants from water
but leave mercury, chlorine and simple compounds like chloroform and
phenol. They have a membrane life of one to four years and are slow.

Because they remove salts they can be used to purify brackish or sea per water.

Distillers also remove most contaminants but, because chemicals like chlorinated hydrocarbons and other organic chemicals have a boiling point lower than water, a fractional type is needed. They are very slow (quart per hour is typical) and most use electricity to heat the water. Some clog quickly in hard water and require frequent cleaning that is difficult to do and that uses a strong acid.

Ultraviolet light units sterilize the water quickly and cheaply but require electricity. Certain spores and viruses are also fairly resistant to UV, and it is not fully effective in water containing large amounts of suspended particles, dissolved iron, or certain organic pollutants. Other pollutants aren't removed at all. Most units also need frequent maintenance.

Ozone is used throughout Europe and Canada to sterilize water rather than the chlorine used in the U.S.A. As effective as it is, however, it does not remove any particulate material nor chemicals and needs electricity to operate.

Backup Sources

In addition to storing water and being capable of purifying it, you should also consider the possibility of having backup sources. This is especially vital if you intend to keep livestock. These sources could include springs, streams, lakes, ponds and wells. Wells should be equipped with manual pumps and artesian wells should be capped and controlled. Be advised, too, that shallow wells are dependent on nearby surface water.

Emergency Reserves

Prior to deciding how to store all that water, it's nice to know that you probably already have some stored right in your house in the hot water heater, toilet tanks (not bowls, that's contaminated) and water pipes. The total amount depends on the size of the water heater, the type and number of toilet tanks, and the volume of the pipes.

There are some things you should know and do to make this water available when needed.

First, install an anti-siphon valve on the water inlet to keep the water from flowing back out of your house if the water pressure drops substantially. Also, have a wrench or valve shut-off tool in a handy location to use to close the main valve whenever you have any warning or notice a large drop in water pressure. This will prevent contamination of the water contained in your water system.

The water in the pipes can be drained by opening the highest faucet to vent the system and then draining the water from the lowest faucet. The water in the toilet tanks should be kept free of scale, rust and organic growth by occasionally cleaning with bleach. The water in the hot water heater can be used if its inlet valve is closed before any contamination enters and if the water is regularly drained to prevent an accumulation of rust and sediment in the tank bottom. When the water pressure drops drastically, the inlet valve should be closed and the gas and electricity turned off. The tank water can be drained from a self- vented tank by simply opening the bottom valve. If the tank is not self vented, then air must be let into the system from the top valve as with the pipe system.

Some believe they can use the liquids contained in canned fruits, vegetables and their juices. To some extent this is true, but the less water you have the less you should eat because eating food increases the need for water. You can melt ice cubes for water. Solar stills can also be used to obtain water from ground moisture and edible plant matter. Rain can be captured in barrels.

Conservation

Realizing just how valuable pure water is, you don't want to waste it. Now is the time to practice conserving it by cutting down your use of it, replacing shower heads with the low-flow type and learning how to recycle gray water.

12

SPROUTING

Fresh vegetables can be hard to come by during a prolonged crisis, particularly if it's not harvest time. Storing a supply of seeds to sprout can help fill that void. Sprouting is easy, can be done year round and provides tasty sprouts in a few days even in complete darkness. It can add needed vitamins and some variety to a sparse survival diet.

Sprouts are the germinated seeds of vegetables, grains, legumes and nuts. Almost any whole seed can be used with the notable exceptions of tomato and potato, which are poisonous. Many can be sprouted in combinations. Grasses can also be grown by sprouting wheat, rye, or triticale in one inch of soil and then cutting it when it grows to seven or eight inches.

Food Value of Sprouts

Sprouts are fairly nutritious, although they do not live up to the exaggerated claims often made for them. Generally, sprouts can be a reliable source of vitamin C and the B vitamins, particularly riboflavin and niacin. Wheat and alfalfa are very marginal sources of vitamin A, but even then only if they are exposed to light for at least a few hours prior to harvesting.

Claims made that sprouts have increased protein and minerals are simply untrue. The ratio of proteins and minerals may well have increased, but the total amount remaining is always less than in the original seed. Increased amounts would require a source for the minerals and nitrogen for the protein and, even then, the sprouts don't yet have the root hairs needed to absorb them. Research by major universities and the United Nations also shows the quality of the protein is generally decreased during sprouting.

Bean sprouts also still contain the protein-binding substances common to all legumes. Cooking the sprouts for at least two minutes will inactivate these substances and make the protein available. This can be by blanching in boiling water or by stir-frying. Sprouts do produce less intestinal gas because the soaking and rinsing leach out the complex sugars (trisaccharides) that produce gas.

Sprouting Procedure

All kinds of equipment and gadgets are sold for sprouting, some convenient, but none necessary. Seeds need moisture, warmth and ventilation to sprout, and there are lots of ways to do it. The most common, and often easiest, method follows:

1. Place a small amount of whole seeds into a wide-mouth jar (see Table 12-1 for recommended amounts or use one to two tablespoons per quart the first time). Add about two to four times that amount of lukewarm water and soak overnight or for the specified time.

2. Cover the jar with any material having small enough holes the seeds can't go through. This could be nylon mesh, net or stocking, gauze, cheesecloth or, more permanently, plastic or stainless steel screens. Even canning lids with small holes punched in them will work. Secure the covering with a canning ring, strong rubber band, or string.

3. Pour off the water, rinse thoroughly and then drain completely. Shake the jar to evenly distribute the seeds, and lay it on its side in a location out of direct sunlight. A 65-80^0 F (18-27^0 C) temperature is best, except seeds like cress, pea and rye like it cooler. Keeping the jar in the dark will increase the vitamin B and make white sprouts, while light will increase the vitamin C and make the sprouts greener.

4. Rinse and drain thoroughly with lukewarm water two to six times each day to keep the seeds moist and prevent mold. Soybeans need lots of rinsing, and all seeds need more rinsing when the environment is hot and dry. Too much chlorine in the water may harm the seeds, but letting the water sit for a day or two will allow most of the chlorine to evaporate. Most prefer to rinse away the hulls on seeds which have them. Lay the jar on its side between rinsings. The last rinse can be with cold water to crisp the sprouts.

5. Harvest by sprout length. Although Table 12-1 suggests some sizes, don't be afraid to experiment and find out what sizes your family prefers of each variety. Wheat and alfalfa generally have their highest vitamin A content after three days in the dark, but with the last few hours spent in light.

Use sprouts within a few days. Raw or cooked, they add crispness to salads, soups, sandwiches and vegetables or can be eaten by themselves. They also can be added to scrambled eggs and omelets, stews, breads, casseroles and meat dishes and liquified by blending for use in beverages, sauces and spreads.

Other sprouting methods use pans, trays, bowls, strainers, colanders, racks, screen frames, and damp towels. Some seeds, like chia, cress and buckwheat, turn into a jelly-like mass with too much water and do better placed on a flat surface, kept moist by sprinkling.

Amount to Store

The recommended amount to add variety to the diet is ten pounds per person, providing about an half cup serving per day. You could store anywhere from five to forty pounds; twenty-five pounds would provide sufficient vitamin C if no other source were available to prevent scurvy. Ignore their calorie contribution to your storage plan because they are very low in calories.

Seeds can be bought from local health food stores, mail order, or other sources (see listing in Chapter 32). They should be raw, clean of foreign matter and sorted to insure few broken ones. Be sure not to buy seeds that have been treated for planting with fungicides or pesticides, but only those that are certified edible. Treated seeds are required to be so labeled by law and are usually dyed to contrast with their normal color to identify them.

Store them where its dry, cool and dark. The older they are, the fewer will sprout, but most still have shelf lives of three-plus years. More than half of some twenty year old wheat sprouted.

By following these simple directions you'll probably do all right without any special books on sprouting. There are a number available, though, if you want more complete directions or desire some special recipes that use sprouts.

TABLE 13-1. SPROUTING GUIDE

Seed	Amount for Quart Jar	Soaking Time	Harvest Length	Growing Time	Sprouting Tips	Comments
Alfalfa and Clover	2 T	2-6 hrs	1-2"	3-6 days	Place in light before harvest to green	Eat raw in salads or sandwiches, cooked in baked goods, soups
Barley and Millet	1½ cups	10-14 hrs	length of seed	3-5 days	Best when less than ¼"	Toasting enhances flavor. Use in salads, breads and casseroles.
Beans not listed elsewhere	¼ cup	12-16 hrs	1-1½"	3-4 days	Don't over-sprout	Casseroles, soups, steamed, base for dips. Best cooked first.
Buckwheat	NA	NA	5-7"	8-12 days	Simple to sprout. Use raw, un-hulled groats	Good as lettuce substitute in salads
Cabbage and Fenugreek	¼ cup	8-12 hrs	¾-1½"	3-6 days	Place in light to develop chlorophyll	Use alone or with alfalfa in salads, steamed, stir-fried
Chia	NA	NA	1-2"	3-6 days	Becomes gelatiny mass when wet	Salads, garnish, in baked goods
Corn	1½ cups	12-20 hrs	½-1"	3-8 days	Try different varieties	Sweet and chewy. Hard to find untreated
Cress	NA	NA	¾-1½"	3-5 days	Becomes gelatiny mass when wet	Strong, hot peppery taste. Use as spice.
Garbanzo beans	1 cup	12-16 hrs	½-1"	3-5 days	Combine with wheat for nutritious mix	Nutty flavor good in salads, steamed, base for dip. Cook first.
Lentil	¾ cup	8-12 hrs	¼-½"	2-4 days	Very easy to sprout	Delicious in soups, steamed, in sauces and dips

TABLE 13-1. SPROUTING GUIDE (Continued)

Seed	Amount for Quart Jar	Soaking Time	Harvest Length	Growing Time	Sprouting Tips	Comments
Mung beans	1/3-1/2 cup	10-14 hrs	1-3"	3-5 days	Use hot water for first rinse, grow in dark	Oriental dishes, stir-fried, omelets, salads, soups, sandwiches
Oat	1½ cups	1-2 hrs	length of seed	3 days	Only un-hulled will sprout, water sparingly	Salads, cereals, baked goods
Pea	1½ cups	8-12 hrs	1/4-3/4"	3-4 days	Become tough if sprout too long	Soups, salads, casseroles. Like fresh peas.
Peanut	1½ cups	12-16 hrs	1/4-1"	3-4 days	Use raw, unshelled nuts	As snack, in desserts, salads, casseroles, stir-fried, steamed
Pumpkin and Sunflower seeds	1½ cups	8-12 hrs	1/4"	2-3 days	Sprout becomes bitter if develops leaves	Delicious as is, in salads, sauces, dips, baked goods
Radish	1/4 cup	8-12 hrs	1/2-1½"	3-5 days	Place in light to develop chlorophyll	Salads, sandwiches, dips. Nippy flavor.
Rye	1 cup	10-14 hrs	length of seed	2-3 days	Sprouts easily	Milder than wheat for salads, cereals, breads
Soybean	1 cup	12-16 hrs	1/2-1"	3-5 days	Grow alone. Don't use soak or rinse water	Cook before eating, use in salads, casseroles, base for cheese
Wheat and Triticale	3/4 cup	8-12 hrs	length of seed	2-3 days	Simple to sprout	Short: salad, soups, baked goods
			1/2-1"	4-7 days		Long: desserts, juices

13

GROWING YOUR OWN

No matter how much food you store, it would eventually run out if the crisis lasted long enough. Being able to grow your own will allow you to not only replace the storage food, but to supplement it and make it last longer. However, as important as growing your own is, it in no way takes the place of your food storage. Like all living sources it is too vulnerable to be your only food source. It requires a lengthy period of suitable weather before producing, and it is quite vulnerable to drought, diseases, pests, and vandals.

Growing fruits and vegetables is an involved process, covering many subjects, and the details will not be covered here. What will be presented are the vital items you should stockpile now, suggested resources for further guidance, and general considerations. Many fine books are available on the details, but you can also get some of the best information for your particular area free or at low cost from your local county extension agent or university.

Gardening

Successful gardening comes from learning skills and gaining experience with your unique combination of climate, seasons, soil, water, insects, disease conditions and preferences. It can't all be learned overnight, nor can some of the techniques be done quickly. So no matter what your circumstances, it is best if you begin now to acquire the necessary knowledge, even if that means just reading about it and planting some vegetables in a window box or pots. You should also stockpile the few necessities mentioned.

Seeds

Priority I. No one can grow a garden without seeds and, during a prolonged food shortage, they would be worth their weight in gold. A small amount of them represent a large amount of potential food.

Get the best seed you can for the best results. If you expect to save any seed for the next year's crops, they should be of the standard variety (non-hybrid). Hybrids produce seed that is unreliable and often

TABLE 13-1.
SEEDS NEEDED FOR ONE YEAR BY FAMILY OF FOUR

Bush beans- 8 oz	Cucumber- 1 oz	Radish- ½ oz
Beets- ½ oz	Lettuce- ¼ oz	Spinach- 1 oz
Cabbage- ¼ oz	Onion- ¼ oz	Squash- ¼ oz
Carrots- ½ oz	Peas- 12 oz	Tomato- ¼ oz
Corn, sweet- 8 oz	Pepper- ¼ oz	Turnips- ⅛ oz

produces plants greatly inferior to the parent. Also, some plants, hybrid or not, cross-breed and may not produce seed suitable for saving. Store at least a year's supply, more would be better, and perhaps some for barter. The amount a particular family needs for one year can vary widely, but Table 13-1 lists the amounts of fifteen different vegetables needed by the average family of four for a year.

Which varieties? Get a good selection of those that grow well in your soil and climate. Choose those that your family likes and that will provide balanced nutrition ,particularly vitamins A and C. Also take into account how quickly they grow, how much they yield for the space, how well they can be stored or canned, and how resistant they are to temperature, drought and disease. I'd certainly consider the following: tomatoes, cabbage, carrots, squash, onions, spinach, peas, green beans, corn and peppers. It won't hurt to add radishes, cucumbers and some melons. Nutritious but less common varieties are kale, collards, chard, broccoli, sweet potatoes and parsnips. Seeds for an herb garden would be a nice addition, too.

Store the seeds where it's dry and cool, the nearer freezing the better. Shelf life varies with the type of seed and the exact conditions. Table 13-2 gives a general idea of the shelf life of various seeds.

Canned seeds

Seeds remaining in the small packets can be saved by placing them in an airtight jar. Although limited in choices and amounts, the best way to store your long-term seeds is by getting the selections specially prepared and sealed in cans. The above shelf lives will be increased substantially. Even with the cans you should rotate the seeds regularly, using them for planting, to keep as fresh as possible. Canned seeds are available from some of the sources listed in Chapter 32.

TABLE 13-2.
PROXIMATE STORAGE LIFE FOR VARIOUS SEEDS

2 Years: field corn, onions, parsnips, soybeans
3 Years: asparagus, green beans, carrots, sweet corn, kale, leeks, lettuce, parsley, peas, peppers, hybrid tomatoes
4 Years: beets, cabbage, cauliflower, chard, okra, pumpkin, radish, spinach, squash
5+ Years: broccoli, Brussel sprouts, celery, collard, cress, cucumbers, endive, kohlrabi, melons, non-hybrid tomatoes, turnips

Fertilizer

Plants need food to grow, and the first step is to find out what is lacking in the soil. You can buy a soil test kit and do it yourself, or have samples tested by the county extension agent, university, or commercial testing service. Once you know what and how much is needed, buy and store enough fertilizer for a year or more. You can also start a compost pile, pit, or barrel to provide organic fertilizer. Animal manure is good fertilizer and you can grow "green manure" crops like the legumes, ryegrass and buckwheat to increase the nitrogen and organic material in your soil.

Pesticides

Vegetables destroyed by pests and diseases can be easily replaced now, but that may not always be true. A selection of pesticides in your storage can help. The EPA-approved list of pesticides is always changing (diazinon will be totally banned by the end of 2003) so heck with your county agent to see which ones you should store. Be sure to store them locked up in a ventilated area away from your house because they are poisonous and, if made with petroleum solvent, a fire hazard.

You can also grow your own organic pesticide by storing seeds for the chrysanthemum cinerariifolium flower. The dried flower, containing the botanical poison phrethrin, is ground up and used as a dust. Sprays made from garlic, onions and other pungent plants also work.

Learn about the beneficial insects and how you can cultivate them. Cut down on your garden's need for pesticides by keeping the area clean, removing places for pests to breed and live, and by promptly and properly disposing of garden refuse. Proper crop rotation will not only

TABLE 13-3. BASIC GARDENING TOOLS

☐ shovel	☐ rake ☐ hoe	
☐ trowel	☐ spading fork	☐ hand sprayer (2-gal)
☐ weeder	☐ gloves	☐ string or twine
☐ hand fork	☐ watering can	☐ hoses and sprinkler
☐ wheelbarrow	☐ extra handles	☐ wheeled cultivator

keep down the buildup of damaging insects and diseases but also balance the use the different soil nutrients.

Weeds can be your biggest pest because they crowd out the desired plants and steal nutrients. Weed early, while they're small, and keep at it.

Mulching will help keep weeds down, maintain more even soil temperatures, retain moisture and build the soil.

Also protect your garden with fencing and other precautions. An entire year's harvest can easily be destroyed in a few minutes by animals or vandals.

Tools and Supplies

Acquire the basic gardening tools listed in Table 13-3. Buy good quality tools that will last, and maintain them properly so they will. Clean them after use, and store where they won't rust or warp.

Rotary tillers are handy for larger gardens, but they'll only run if they have fuel.

Location

The garden site must receive at least four to six hours daily of direct sunlight. Fruit-bearing vegetables need the most, while leaf vegetables can use less. The afternoon sun is better than the morning sun. The soil should be well-draining, and the top six to eight inches should have a loose, crumbly texture. Poor soil can be gradually improved by adding humus, but it can take years. Obviously, you'll need a source of water.

The amount of space you'll need will depend greatly on the methods you use, your skills and your resources in way of climate, soil and seed varieties. In general, however, you can provide a year's supply of vegetables from a couple of hundred square feet per person with good gardening techniques. Some sources offer tables of projected yields but, although they can be helpful, they are very approximate and your experience will be a much better guide.

Planning

The first step in planning a garden is to plan it on paper. Place taller crops on the north side, and have rows running north and south to cut down on shading of other plants. Perennials and fall-bearing crops should be located in separate plots or on the edges so that they won't be disturbed when the rest is turned under. Make the most of your space by allowing climbing vegetables like tomatoes and beans to grow upward on stakes and trellises.

Methods have been developed that produce up to five times as much while using less water and allowing better weed control. You should be aware of and consider them:

1. Wide row or plot method. Uses three to four foot wide rows or plots, either indented or raised with a six inch dike around and one to two foot paths between.
2. Biodynamic/French intensive method. Uses bed well prepared by deep double digging. Method is outlined in the book *How to Grow More Vegetables and Fruits, Nuts, Raising Grains...* by John Jeavons.
3. Raised bed or grow box method. Outlined in the book More Food from *Grow-Box Gardens* by Jacob R. Mittleider.
4. Square foot gardening method. Uses small grow boxes divided into one-foot squares. *Square Foot Gardening* and *Ca$h from Square Foot Gardening* by Mel Bartholomew.

Planting various plants together, called companion planting, can increase yields, better utilize nutrients and ease care requirements. Certain plants also help others repel insects.

Watering deeply two to three times per week helps the plants develop a healthy root system that makes them more drought resistant. Certain varieties are naturally more resistant to drought and, as mentioned, mulching also helps. A drip irrigation system can also cut down drastically on the amount of water needed.

Extending the Season

Your garden can produce more if you use various techniques to lengthen the season. Succession planting, where an early-maturing crop is replaced with a later one, can double your yield. Growing seedlings inside for later transplanting, using hardy varieties and warding off frost with hot caps, hot beds and cold frames gives the plants more growing time. Tomatoes can be started about two months earlier by placing them inside a Tomato Tepee (much better built than a similar Wall O' Water). Row covers can be used to not only extend the season by keeping the plants warmer, but they can also keep insects and other predators off. Greenhouses allow year-around gardening no matter what the weather is outside.

Hydroponics allows gardening all year in a completely enclosed spaces without soil. It does require a suitable light source, though.

Keep Records

No matter how or where you garden, you should keep good records. Write down how much of what was planted, when planted, how it was cared for (weeding, water and fertilizer), insect and disease problems, time of harvest and the yield. These records will become a valuable planning tool for following years.

Fruits, Nuts, Berries And Grapes

Cultivating orchards, vineyards and berries are a long-term investment well worth considering.

You should store the necessary fertilizers and pesticides, particularly for fruit trees. You'll want some spray oil, diazinon (or whatever replaces it), lindane, malathion and thiodan. Tools to store include pruning shears, lopping shears with long handles for trees and a pruning saw.

When choosing nut and fruit trees, consider the different varieties, their hardiness and pollination requirements. Dwarf or semi-dwarf trees can be a good choice and will often bear fruit in two to three years. To get the most from your trees and vines you'll need to learn how to prune them properly. Trees are also useful for fuel, windbreaks and shade. Books that may be of interest are:

Backyard Fruits and Berries by Miranda Smith
The Backyard Berry Book by Gene Logson
The Farmer's Wife Guide to Fabulous Fruits and Berries by Doyen
The Backyard Berry Book by Stella Otto
Planning and Planting Your Dwarf Fruit Trees by L. Southwick
Pruning Simplified by Lewis Hill

TABLE 13-4. NEEDED SEED AND CROP YIELDS

	Pounds seed per acre	Yield per acre
Alfalfa		3-4 tons
Barley	100	40-50 bushels
Buckwheat	50	25-35 bushels
Field corn	8	65-90 bushels
Grain sorghum	6	55-80 bushels
Oats	80	35-50 bushels
Rye	85	25-35 bushels
Wheat	90	15-35 bushels

Field Crops

Often overlooked in preparation, you should consider growing your own grains and grasses. If you do, you'd better store some scythes to harvest them with (grain cradle is handy for anything over an acre). Using Table 13-4 will help determine the area needed for a particular yield and how much seed must be stored. \

Some corn matures within weeks while fall-planted wheat takes almost eight months. Potatoes are a good food crop and yield ten to twelve tons per acre. You could consider some unusual varieties like amaranth, too. A book that may be of help but currently has limited availability is:

The Scythe Book by David Tresemer

Remember that you'll have to grow field and forage crops for any livestock you plan on raising, too.

14

RAISING YOUR OWN

Raising your own domestic animals is a good way to provide an on-going supply of fresh meat, eggs, milk, fertilizer and even leather. However, before you start buying a lot of animals, you should be aware that it takes a lot of time and effort. Daily attention is usually necessary, often two to three times per day with dairy animals. It requires a long-term commitment for success. Animals are also vulnerable to disease, starvation and being killed or stolen. I certainly am not trying to discourage you from raising animals, but I do think you need to know the negative side, too. If you really want to do it, then start with a few animals, experiment a bit and work your way up.

Successful animal husbandry requires a good deal of experience and knowledge. You should either learn it first-hand from someone who does it or get a number of good books and read about it in depth. This chapter will discuss the basic considerations to get you pointed in the right direction.

The best animals for you will depend on your situation. The first thing you should consider are the zoning laws. And, no matter what the laws, you'll be better off if you don't annoy any neighbors and keep the area sanitary so that you won't have any problems with the local Department of Health. In a really bad crisis zoning laws won't mean much anyway.

If you're just starting out or have a limited space, you're probably better off with smaller animals like rabbits, chickens and perhaps goats. They require not only less space, food and care, but they generally produce less odor. Most backyards can support some rabbits and chickens; in postwar Germany they were even kept by people living in large cities. They are relatively easy to care for, require minimal protection and can be kept in pens or allowed to run free in fenced yards. More space and more commitment will allow you to consider the larger animals like sheep, pigs and cows.

Whatever animals you choose to raise, you'll need to know their food requirements and store enough to last you through a crisis. You'll need to provide them with adequate shelter and learn how to keep them healthy and free from disease. You should also know how to protect them from predators and fallout. If you want them to reproduce, you'll need both sexes. Keeping records for each animal will allow you to know which are the best so that you can cull out the others. Finally, you'll need to know how to slaughter, butcher and carve them for use.

Equipment

Each animal requires its own particular tools, equipment and supplies that you will need to store. There are other items that will be needed for accomplishing certain chores, no matter what the animal. Milk animals need milk pails or other containers, pasteurization equipment if desired, a cream separator, butter churn and butter molds. Meat saws, cleavers, knives and scrapers are used in slaughtering and butchering animals.

Veterinary Supplies

Medicines for animals could be impossible to get during a crisis, so you should store some now. To find out which might be needed for each animal, you'll have to learn about the diseases they are likely to get. If you can't find the supplies locally, you can order from the sources listed in Chapter 32. Be sure to store the necessary instruments as well as the serums, ointments, sprays and antibiotics. Most medicines have an expiration date on the bottle.

Books

There are a number of books, some covering raising animals in general with others for one specific animal. Some you might consider are:

Backyard Livestock by Steven Thomas
Chickens in Your Backyard by Luttmann and Luttmann
Try the Rabbit by S.O. Adajre
The New Goat Handbook by Jaudas and Vriends
Animal Husbandry by Laura Zigman
Merck Veterinary Manual by Susan Aiello
Veterinary Guide for Animal Owners by Spaulding and Clay

Specific Animals

Here is a capsule review of the more popular animals so that you can make some informed decisions:

Rabbits

Comments: Rabbits produce more meat for the amount of feed than any other domestic animal. It is a high-protein meat tasting similar to chicken. Rabbits can be taken care of in a few minutes a day, are relatively odorless if properly cared for and are quiet and unobtrusive. They require only a small money investment, take less space than chickens, can be kept indoors and are easy to keep in good health.

Production: Ten does and two bucks will provide about one and a half to two pounds of meat per day. Their productive life is two to four years. They also produce fur and the best natural fertilizer (about 40% of the total weight of their food).

Space and shelter requirements: Hutches should have eighteen inches headroom and allow eight square feet for each doe with liter. Bucks need four to five square feet. They are best made of mesh wire that allows droppings to fall through.

Equipment: Feeders, water bottles, nest boxes.

Food requirements: Feed should be at least 15-17% protein and can be homemade from corn, grain sorghum, hay, oats, soybeans and wheat. A dozen rabbits and their young require about three and half tons of commercial pellets in a year. They also need a salt lick.

Varieties: New Zealand White and Californian for meat and fur; Rex for fur.

Chickens

Comments: Chickens require a small money investment, and will help keep your garden free of bugs. A rooster is noisy but needed to reproduce.

Production: A dozen hens will provide nearly four dozen eggs a week. They start laying at four and a half months and their productive life is two to three years. Brown eggs are as nutritious and tasty as white. They also provide meat, feathers and an excellent fertilizer.

Space and shelter requirements: A dozen chickens need a fifty square foot coop with nesting boxes, feeders and roosts plus a pen at least as big. The coop should be water and predator proof and a concrete floor is easier to keep clean. The pen should have a five or six foot poultry wire fence and be covered to keep out hawks. Chickens need fourteen hours of light per day and, in the winter, a lightbulb will help and also provide some heat.

Equipment: Waterers, feeders, incubator, brooder.

Food requirements: Feed should be at least 15% protein. A homemade mash from grains and soybean meal should contain well-ground eggshell or bone meal to provide enough calcium. Milk and scraps of fish and meat can also be added. Commercial mash becomes stale within a few months. A dozen laying hens would require about 1,200 pounds of mash a year. Garden greens shouldn't exceed one-third by weight of the diet. Strong-flavored food will result in strong-flavored eggs.

Varieties: Rhode Island or New Hampshire Reds and Plymouth Rocks for both eggs and meat; White Leghorns are highest egg producers. Make sure they have been vaccinated and are free from pullorum and typhoid diseases.

Other Poultry

Turkeys: Larger than chickens, they are nervous and must be protected from their own stupidity. They are also smelly and produce virtually worthless manure. You should provide a shelter with five to ten square feet per bird that is well-ventilated and shades them from the sun.

Ducks and Geese: both are extremely hardy, will forage for most of the food they need, and will provide feathers and down as well as meat and even eggs. Geese make excellent watchdogs, will weed for you, and are exceptionally healthy and disease resistant. An acre can support about twenty birds. Obviously they would like a pond but its not absolutely necessary. They should be protected from predators and their nests particularly from skunks. Muscovy ducks and Emden geese are good for meat while the Khaki Campbell duck is a good egg producer.

Goats

Comments: Goats are excellent foragers and ideal for a smaller area. Their milk is used by more people in the world than cow milk and is easily digested. It's simply a matter of getting used to its taste.

Production: Two nannies will produce from one to two and a half gallons of milk per day year around. That means cream, butter and cheese. Average productive life is ten to twelve years. Kids can be killed when three months old and will provide twenty to twenty-five pounds of meat.

Space and shelter requirements: They require a twenty to twenty-five square foot shed with a two to three hundred square foot fenced area per goat. A larger area is needed for grazing.

Equipment: Milking stand with stanchion.

Food requirements: Goats need two to four pounds of a high-grain dairy ration and five pounds of hay per day. That means two would require about one and a half tons of the ration and almost two tons of hay in a year. A ration can be homemade from grains and soybean meal, and root crops can also be fed. Rock salt is also needed.

Varieties: Saanen for milk and Nubian for milk and meat. Make sure they are free of brucellosis and tuberculosis.

Sheep

Comments: Sheep are easy to handle, have gentle dispositions and subsist on a wide variety of forage. They need protection from predators and sometimes from themselves.

Production: A hundred pound lamb yields thirty-five pounds of meat and a shearling skin. Sheep must be sheared every year and provide about eight pounds of wool each time.

Space and shelter requirements: Only minimal shelter is needed in the most extreme weather and when lambing. About twelve to fifteen square feet per sheep will do.

Equipment: Hand shears, hoof trimmers.

Food requirements: An acre will graze two to four sheep. A pregnant or nursing ewe needs a grain and hay supplement. Figure on two hundred pounds of grain and eight hundred pounds of hay per year each. Need salt blocks.

Varieties: Merino for wool, Corriedale and Columbia for meat and wool. Should be vaccinated for tetanus.

Pigs

Comments: Pigs are foragers, intelligent and cleaner than commonly believed although they do produce offensive odors.

Production: A good sow will raise two liters a year of five to twelve plus pigs each. A two hundred pound hog dresses out to about one hundred forty pounds of bacon, ham, sausage, chops and roasts as well as valuable lard. Their hide is some of the toughest yet softest leather around. Their productive lives average eight to nine years.

Space and shelter requirements: Pigs need a shed for shade within a one hundred square foot minimum per pig pen surrounded with a strong fence. A wallow is necessary to cool them in the summer.

Food requirements: An acre will support five to six pigs if they are supplemented with two to four pounds of coarsely-ground grains daily. Figuring three pounds of grains per pound gained shows you'll need six to seven hundred pounds of grain per hog slaughtered. Excess milk, eggs, vegetables and table scraps can also be used.

Varieties: Duroc, Chester White, Hampshire and Yorkshire. All should be inoculated against hog cholera.

Cows

Comments: Cows are a large animal requiring daily care. They also produce three to four times as much milk as a goat.

Production: A good dairy cow will average two to three gallons of milk daily for ten months of each year. A six hundred pound beef cow will yield about three hundred pounds of meat.

Space and shelter requirements: A shed open on one side with one hundred square feet per cow is best. Calves need at least thirty square feet each. About forty to fifty bails of straw are used yearly for bedding.

Equipment: Stanchion, manger, water trough.

Food requirements: One to three acres are needed to graze each cow unless supplemented with hay. With adequate summer pasture you will need to have about a ton of grain and two to four tons of hay per cow for winter. Raising a beef will take about five hundred pounds of grain and a like amount of hay.

Varieties: Jersey, Guernsey and other smaller breeds best for milking; Hereford and other varieties for meat. All should be free from brucellosis and tuberculosis.

Bees

Bees require minimal attention and, after the first year, will produce thirty to one hundred pounds of surplus honey per hive. You start them in the spring when blossoms appear. It's best to have at least two hives and you should have ample supers for the bees to store the honey in. The hives need to be placed where they will get adequate sunlight and be protected from winter winds. You'll want bee gloves, veil, smoker, hive tool, uncapping knife and a honey extractor. Italian bees are best for beginners.

Aquaculture

Raising fish or other aquatic life in ponds or holding tanks can be an excellent source of high-quality protein. Varieties of fish you might want to grow depend largely on the amount of fresh water you have available, its quality and oxygen content, and its temperature. Popular varieties include trout, bluegill, carp, largemouth bass, channel catfish and tilapia.

A solar-powered twelve foot diameter by three foot deep vinyl-lined above ground swimming pool with a dome cover and a filter-aerator can produce forty to one hundred pounds of fish per year. Ponds will produce from one hundred pounds per year naturally to ten to twenty times that if supplemented. Figure on two pounds of high-protein supplementary ration per pound of fish harvested.

There are a number of books on aquaculture and you should read about it before you plan anything. For more information on fish ponds, contact your state wildlife department or a local fish hatchery. A pond will also attract migratory waterfowl, especially if you plant wild rice and other food for them.

15

FINDING YOUR OWN

Some people question the need for storing food, saying if they ever had to they could just gather all their food from the wilds. They see themselves digging a few wild onions, picking a handful of berries, perhaps catching and eating a fish, and lying back under a tree, full and contented. This notion is mostly an illusion, however, and you should not base your survival planning on it.

In reality, foraging food from the wilds would provide bare subsistence at best.

First, consider the amount of wild food that would probably be available. In any major crisis hordes of unprepared people, having the same idea, would converge on the areas, quickly killing, gathering and eating nearly everything edible. It would be dangerous just to be there. If the crisis were nuclear war, fallout would kill many of the animals. In any event, the natural resources would soon be depleted. And that doesn't even take into account herd migration or winter when game is scarce and edible plant life is negligible. Even in the real back country with minimal human population, it would be a desperate struggle to keep from starving to death.

Nevertheless, foraging could be used to stretch and add some variety to the survival diet or to keep you alive temporarily. But keep in mind that the first rule of obtaining food from the wilds is that you mustn't expend more energy getting it than it will give you in return.

Wild Edible Plants

There are a large variety of plants that humans can eat but they have their limitations. The problems are in two areas: 1) most are very low in calories and it would take large quantities to survive, and 2) many are not exactly what you've been used to and are not considered by most to be great delicacies for either your taste buds or your stomach. And that all assumes you didn't choose some that are poisonous!

Edible greens are simply wild vegetables and most contain fewer than one hundred calories per pound. You would need to eat from fifteen to more than fifty pounds per day to meet your energy needs! Even berries only average about 250 calories per pound and nuts aren't always available. Although you can acquire a taste for wild greens and they can be tasty if properly prepared, they contain a lot of indigestible roughage. The adjustment period would commonly bring bouts with diarrhea.

Then there is the problem of not eating the poisonous plants. Some poisonous plants look quite similar to good ones, and often some parts of the same plant are safe while other parts are not. Although some edible plants are easily distinguished by nearly anyone, others take great skill to tell. The best way to develop this skill is by learning in the field from someone already knowledgeable. If that isn't possible, books can help. Each area of the country has its own indigenous edible plants, and you will need a guide to the plants common to your local area. Many of the books are worthless, but following these guidelines will help you choose a good one:

1. Look for numerous clear illustrations of the plants and their edible parts at harvest time. Color pictures are best.
2. Descriptions should include the plant's range, habitat, when and how to collect, and how to use it. Poisonous species that might be confused with it should also be mentioned with details on how to tell them apart.
3. There should be enough species for your locale to make it a valuable reference source. Recipes telling you how to prepare the plants to make them palatable are also very helpful.

Books you might consider are:

Plants of the Rocky Mountains by Kershaw, Pojar and Alaback
Feasting Free on Wild Edibles by Bradford Angier
Field Guide to Edible Wild Plants by Bradford Angier
Tom Brown's Guide to Wild Edible and Medicinal Plants
Guide to Wild Foods and Useful Plants by Christopher Nyerges
Field Guide to Edible Wild Plants by Peterson and Peterson

There are also decks of cards you can carry in your pocket. Each has fifty-two cards with color pictures, descriptions, habitats and uses. Both are available from Knowledge Brokers International, 340 Rogers Lane, Calimesa, CA 92320, 909-795-8287, info@freeoutdoors.com:

Edible and Poisonous Plants of the Western United States
Edible and Poisonous Plants of the Eastern United States

Most green plants are not poisonous but there are some general guidelines that may be helpful. First, just because an animal safely eats a plant doesn't prove it's safe for humans. White berries are almost always poisonous while red ones are sometimes. Avoid plants resembling cucumbers, melons, or parsnips unless you are positive they are safe. And mushrooms should be left alone unless you are an expert on them. It's often most difficult to distinguish between the safe and toxic varieties.

If your very life depends on eating some unknown plants or not, there is a test you can perform. Follow these steps in sequence:

1. Smell. Check for any odor and discard if found.
2. Look. See if any milky substance comes from the plant when it is cut, squeezed, or crushed. Don't continue if there is.
3. Taste. Bite off a very small piece. If it doesn't taste bitter, stinging, or soapy, place inside lower lip for five minutes. If it still doesn't have a foul taste or burn, you can continue.
4. Wait. Swallow a small piece of the plant and wait for three to five hours. If no stomach cramps, headache, or general achiness or sickness occurs during that time, the plant is probably safe to eat. Never eat great quantities of any new plant.

Hunting, Fishing and Trapping

Normally hunting and fishing are "sports" with accepted methods and are governed by laws and regulations. In time of dire need, however, that will quickly change. Sporting methods and regulations are mostly to give the wild animals a chance. Poaching methods are designed to provide food. Mostly unknown now, you can learn about some of these methods from the following books:

Modern Hunting with Indian Secrets by Allan A. Macfarlan (used)
Live Off the Land in the City and Country by Ragnor Benson
Survival Poaching by Ragnor Benson

Fishing

Fish are also low-calorie food, averaging 150 to 400 calories per pound as caught. You'd need five to more than fifteen pounds per day to survive. And, unless you fish in the ocean, much of what you can catch today came from a hatchery that probably won't be stocking fish then. While it would be nice to have a stockpile of line, leaders, sinkers, lures and especially hooks, the best way to catch the most fish quickly is with nets and, particularly, traps. You can also stun them by throwing the crushed leaves, seeds and stems from mullet into a dammed-off stream or kill them with bleach. A fillet knife is handy for preparing fish.

Ocean shorelines can supply various kinds of shellfish like mussels, clams and oysters.

Small animals

Survival courses show you how to live off of rodents, lizards, snakes, frogs, turtles ,and bird eggs. Indians often ate beetles and grasshoppers. Obviously there are rabbits, porcupines, birds and other small animals. Sling shots with #9 buck shot will work if you practice a lot and pellet guns are quiet, accurate at short ranges and cheap to shoot. Shotguns are very useful, with #6 shot being an all-around selection. Store wire of different sizes for snares. And traps are the most efficient way of obtaining small animals. They work quietly twenty-four hours a day with little attention.

Again, like most wild things, small animals are low in calories and you would need quite a few to stay alive. Most are also very low in fat content, too. Rabbit meat, for instance, is only 610 calories per pound and has so little fat that if it were all you ate, you would eventually die of fat starvation.

Game animals

Venison has 570 calories per pound and is still only 4% fat. I'd definitely prefer a rifle to the ancient bow and arrow. Store plenty of ammunition, a hunting knife and a skinning knife. It's best to learn the basic skills now from an experienced hunter. Using a red filter over a light will allow you to see the game at night without them seeing you. Close observation of their feeding and watering habits will help you have success. A guide to animal tracks will help you identify what it is you're following and what it is doing.

Fur animals

If you will want to trap fur animals like muskrat, beaver, otter and mink, store six to twelve steel traps. Sizes #1 and #1½ are the best all-around with #4 for beaver. Get a book or two on trapping to tell you about the animals' habits, how to trap them and how to properly prepare the traps to get rid of human scent.

Wild Game Recipes

After you've caught whatever game you were after, it will help if you know how to take care of it and to prepare it for the table. Some books that could help:

Wild About Game by Jane Hibler and Janie Hibler
Wild Game Cooking Made Easy by John Schumacher
Wild Game Cookbook by Judity Bosley
Wild Game Cookery by J. Carol Vance, et al
America's Favorite Wild Game Recipes (Hunting & Fishing)
Native Indian Wild Game, Fish & Wild Food Cookbook
500 Wild Game and Fish Recipes by Galen Winter
A Guide to Canning, Freezing, Curing and Smoking of Meat, Fish and Game by Wilbur F. Eastman, Jr.
Getting the Most from Your Game and Fish by Robert Candy
Home Book of Cooking Venison and Other Natural Meats by Bradford Angier (used)

16

COLD STORAGE

Many fresh, unprocessed fruits and vegetables can be preserved without refrigeration by using cold storage methods. These methods were used long before refrigeration and are the easiest and least expensive ways of prolonging the harvest where there isn't a year-around growing season. This allows more variety in the survival diet. Some fruits and vegetables are also more suited to cold storage than other methods of preservation.

Fruits and vegetables can be either home-grown or purchased during the harvest season. Cold storage will allow many to be kept up to eight or more months with the right conditions.

Storage Conditions

Optimum shelf lives are achieved by maintaining the proper temperatures and humidity. Basically, fruits and vegetables can be divided into two groups: 1) those needing cool and dry (45-60^0 F, 70% or less humidity) conditions, and 2) those needing cold and moist (32-45^0 F, 80% or above humidity) conditions. Adequate ventilation is needed to properly control the temperatures and moisture levels and to remove the gases given off by ripening fruit. Table 16-1 lists the ideal temperature and humidity ranges for the more common fruits and vegetables. Whether the temperature or humidity is more critical depends on the produce. The shelf life of onions, for instance, is more dependent on the humidity.

Higher temperatures cause sprouting, ripening and deterioration of the produce. Wide fluctuations in temperature should be avoided, and alternating freezing and thawing cycles are particularly damaging. Keep a record of temperatures both inside the storage area and outdoors with daily monitoring recommended during the coldest periods of winter. That allows adjustments to be made to correct for temperature extremes. Two thermometers are handy for the two different locations, and the minimum-maximum type of thermometer are the most useful. When the temperature approaches freezing inside, a low-wattage light bulb or a small kerosene lantern can be used to keep the space above freezing. Heaters may produce too much heat.

Too much moisture allows the produce to rot, while too little makes it shrivel and dry out. Moisture levels can be accurately checked with a hygrometer. High humidity can be maintained by placing large pans of water near the air-intake vents and by sprinkling water directly on the produce or the floor. A three-inch layer of clean sand, sawdust, or coarse, well-washed gravel covering on the floor will help retain moisture. Normally this will not be enough for root crops which are best kept in perforated polyethylene bags or box liners.

Windows or other vents help regulate the temperature and humidity. Outside air that is colder or warmer can be allowed in or shut out to cool or warm the space. Excess moisture can be vented, or high outside humidity can be used as needed. Two vents are needed for each separate space to allow flow. Daily adjustments frequently will be necessary.

Normally the ideal conditions are not always available. Try to come as close as you can with the space and temperature ranges you have.

The shelf lives listed in table 16-1 are estimates for the various varieties of fruits and vegetables. Exact shelf lives will depend on the facilities you have, the temperature and moisture fluctuations and the variety of the produce. Late-maturing varieties usually store best but check with growers in your area. Some apples, like Jonathan for example, may last only a few months, while varieties like Winesap will keep for six months or longer under the same conditions. Selecting the best keeper varieties for growing at home and buying produce to store in late fall and early winter will help.

Preparation and Storage

Shelf lives are also dependent on the condition of the produce prior to storage. The better the quality to begin with, the longer the shelf life. With the exception of tomatoes, all produce should be picked when it is mature. Pears should be fully mature but still hard and light green.

Harvest produce when it is cool and dry. Pick in the morning or allow it to sit overnight after picking to cool. Cut off all leafy tops right after digging. Cut root crop tops off one inch above the crown. Leave stems on squash and pumpkin. Don't trim roots because it may cause spoilage. Root crops should also not be exposed to the sun or wind.

Don't wash dirt off prior to storage unless there is an excess. Then brush it off gently with a soft, dry cloth. The produce should be handled

TABLE 16-1. COLD STORAGE OF FRUITS AND VEGETABLES

Fruit	Where to Store	Storage Conditions Temperature	Humidity	Storage Life (in months)
Apples	RC-F	32-40° F	80-90%	4-6+
Grapefruit	RC-F	32-40° F	80-90%	1-2
Grapes	RC-F	32-40° F	80-90%	1-2
Oranges	RC-F	32-40° F	80-90%	1-3
Pears	RC-F	32-40° F	85-90%	2-5
Vegetables				
Beets	BSR,M/B,RC	32-40° F	90-95%	4-6+
Broccoli	BSR,RC	32-40° F	90-95%	1-2
Brussel sprouts	BSR,IG,RC	32-40° F	90-95%	1-2
Cabbage	M/B,RC,T	32-40° F	85-90%	3-6+
Carrots	BSR,IG,M/B,RC	32-40° F	90-95%	4-6+
Cauliflower	BSR,RC	32-40° F	80-90%	1-2
Celeriac	BSR,MB,RC	32-40° F	90-95%	3-6+
Celery	BSR,IG,M/B,RC,T	32-40° F	85-90%	1-5+
Chinese cabbage	BSR,RC	32-40° F	95-98%	2-4
Collard greens	BSR,RC	32-40° F	90-95%	1-2
Eggplant	BSR,RC	40-50° F	90-95%	1-2
Endive/Escarole	BSR,IG,RC	32-40° F	85-90%	2-3
Garlic	A,BSR,DS	32-40° F	60-70%	6-8+
Horseradish	BSR,IG,M/B,RC	32-40° F	90-95%	4-6+
Jerusalem artichoke	BSR,IG,M/B,RC	32-40° F	90-95%	4-6+
Kale	IG	32-40° F	95-98%	1-2
Kohlrabi	BSR,M/B,RC	32-40° F	90-95%	2-3
Leeks	BSR,IG,M/B,RC	32-40° F	80-90%	2-5
Onions	A,BSR,DS	32-40° F	60-70%	5-6+
Parsnips	BSR,IG,M/B,RC	32-40° F	90-95%	4-6+
Peppers, green	BSR,DS,RC	45-50° F	80-90%	1-2
hot chili	BSR,DS	50-55° F	60-65%	4-6+
Potatoes, sweet	BSR,DS	55-60° F	60-70%	4-6+
white	BSR,M/B,RC	35-40° F	80-90%	4-6+
Pumpkins	A,BSR	55-60° F	60-70%	4-6+
Radish, winter	BSR,IG,M/B,RC	32-40° F	90-95%	2-5
Rutabagas	BSR,M/B,RC	32-40° F	90-95%	3-6+
Salsify	BSR,IG,M/B,RC	32-40° F	90-95%	4-6+
Squash, winter	A,BSR	50-60° F	60-70%	4-6+
Tomotoes, green	BSR,DS	55-60° F	60-70%	1-3+
Turnips	M/B,RC	32-40° F	90-95%	3-6+

KEY: A = attic, BSR = basement storage room, DS = dry shed, IG = mulched in ground, M/B = outdoor mound or buried barrel, RC = root cellar, RC-F = root cellar for fruit, T = covered trench or pit.

as little as possible and carefully to prevent cutting and bruising. Any that is bruised or shows any signs of disease or spoilage should be culled out. You must also inspect on a regular basis once it is stored because spoilage will quickly affect adjacent produce unless removed. Mold on squash can be removed by rubbing softly with a cloth with a little vegetable oil on it.

Garlic, onions, potatoes, pumpkins and squash should be cured prior to storing to harden their skins and prolong their shelf life. Cure pumpkins and squash by leaving them in the field for two weeks after picking to be exposed to the sun and air. If it is rainy weather they can be placed in a room at 80-85^0 F for ten days (near the furnace may be good). Acorn squash doesn't need curing and will store at 45-50^0 F for one to one and a half months. Sweet potatoes are cured by placing them in a humid room at 80-85^0 F for ten days to two weeks. White potatoes should be cured for seven to fourteen days at 60-75^0 F, and onions and garlic should be placed in the sun for five to seven days.

Produce will last longer if properly packaged for storage. Tomatoes are best individually wrapped in wax paper. Apples can be wrapped in oiled or shredded paper. Cabbage, pears, pumpkins, squash and sweet potatoes can be individually wrapped in newspapers or dry burlap. Layers of produce can be separated from each other by layers of newspaper, straw, dry leaves, moss, or grass. This may all seem like a lot of effort, but it may extend the time you have food available.

Containers can often be recycled, but be sure they have smooth inner surfaces without protruding staples to puncture the produce. For dry areas open containers are best to promote air circulation. Crates and similar containers can be stacked by placing wooden burring strips between them. There should also be about 4 inches of space beneath the containers. Containers for humid storage should be relatively closed and can be covered with moist burlap or old rugs.

Produce you might consider for cold storage include apples, pears, beets, cabbage, carrots, garlic, horseradish, Jerusalem artichokes, onions, parsnips, white potatoes, pumpkins, rutabagas, squash, sweet potatoes and turnips.

Storage Facilities

The local climate will determine what facilities will be adequate for cold storage in your area. A cool and dry area can readily be found in most homes but an outside root cellar or other special structure must often be constructed to provide a suitable cold and moist area. All storage areas must be dark and windows should be screened. Large slatted louvers over windows will shade them while allowing air circulation.

The two common storage areas are simple and effective:

Basement storage rooms. Work best located in coolest part of unheated basement, usually the northeast or northwest corner. Should be away from furnace, chimneys, heating ducts and hot water pipes. Ceilings should be insulated and the door should be tight and secure. The room must be rodent proof. In heated basements, the room can be used for ripening tomatoes and for short-term storage of onions and potatoes, or it can be insulated. Concrete outside walls should not be insulated. The room can be partitioned into the two areas necessary. Removable heavy-duty slatted shelving and flooring is preferred to make air circulation and cleaning easier. Shelving three feet deep allows storing squash and pumpkins without them touching. Average needs can be handled by fifteen to twenty square feet per person.

Outside root cellar. Root cellars take more time and money to build but, once built, require minimal upkeep and work well keeping fairly large amounts of produce. They can be built entirely underground, into a slightly sloping hillside, or bermed on three sides. Like the basement storage areas, they can do double duty as a storm or fallout shelter if planned for ahead of time. The best root cellars are from reinforced concrete but they can also be made from cinder blocks, bricks, stones, or even wood. A firmly tamped dirt floor helps maintain the proper humidity levels and the roof and walls should be waterproof. Doors are best when located on the northerly sides.

Cheaper but less effective methods abound:

Buried barrels, crates, boxes, garbage cans, discarded refrigerators or freezers. The container is filled with alternating layers of straw, leaves, or similar packing and produce. When filled to the top, the container is covered with straw and then earth.

Outdoor mounds. Cabbage and root crops are often stored in these where it isn't too cold. A bottom layer of straw or leaves is covered with a cone-shaped pile of produce which is then covered with more straw. About three to four inches of soil is then placed over the straw, allowing the straw to protrude in the center to act as a ventilation flue. A cap of boards, sheet metal, or plastic is placed on top to keep the water out. The mound can be covered with a one-inch mesh chicken wire or hardware cloth to keep out rodents. If the area is not well-draining, a shallow drainage ditch can be dug around the perimeter. Because the entire mound should be used upon opening, it is preferable to make a number of smaller mounds rather than one large one. A variety of vegetables is stored in each.

Covered pits or trenches. These can be handier than the mounds because you need only use the portion uncovered at one time. They are about two feet deep and as wide as necessary to store the produce without crowding. As for any buried container, it is best to line the hole or trench with rocks to aid in proper drainage. This is then covered with alternating layers of straw or similar material and produce. The top can be covered with bales of straw or hay for easy access. A slanted roof helps prevent rain and snow from getting inside. Cabbage is normally stored roots up while celery is replanted in the bottom dirt.

All mounds, pits and trenches should be made in a different location the next year because the area used is usually contaminated by the leftovers.

Other areas that can be used for storage include insulated crawlspaces under porches, covered window wells, outside basement entry steps, enclosed porches, balconies, fire escapes and unheated pantries, halls, attics, garages or spare rooms.

Hardy root crops like carrots, horseradish, Jerusalem artichokes, kale, parsnips and salsify can often be left right in the ground. They can be covered with an eighteen inch to two foot blanket of mulch topped with chicken wire and weighted down with a rock or covered with bales of hay or straw. They can then be dug until the ground is too frozen, and the remainder dug in the spring.

Fruits give off gases and are best stored away from vegetables. Vegetables like cabbage, rutabagas ,and turnips have strong odors and should not be stored with potatoes or fruits. Most people also prefer those vegetables stored outside the house.

Whatever the storage facility, like all storage areas, it must be kept clean. Each summer it should also receive a thorough cleaning. All containers, bins and shelves should be removed, and the entire area disinfected, aired out and repainted if needed to eliminate mold and disease. Any necessary repairs can be made at this time. Packing materials and cardboard boxes should not be reused because they become contaminated.

For more detailed information on particular produce or for plans and ideas on building storage facilities, consult these books:

Root Cellaring by Mike Bubel, Nancy Bubel and Pam Art
Keeping the Harvest by Nancy Chioffi, et al

Keeping Other Items Cool

Dairy products and other produce can be kept cool for short periods of time by using methods like ice boxes, evaporative coolers, spring houses and cooling cabinets. Ice for the iceboxes can be harvested during the winter from ponds and streams and then stored for summer use.

17

HOME CANNING

The best method of home food preservation is determined by the nature of the particular food, the climate and storage conditions and the space and equipment available. No single method solves all storage problems and a combination of methods is often best. To help you decide which methods you will use, Table 17-1 gives comparisons of the relative costs, energy needs, work necessary, time it takes and the vulnerability to damage by crises.

TABLE 17-1.
COMPARISON OF HOME FOOD PRESERVATION METHODS

Method	Cost	Energy	Effort	Time	Vulnerability
Cold storage	Low	Low	Moderate	Low to Moderate	Moderate
Canning	Moderate	Moderate	High	Moderate	Moderate
Drying	Moderate	Moderate	Moderate	High	Low
Freezing	Very high	High	Low to Moderate	Low	High
Pickling	Varies	Low	Moderate	High	Moderate

Canning

Canning is very inexpensive and is the most prevalent way to preserve produce at home. It does involve a moderate amount of labor and is likely to be done during the summer, when it is already hot. It is an excellent method for foods that are normally thoroughly cooked, and it works best with fruits, tomatoes, asparagus, green beans, lima beans, beets, carrots, corn, peas, potatoes, pumpkin, spinach and squash.

Some people fear doing their own canning because of its safety. Perhaps they have heard the horror stories of botulism poisoning. In actuality, home canning is safe if the proper steps are carefully followed. This chapter is too short to give you anything other than an overview and list the equipment and supplies you'll need, so be sure you have one of the books listed. Any one of them will give all the detailed information necessary to safely can a large variety of produce.

Processing equipment

Even if you aren't presently canning, or even planning to, it would be best to have the necessary equipment and supplies stored. It could come in very handy some day and, at the worst, would be valuable for barter.

The most important canning tool is a <u>pressure cooker/canner</u>. There are a variety of brands and all should work safely. Store extra pressure release valves and gaskets for those that use them. Whichever brand you have, make sure the pressure gage is checked regularly to verify its accuracy. If it uses fixed weights instead of a gage, have it properly adjusted to the correct altitude. One which uses fixed weights (e.g. Mirro) may be better for long-term survival use because it does not require periodic calibration like the gage type does. And, to work as they should, clean the petcock and safety valve openings at the beginning of and throughout each canning season.

Another tool is a boiling water bath canner. It should include a rack to hold the jars and keep them off the bottom and be deep enough to allow two to four inches of space over the jars. A pressure cooker/canner can also be used as a bath canner but it's much heavier.

The steam canner processes fruits and tomatoes with steam rather than boiling water. This allows it to use about half the energy and take half the time. It also uses much less water, keeps the kitchen cooler and eliminates most boil-over mess. Best of all, the product quality is superior. It can also be used to blanch vegetables for drying and freezing.

Steam canner

Get a strainer; you'll never regret it. They make processing apples and tomatoes easy. Two well-known brands are Victorio and Squeezo. Buy the berry and pumpkin screens, too.

Finally, you will want a steam juicer, in either aluminum or stainless steel. It will effortlessly extract the juice from grapes, apples, etc. with no straining at all.

Other inexpensive equipment you should have:

☐ food grinder	☐ food chopper	☐ colander
☐ dipper or ladle	☐ canning funnel	☐ jar wrench
☐ canning tongs	☐ jar lifter	☐ slotted spoon
☐ measuring spoons	☐ measuring cups	☐ cutting board
☐ thermometer	☐ cooling racks	☐ timer
☐ pot holders	☐ knives	☐ kitchen scale

☐ kitchen shears   ☐ manual food mill/press

Some canning equipment is also useful for other preservation methods as well:

☐ apple corer   ☐ apple parer   ☐ bean slicer
☐ cabbage shredder   ☐ cherry pitter   ☐ corn cutter
☐ pea sheller   ☐ pear corer   ☐ potato peelers

If you want to do any canning with tin cans, you will also need a hand-operated can sealer. The sealer will also allow you to seal seeds, ammunition and other things in tin cans. They normally handle can sizes #1 through #3. Tin cans also require a glass food thermometer. A capper is needed if you anticipate capping bottles.

Doing jellies without a steamer will require a muslin or canvas jelly-bag strainer—or you can make your own from cheesecloth. For jellies, jams and other preserves, a jelmeter will give you a rough estimate of the amount of pectin in the fruit (or you can use an alcohol test but, if you use denatured alcohol, remember it is poisonous). A large (eight to ten quart) flat-bottomed kettle works fine and a double boiler and a thermometer come in handy. Some way to mash the fruit (food press, mill, grinder, or chopper) helps.

Pickles require utensils of unchipped enamelware, stainless steel, aluminum, or glass to avoid reactions with acids or salts. Fermenting (brining) is done in a crock or stone jar, plastic food storage bucket, unchipped enamel-lined pan, large glass jar, bowl, or casserole. All need covers and a weight to hold it down and keep the produce below the brine's surface. A simple cover is to use a plastic bag filled with water.

A fruit press may come in handy if you anticipate making a lot of fruit juices. Juices can be strained through the same bag used for jelly.

Supplies

Stockpile all the glass jars you'll need for your family. The information in Chapter 8 combined with Table 17-2 might be useful here. Store extras to replace any that might get broken. You'll want a selection of sizes, mostly pint and quart, but foods should be canned in sizes your family can eat at one meal. Wide-mouths are more expensive but best for larger fruits and easier to clean, while the narrow-mouths are fine for smaller produce and purees. Mayonnaise and similar jars can often be re-cycled if their lips are not chipped. They are not as sturdy as regular jars and are best for products requiring short processing times. Obviously, you'll want to store extra sugar for canning.

Store at least two seasons worth of lids and enough rings for your jars; more if you use a freezer. They could be in extremely short supply when most needed. Kept cool and dry, they will keep five years or longer.

I have found that the normal lids can also be reused a time or two if they are carefully removed without bending, have the rubber sealing compound intact, have not been corroded by an acidic food like tomatoes and are carefully cleaned; Ball is the best brand for this.

There are also jars that come with their own attached reusable lid. They are the Luminarc wide-mouth glass storage jars imported from France. They are heavy glass with a hinged glass lid containing a red rubber "o-ring" seal and are more expensive than regular jars.

Obviously, if you want to do tin canning, you will need some cans and lids. The most handy sizes are normally the #303, #2 and #2½ ones. They come in different qualities, too, with the better lasting much longer in storage. There are three varieties of cans and you'll probably want some of each. The enamel prevents discoloration of the food. The types and their uses are:

C-enamel (corn enamel): corn, hominy
R-enamel (sanitary or standard enamel): beets, red berries, red or
       black cherries, plums, pumpkin, rhubarb, winter squash
Plain tin: everything else including meat

For making jams, jellies and other preserves, store pectin (powder or liquid), ascorbic or citric acid crystals, paraffin wax and sugar. You can make your own pectin from tart apples if necessary. Powdered ascorbic acid compounds should be stored in a cool place where they won't absorb moisture and cake. They will keep at least two years.

Pickles and relishes take vinegar with forty to sixty grain acidity (4-6% acid), pickling or canning salt, sugar and spices. Salt is also used as a flavoring in canned meat.

Canning Methods

Water bath canning is suitable for high-acid (4.6 pH or below) produce. That includes all fruits, tomatoes (you can add two tablespoons of lemon juice or a half teaspoon of citric acid per quart to increase the acidity of low-acid tomatoes) and pickled vegetables. The two ways to do water bath canning are raw pack and hot pack. In raw pack the uncooked produce is placed in the container and then processed in the canner. In hot pack the produce is first heated and then placed in the container and processed. Some produce can be done either way while others are best done with a particular one (see Table 17-3). Times given in the tables should be increased at altitudes over one thousand feet according to Table 17-5. Fruits are normally canned with a sugar syrup (see Table 17-4).

Pressure canning is required for all low-acid vegetables and meat (4.5 pH or higher). This is because dangerous bacteria in low-acid foods are only killed completely at 240^0 F (116^0 C). That temperature can be attained only under pressure. As altitude increases, so must the pressure necessary to attain the correct temperature. If you are canning at altitudes above one thousand feet see Table 17-5 for the adjustment you should make. Pressure canning can be done with either glass jars or tin cans. Using pressure canning rather than water bath for high-acid produce will result in a lower quality product due to the longer total time spent at high temperatures.

Tin cans are more durable than glass jars and can be stored in the light, but they can't be reused and involve the extra step of sealing. Because the tin cans are sealed prior to processing in the canner, the air must be exhausted before sealing. To achieve the necessary vacuum, the food in the can must be at 170^0 F (77^0 C) or higher. The can is then sealed, processed in the canner and then cooled in cold water. The quicker cooling allowed by the tin can results in slightly better produce texture and less heat damage to the food's vitamins.

With all methods, some fruits and vegetables are scalded prior to packing to loosen their skins so they can be removed. The normal head space left in the containers before processing is one-half inch for jars and one-quarter inch for tin cans. Corn, lima beans ,and peas expand on cooking and should not be packed too tightly.

Jams, Jellies and Preserves

Fruit that is too large, too small, or irregularly shaped can be made into jams, jellies, conserves, marmalades, or preserves. All will add variety to your meals.

The proper amounts of pectin and acid are necessary to make jellied fruit products. Some fruits are high in natural pectin but you will have to add it to others. Lemon juice or citric acid is added for flavor and for gel formation; there is more natural acid in under-ripe fruit. Sealing the jar with paraffin is only recommended for jellies; the others should all be canned normally. Processing five minutes in a water bath is the usual time suggested.

Juices

Juices are the best way to use bruised and overripe fruits and vegetables. Obviously, the bruised or spoiled portions are removed first. Juices can be stored as concentrates or made into ciders, vinegars and wines.

Pickles & Relishes

Pickles and relishes can be made from many different fruits and vegetables and may be real treats in the survival diet. Pickling can be by fermentation or by fresh-pack. Both use brine and vinegar as preservatives with sugar, herbs and spices added for flavor. Pickles must be canned by the water bath method unless they will be eaten soon after being made.

Meat, Poultry and Fish

All types of meat, poultry and fish can be preserved at home by canning in a pressure cooker/canner. Combinations like stews, soups, chili sauce, etc. may also be canned. Either glass jars or tin cans will work. Use the C-enamel tins when canning smoked salmon in tin cans.

Further Information

There are many books on canning, and often they go into some of the other preservation methods as well. The best books I've found are:

Stocking Up by Carol Hupping
Putting Food By by Janet C. Greene, et al
A Guide to Canning, Freezing, Curing and Smoking of Meat, Fish and Game by Wilbur F. Eastman, Jr.
Ball Blue Book
Kerr Home Canning Guide

The *Complete Guide to Home Canning, Preserving and Freezing,* Bulletin #539 by the USDA is also available from Dover Publications and on the Internet at http://extension.usu.edu/publica/foodpub2.htm.

TABLE 17-2. YIELD OF CANNED FROM FRESH PRODUCE

The actual number of quarts will depend on the variety, size, maturity and quality of the produce and the way it is prepared. The standard weight of the fresh produce quantities is not the same in all states. Multiplying the quarts by two will give you the number of pints. The number of #2 and #2½ cans can be found by adding 60% and 14% respectively to the given numbers.

	Fresh quantity	Quarts
Fruit		
Apples, whole or sliced	1 bushel (48 lbs)	16-20
juice	1 bushel (48 lbs)	10
applesauce	1 bushel (48 lbs)	14-18
Apricots	1 bushel (50 lbs)	20-24
	1 lug or crate (22 lbs)	9-11
Berries (except strawberries)	1 crate (24 qts)	12-18
Cherries (un-pitted)	1 bushel (56 lbs)	22-28
	16 qt crate (22 lbs)	8-11
Peaches	1 bushel (48 lbs)	18-25
	1 lug (20 lbs)	8-10
Pears	1 bushel (50 lbs)	20-25
	1 western box (46 lbs)	18-23
	1 peck (14 lbs)	5-7
Plums	1 bushel (56 lbs)	24-30
	1 lug or crate (20 lbs)	9-11
Rhubarb	15 lbs	7-11
Vegetables		
Asparagus	1 crate (12 lbs)	3-4
Beans, green and wax	1 bushel (30 lbs)	14-18
lima (in pods)	1 bushel (32 lbs)	6-9
Beets (without tops)	1 bushel (52 lbs)	16-20
Cabbage (sauerkraut)	50 lbs	16-18
Carrots (without tops)	1 bushel (50 lbs)	16-20
Corn, sweet (in husks)	1 bushel (35 lbs)	7-9
Greens, chard, collard and		
mustard	1 bushel (12 lbs)	4-6
beet	1 bushel (15 lbs)	5-8
kale and spinach	1 bushel (18 lbs)	6-9
Okra	1 bushel (26 lbs)	16-18
Peas, green (in pod)	1 bushel (30 lbs)	6-8
Potatoes, white	1 bushel (50 lbs)	18-22
Pumpkin	50 lbs	14-16
Squash, summer	1 bushel (40 lbs)	16-20
Sweet potatoes	1 bushel (50 lbs)	18-20
Tomatoes, whole	1 bushel (53 lbs)	15-20
juice	1 bushel (53 lbs)	14-17
sauce	1 bushel (53 lbs)	8-11
paste	1 bushel (53 lbs)	4-6

TABLE 17-3. PROCESSING METHODS AND TIMES

		Processing Time in Minutes			
		Jars		Cans	
Boiling Water Bath					
Fruit	Method	Pint	Quart	#2	#2½
Apples	hot	15	20	10	10
Applesauce	hot	20	20	20	20
Apricots	raw	25	30	30	35
	hot	20	25	25	30
Berries (except strawberries)	raw, hot	10	15	10	15
Cherries	raw	20	25	20	25
	hot	10	15	10	20
Fruit juices	hot	5	5	5	5
Fruit purees	hot	20	20	20	20
Peaches	raw	25	30	30	35
	hot	20	25	25	30
Pears	raw	25	30	30	35
	hot	20	25	25	30
Plums	raw, hot	20	25	15	20
Rhubarb	hot	10	10	10	10
Vegetables					
Pickled beets	raw	30	30	—	—
Sauerkraut	raw, hot	15	20	20	20
Tomatoes, whole or juice	hot	40	45	45	45
Pressure Cooker (normally 10 lbs pressure at sea level)					
Vegetables					
Asparagus	raw, hot	25	30	20	20
Beans, kidney and navy	hot	65	75	65	75
baked	hot	80	100	95	115
lima	raw, hot	40	50	40	40
snap	raw, hot	20	25	25	30
Beets	hot	30	35	30	30
Carrots	raw	25	30	25	30
	hot	25	30	20	25
Corn, cream style	raw	95	—	105	—
	hot	85	—	105	—
whole kernel	raw, hot	55	85	60	60
Hominy	hot	60	70	60	70
Mushrooms	hot	30	—	30	—
Peas, blackeye	raw	35	40	35	40
	hot	35	40	30	35
green	raw, hot	40	40	30	35
Potatoes, cubed	hot	35	40	35	40
whole	hot	30	40	35	40
Pumpkin, cubed	hot	35	90	50	75
Spinach and other greens	hot	70	90	65	75
Squash, summer	raw	25	30	20	20
	hot	30	40	20	20
winter, cubed	hot	55	90	50	75
Sweet potatoes, dry pack	hot	65	95	80	95
wet pack	hot	55	90	70	90

TABLE 17-3. (Continued)

		Jars		Cans	
Pressure Cooker (continued)					
Meat, Poultry and Fish	Method	Pint	Quart	#2	#2½
Beef, lamb and pork	raw, hot	110	120	100	110
Sausage	hot	75	90	65	90
Corned beef	hot	75	90	65	90
Stew	raw	60	75	40	45
Soup stock	hot	20	25	20	25
Poultry and rabbit					
with bone	raw, hot	65	75	55	75
without bone	raw, hot	75	90	65	90
giblets	hot	75	—	65	—
Fish	raw, hot	110	120	100	110

Processing Time in Minutes

TABLE 17-4. SUGAR SYRUPS

Light: 2 cups sugar in 4 cups water   =   5 cups syrup
Medium: 3 cups sugar in 4 cups water   =   5½ cups syrup
Heavy: 4¾ cups sugar in 4 cups water   =   6½ cups syrup

TABLE 17-5. ADJUSTMENTS FOR HIGH ALTITUDE CANNING

Altitude above sea level	For Boiling Water Bath: of 20 min or less, add:	of more than 20 min, add:	For pressure canning, add:
1,000 feet	1 minute	2 minutes	½ lb
2,000 feet	2 minutes	4 minutes	1 lb
3,000 feet	3 minutes	6 minutes	1½ lb
4,000 feet	4 minutes	8 minutes	2 lbs
5,000 feet	5 minutes	10 minutes	2½ lbs
6,000 feet	6 minutes	12 minutes	3 lbs
7,000 feet	7 minutes	14 minutes	3½ lbs
8,000 feet	8 minutes	16 minutes	4 lbs
9,000 feet	9 minutes	18 minutes	4½ lbs
10,000 feet	10 minutes	20 minutes	5 lbs

18

HOME DEHYDRATING

Drying food is the oldest method of food preservation and is easy to do. It is inexpensive, particularly if done with a solar dryer, but takes a fair amount of time and is not well suited to some produce. Most fruits are easily and satisfactorily dried, while dried corn, onions, peas, peppers and herbs are particularly good.

Equipment

Basically, you'll need some type of dehydrator. An electric dehydrator is easiest and does the best job, but a solar drier would be a good backup. There are many brands available and most do a credible job. The best have a thermostat heat control and keep dehydrating heats low. A fan is normally used to force air across the food and carry off the moisture. Solar driers need an insect-proof cover and don't work too well on rainy days or in high-humid climates. Oven drying is expensive and relatively hard to control.

If you expect to do purees for leathers, teflon sheets the size of the dehydrator trays are great. There are also heavy plastic sheets you could use. Otherwise, you're stuck with oiling the trays or lining them with plastic wrap. A manual food slicer can help, as can a plastic bag sealer. It is assumed you have stored the items needed for basic canning. Otherwise you will also need a blancher. A wire basket is useful for scalding and blanching produce. If you have the vacuum packing equipment and/or oxygen absorbers mentioned in Chapter 6, you'll be able to use it to provide an oxygen-free storage environment.

Supplies

Store ascorbic acid and sulfuring products (flowers of sulfur, sodium sulfite, or sodium bisulfite) for use in retarding oxidation. A pound of sulfur will do about sixty-four pounds of fruit. Be sure to keep the products cool and especially dry. You'll need plastic bags for the bag sealer, and you can reuse #10 cans if you have extra lids for them. Cheesecloth can be used to cover trays to prevent sticking, scorching, or falling through. Plastic wrap or wax paper is used to roll leathers in to keep the layers separated.

How to Dehydrate

After larger produce has been initially prepared and sliced, it is ready for pre-treatment. Oxidation and darkening of the fruit can be prevented by dipping it in an ascorbic acid or sulfite mixture or by burning flowers of sulfur in an enclosed space (sulfuring). Tough skinned fruits like grapes, plums, cherries and some berries can be water blanched to speed up drying. Sulfuring, because the fumes are smelly and dangerous, should be done outside. Vegetables should be water or steam blanched with the steam method preferred to retain more nutrients. The blanching deactivates enzymes, speeds up drying by relaxing the tissue, preserves vitamins, and flavors and sets colors.

Recommended blanching and sulfuring times are listed in Table 18-1.

The best temperature for dehydrating most produce is 135-140^0 F (57-60^0 C), but drying times will vary widely according to the individual item, the size of the pieces and the dehydrator used. Drying in the sun takes considerably longer than drying in a dehydrator. Fruit is dry when it is leathery and pliable and retains its characteristic color. Vegetables should be brittle, and leathers should no longer be sticky in the center. Produce should be allowed to cool prior to testing. It's also better to over-dry than to under-dry and long-term storage requires drier produce.

The most accurate test for dryness is to compare the weight of the dried product with its pre-dried weight. Some of the best sources have used this idea, but they didn't understand it and got the numbers all mixed up. They thought if produce should have only 15-20% water when it is dry, then one could calculate the water that must be removed by taking 80-85% of the original water. However, that figure leaves way too much water in the dried product. Table 18-2 helps you avoid this problem by giving you ratios. For example, if you start with twenty-five pounds of apricots and want to dry them to the 25% listed for dry produce, you would multiple the twenty-five pounds times the ratio of .196 and find 4.9 pounds. This means that twenty-five pounds of apricots dried to 25% moisture content will weigh 4.9 pounds. Doing the same for 3.5% dehydrated (ratio .152) gives only 3.8 pounds.

Produce should be cooled after dehydrating. Then it can be sealed in a plastic bag and placed in a #10 can with a plastic lid or in a glass jar. Store all dehydrated products in a cool and dry location. Jars should be kept in the dark.

TABLE 18-1. SULFURING AND BLANCHING TIMES

Produce	Sulfuring Time	Blanching time	
		Steam	Boil
Fruits			
Apples	45 min	5 min	2 min
Apricots	2 hrs	3-4 min	4-5 min
Nectarines	8 min	8 min	8 min
Peaches	8 min	8 min	8 min
Pears	5 hrs	6 min	—
Plums	1 hr	—	—
Rhubarb		2-3 min	—
Vegetables			
Asparagus		3-5 min	2-3 min
Beans		2-2½ min	2 min
Beets		6-8 min	—
Broccoli		3-3½ min	2 min
Brussel sprouts		6-7 min	—
Cabbage		2½-3 min	1½-2 min
Carrots		3-3½ min	3½ min
Cauliflower		4-5 min	3-4 min
Celery		2 min	2 min
Corn		2-2½ min	1½ min
Eggplant		3½ min	—
Parsnips		3-5 min	—
Peas, green		3 min	—
Potatoes, white		6-8 min	—
Pumpkin		2-3 min	—
Rutabagas		3-5 min	—
Spinach		2-2½ min	1½ min
Squash, summer		2½-3 min	1½ min
Sweet potatoes		2-3 min	—
Tomatoes		3 min	1 min
Turnips		3-5 min	—

Dried Meat

Lean beef and similar meats can be cut into thin strips and dried into jerky. Pork should not be used because the low heats of dehydration will not kill the trichinosis bacteria. Unless you live in a hot and dry climate, you risk losing a lot of the meat to spoilage by drying it in the sun. Meat for jerky should be parboiled for fifteen to thirty seconds prior to drying. Jerky will keep a year or so if properly protected. It can also be pounded into a powder and mixed with dried powdered berries, nuts and suet to make pemmican.

Fish containing less than 5% fat can also be dried if done quickly. It should keep at least three to four months if made without salt and even longer with it.

TABLE 18-2. WATER CONTENT OF PRODUCE
AND DEHYDRATION RATIOS

This table gives the percentage of water contained in fresh, dry and dehydrated produce according to the USDA Handbook #8. The ratios for dry and dehydrated have been calculated from the given water content. Where no content was listed, the ratios were calculated using 20% for dried fruits and 4% for all dehydrated items. The ratios can be used to accurately estimate when the produce is dried or dehydrated to the listed percentage. For example, if you wanted to dehydrate 10 pounds of sweet cherries to the 20% moisture content, multiplying 10 by the given ratio of .245 would tell you that the 10 pounds of cherries would weigh only 2.45 pounds when they are dehydrated to that percentage. The ratio means that one pound of sweet cherries would only weigh .245 pound (less than ¼ pound) when dried to a 20% water content.

Fruit	Fresh %	Dry %	Ratio	Dehydrated %	Ratio
Apples	84.8	24	.200	2.5	.156
Apricots	85.3	25	.196	3.5	.152
Bananas	75.7	—	.304	3.0	.251
Cherries, sour	83.7	—	.204	—	.170
sweet	80.4	—	.245	—	.204
Cranberries	87.9	—	.151	4.9	.127
Currants	84.2-85.7	—	.188	—	.157
Figs	77.5	23	.292	—	.234
Grapes and raisins	81.5	18	.226	—	.193
Nectarines	81.8	18	.226	—	.190
Peaches	89.1	25	.145	3.0	.112
Pears	83.2	26	.227	—	.175
Pineapples	85.3	—	.184	—	.153
Plums	81.1-86.6	—	.202	—	.168
Prune plums	78.7	28	.296	2.5	.218
Rhubarb	94.8	—	—	—	.054
Strawberries	89.9	—	.126	—	.105

Vegetables	Fresh %	Dry %	Ratio	Dehydrated %	Ratio
Beans, green	90.1	—	—	—	.103
Beets	87.3	—	—	—	.132
Cabbage, regular	92.4	—	—	4.0	.079
Chinese	95.0	—	—	—	.052
Carrots	88.2	—	—	4.0	.123
Corn, sweet	72.7	—	—	—	.284
Eggplant	92.4	—	—	—	.079
Horseradish	74.6	—	—	—	.265
Mushrooms, domestic	90.4	—	—	—	.100
Onions	89.1	—	—	4.0	.114
Parsnips	79.1	—	—	—	.218
Peas	78.0	—	—	—	.229
Peppers, red & green	90.7-93.4	—	—	—	.083
chili	74.3-88.8	—	—	—	.197
Potatoes	79.8	—	—	5.2-7.1	.215
Pumpkin	91.6	—	—	—	.088
Rutabagas	87.0	—	—	—	.135
Squash, summer	94.0	—	—	—	.063
Tomatoes	93.5	—	—	1.0	.066
Turnips	91.5	—	—	—	.089

More Information

There are a number of books on just dehydrating with the following being among the best:

How to Dry Foods by Deanna DeLong and Lara Gates
The ABC's of Home Food Dehydration by Barbara Densley
Dry It, You'll Like It by Gen MacManiman

19

OTHER FOOD
PRESERVATION METHODS

The food preservation methods covered in this chapter should not be your main ways of preserving food but they can be used to supplement other methods.

Freezing

Freezing is an excellent and easy way to preserve many fruits, vegetables and meats, but it is very expensive compared to canning and dehydrating. However, from a survival standpoint, its major disadvantage is vulnerability. Even with an alternate source of power, the freezer can malfunction and put your frozen food storage in immediate peril. If that happens, you can prolong its frozen life with the techniques outlined in Chapter 7. You'll still have only a few days to preserve the food by another method or loose it.

Besides meats and seafood, the produce preserved well by freezing includes applesauce, asparagus, green beans, lima beans, broccoli, carrots, cauliflower, corn, peas, peppers, potatoes, spinach, strawberries ,and summer squash. Approximate yields of frozen foods from fresh is listed in table 19-1. Recommended storage times are given in table 19-2.

Obviously, a freezer is necessary. A chest freezer is better at retaining cold when opened, and a lock will prevent accidental opening. About six cubic feet per person is often recommended. A cooler or ice chest may come in handy if the power goes off, and you'll need a blancher to prepare produce for freezing. Freezer bags with a bag sealer, plastic containers, freezer wrap with twists and freezer tape, and heavy- duty aluminum foil will provide adequate protection for the food. Proper wrapping prevents freezer burn. Ascorbic acid is used as an anti-oxidant and to prevent discoloring of fruits and fish. Sugar is used to wet-pack fruits for added flavor.

Flash-freezing will prevent the formation of large ice crystals which rupture the cells and harm texture and flavor. You can do this at home if your freezer will get to -20^0 F (-29^0 C) or below. A single layer of

TABLE 19-1. YIELD OF FROZEN FROM FRESH PRODUCE

The actual number of quarts will depend on the variety, size, maturity and quality of the produce and the way it is prepared. The standard weight of the fresh produce quantities is not the same in all states.

Fruits	Fresh quantity	Pints
Apples	1 bushel (48 lbs)	32-40
Apricots	1 bushel (50 lbs)	58-70
	1 lug or crate (22 lbs)	28-33
Berries (unless listed)	1 crate (24 qt)	32-36
Cantaloupe	1 dozen (28 lbs)	20-24
Cherries (un-pitted)	1 bushel (56 lbs)	36-44
	16 qt crate (22 lbs)	14-17
Cranberries	1 box (25 lbs)	46-54
Currants	2 qt (3 lbs)	3-5
Peaches	1 bushel (48 lbs)	32-48
	1 lug (20 lbs)	13-20
Pears	1 bushel (50 lbs)	40-50
	1 western box (46 lbs)	37-46
	1 peck (14 lbs)	11-14
Pineapple	5 lbs	3-5
Plums	1 bushel (56 lbs)	38-56
	1 lug or crate (20 lbs)	13-20
Raspberries	1 crate (24 pt)	22-26
Rhubarb	15 lbs	15-22
Strawberries	1 crate (24 qt)	36-40
Vegetables		
Asparagus	1 crate (12 lbs)	15-22
Beans, green and wax	1 bushel (30 lbs)	30-45
lima (in pods)	1 bushel (32 lbs)	30-45
Beet greens	1 bushel (15 lbs)	30-45
Beets (without tops)	1 bushel (52 lbs)	35-42
Broccoli	1 crate (25 lbs)	22-26
Brussel sprouts	1 box (4 qt)	5-7
Carrots (without tops)	1 bushel (50 lbs)	32-40
Cauliflower	2 medium heads	3
Corn, sweet (in husks)	1 bushel (35 lbs)	14-17
Peas, gren (in pod)	1 bushel (30 lbs)	12-15
Peppers	3 peppers (⅔ lb)	1
Pumpkin	50 lbs	30-34
Squash, summer	1 bushel (40 lbs)	32-40
Sweet potatoes	1 bushel (50 lbs)	33-44
Tomatoes, whole	1 bushel (53 lbs)	15-20

produce is placed on a tray and then put in the coldest part of the freezer for twenty-four hours. After that the freezer can be turned back up to the normal -10 to 0^0 F (-23 to -18^0 C).

Salt Curing

Small amounts of salt can be used to ferment and pickle various fruits and vegetables. Eggs, olives and fish may even be pickled. However, none will keep more than a few months unless canned. Larger amounts of salt will permit storage for longer periods of time.

Pickling salt can be used for brine and dry curing of meat. Brine curing results in a more consistent and milder flavor, but dry curing is faster. A strong brine is necessary to preserve the meat for very long. A brine pump is commonly used on hams and other large pieces of meat to inject the brine throughout the meat and speed the process. Both methods result in extremely salty meat. Excess salt can be washed off or soaked out before eating. Saltpeter (potassium nitrate or

---

TABLE 19-2. STORAGE PERIODS FOR FROZEN FOODS

Maximum storage in months at 0^0 F (-18^0 C) or below

Meat		Vegetables	
Beef, ground and stew	2-3	Asparagus	6-8
roasts and steaks	8-12	Beans	8-12
Fish, fat	2-3	Beets	12
lean	6-9	Broccoli	12
Lamb, chops	3-4	Brussel sprouts	8-12
ground and stew	2-3	Carrots	12
roasts	8-12	Cauliflower	12
Pork, chops	3-4	Corn	8-12
ham and sausage	1-2	Eggplant	8-12
roasts	4-8	Kohlrabi	8-12
Veal, cutlets or chops	3-4	Okra	12
ground	2-3	Parsnips	12
roasts	4-8	Peas	12
Organ meats	3-4	Peppers	8-12
Miscellaneous		Pumpkin and winter squash	12
Baked goods	2-3	Rutabagas	12
Butter and lard	6-8	Spinach and other greens	12
Cheese	6-8	Summer squash	8-12
Coconut, shredded	8-12	Turnips	12
Cookies	8-12	Fruits	
Cream	3-4	Citrus fruits and juices	4-6
Eggs (not in shell)	8-12	Juices (except citrus)	8-12
Fruit cake	8-12	Mixed fruits	6-8
Fruit pies	6-8	Other fruits and berries	12
Nuts	6-12		

sodium nitrate) can be used to preserve color. Sugar can be used as a tenderizer and to improve flavor. There are also commercially-prepared cures you could store. After curing, the meats are usually smoked.

Lean fish that have been salted and properly dried will keep for a year or longer. Fat fish pickled in a strong brine may keep up to three months or longer.

Smoke Curing

Smoking is a type of drying and greatly changes the original flavors of the product. The meat is salt cured before it is smoked. Hams, bacon, meat and fish can be kept by preserving this way. Cold smoking (70-90^0 F) preserves the best, while hot smoking (170-210^0 F) is used solely to flavor and slow-cook the meat. The smokehouse must be built with the proper distance between the fire and the smoke chamber for the type of smoking preferred.

Cold smoking is best done in the late fall and early spring when daytime temperatures are cold enough to keep the meat from spoiling and nighttime temperatures are above freezing. Don't use resinous woods for the fire because they impart unpleasant flavors to the meat. Cold smoked hams will keep longer than a year. All meat that has been salted and cold smoked is still raw and should be cooked prior to eating.

Sausage Making

Meat, poultry and game scraps can be ground up and made into sausage. All you need is a manual cast-iron meat grinder with cutter plates and an attachment for stuffing sausages. A funnel will work in an emergency. Artificial casings may be stored, or you can use the small intestine from a hog or sheep. Light-weight muslin is normally used for sausages over one and a half inches in diameter. A selection of spices will help make sausage to your taste preferences. Good sausage has a balance of fat and lean meat in it. Sausage will keep for six months to more than a year if smoked. Otherwise, it must be canned or frozen for long-term storage.

Further Information

Detailed information on freezing, salt curing, etc. is contained in some of the books listed in Chapter 17. Other books on making sausage, jerky and smoking meats are listed in Chapter 32.

20

EMERGENCY EVACUATION

Without warning, a local disaster like an earthquake, flood, or a chemical or nuclear accident may force you and your family to quickly leave your home. Temporarily relocated, you may find you must rely on yourselves for some period of time until the civil authorities can effectively respond. If you are prepared with an Emergency Evacuation Kit (EEK, sometimes referred to as a "72-Hour Kit"), you will be ready to provide the bare necessities and a minimal level of comfort during that period. Being so prepared will also leave you more in control of the situation and help keep up your morale.

What about national disasters, like a nuclear, biological, or chemical attack? In a major crises the civil government might be totally unable to effectively help you at all. You might be on your own for substantial periods of time.

The Emergency Evacuation Kit (EEK)

When thinking about an emergency evacuation kit, some individuals want to play mountain man and only want "the basics" they can carry in a pocket or two. Others consider basic survival to require a fully-equipped, self-sufficient RV! I don't think either view fits the bill for an EEK.

To function adequately, the EEK must fulfill some well-chosen criteria. The first is to match the anticipated crises. Ideally we would like to be prepared for all possible crises, but that is seldom possible due to cost, space and weight limitations. The EEK should be prepared to handle the high-probability, high-risk crises.

To determine these you are going to have to evaluate your particular situation. It doesn't make much sense to prepare for a possible nuclear accident if the closest reactor is five hundred miles away, but it certainly does make sense for the family living only miles downwind from one. Nearly everyone lives fairly close to a chemical plant or an interstate highway or railroad where chemical spills could occur. Flooding can occur in most areas, and I wouldn't rule out earthquakes whether I lived in an "active" zone or not. You probably have a good idea whether you live where volcanoes could be a problem. Fires, hurricanes, typhoons and tidal waves (more accurately called tsunamis) happen, too.

Once the kinds of probable crises are determined, the criteria of portability comes up. There is an endless list of items that "would be good to have", but you'll have to make some tough compromises. The EEK must be kept handy and ready to go at a moment's notice to be useful. And it needs to be the right size. If it's too large, you will probably find it stored somewhere out of the way and perhaps not complete when needed. Too little, on the other hand, will mean it doesn't contain enough to be effective.

How are you going to transport it? You would need a truck for all the equipment I've seen on some lists. Perhaps you will be able to use a vehicle, but earthquakes can quickly make roads worthless, and automobiles also need fuel to run. But carrying everything on your back can severely limit what you can take. The best alternatives seem to be a decent sized backpack or some container that can be mounted on a pack frame. Then it can be transported either by vehicle or by foot. A person in average shape can carry about one-fourth to one-third his body weight fairly comfortably, and you should try not to exceed that in your planning. The large duffle bags so often seen used for these type kits are just fine for carrying in a vehicle but are hard to carry for any appreciable distance on foot.

Now you can start planning the specific makeup of your EEK. I recommend you put your own together rather than simply purchasing a commercial kit. I've seen a number of them running from under $100 to more than $1,000, but chances are none of them will fit your particular needs. Buying one of them also means making do with their selection and quality.

There is no magic list of the "23 items guaranteed to get you through any situation" so you'll just have to make up your own. To help you, suggested items have been divided into the following ten categories. Go through and choose those that best fit your specific needs.

1.   **Container**. The container should be sturdy and large enough to hold everything. It also helps if it is waterproof and items can be organized and are easily accessible. While a backpack will work fine, one container you might consider is the plastic bucket with a handle and tight-fitting lid. The bucket can do triple duty: it can not only hold the EEK items, but will also serve to carry and hold water and works fine as an expedient toilet and waste holder. Buckets can be strapped on pack frames to be carried.

A large fishing tackle box can help organize items but is awkward to carry far by hand. Improvised containers might be suitcases, ice chests, garbage cans, etc., but remember it must be small enough to fit into a vehicle if you will use one.

One idea I recommend is to have one container per person for individual gear and perhaps some food and water with the remaining items stored in a communal, group, or family container. This will lessen the impact in case of separation.

2.   **Water.** Unfortunately, water is bulky and heavy, weighing over eight pounds per gallon. Have a one to two-quart canteen in each individual's container and some purification tablets and/or a filter in the communal one. A two and a half or five-gallon collapsible bucket or jug with spigot would be a good idea if you aren't using buckets for your EEK containers. In the desert you might want a solar still. Store a five-gallon container of water near the vehicle you would likely use.

3.   **Food.** It's best to store foods that do not need refrigeration and can be eaten without cooking. Don't worry about having it nutritionally balanced; for the short-term just have enough palatable calories (see Chapter 8 to find amount of calories for your family; enough for three days is usually recommended). Store foods like canned meats (Vienna sausage, tuna, etc.), stew, jerky, pork and beans, peanut butter, cheese, soda and graham crackers, canned and dehydrated fruits, hot chocolate, powdered milk, fruit juices, chocolate bars, nuts, hard candy, soup, bouillon cubes, protein bars and sugar. Many are available in pull-tab cans or small packets. If you have babies, remember some baby food, formula and baby bottles with nipples. Also store some salt tablets.

Each individual container should have a spoon, fork and a sharp knife. A plate and a stainless steel camping cup would also be excellent. And each container should have a P-38 G.I. can opener in it; they're exceptionally inexpensive and very handy. Keep some detergent and a dishpan to clean the utensils after use.

4.   **Clothing and Bedding.** Have a change of warm, durable work or outdoor clothing suitable to the coldest weather you can expect. Don't forget outerwear like a coat and rain wear. Extra socks and underwear help along with work gloves, a good hat for

shade and a wool cap for warmth. Keep a pair of well-fitting work shoes or hiking boots near your bed for instant access.

The lightest bedding would be one "emergency" blanket per person. It is a reflectorized metallic blanket that reflects back 90% of the body heat. More substantial bedding could be a sleeping bag or a wool blanket with blanket pins.

5.   **Shelter.** To protect from exposure to the elements, it can range all the way from a plastic drop cloth or "space" blanket up through a nylon tarp or tube tent all the way to a full-fledged backpacking tent. A space blanket is similar to the "emergency" blanket but thicker, and it is the recommended minimum. Get the heavy-duty kind with grommets in the corners so you can improvise a shelter with a piece of rope.

6.   **Sanitation.** If your EEK uses plastic buckets as containers, you're all set. Use one for a toilet and another for waste storage. Otherwise, get a portable camping toilet with plastic bags. Hand soap, facial tissue, packets of wet towelettes, feminine hygiene and shaving needs might be considered. Babies will need disposable diapers. Don't forget toilet paper!

7.   **First Aid Kit**. Have a good basic first aid kit with a good instruction booklet and plenty of large sterile bandages, pads, gauze and adhesive tape. Include a supply of special medications with prescriptions anyone in your group or family would need and some moleskin or Spenco Second Skin to protect feet from blisters.

8.   **General.** You'll definitely want a transistor radio so you can tell what's going on as far as the weather, your rescue, or relief, etc. is concerned. Get either an AC/DC radio with fresh and regularly- checked batteries or a solar-powered radio with rechargeable batteries. You should also have fifty to one hundred feet of nylon rope, parachute cord, or climbing rope for making shelters and other things. Other items to consider are a Swiss army knife or survival knife, a cable saw, insect repellant, duct or electrical tape, folding shovel with serrated edge and maps covering the anticipated evacuation routes.

A pocket survival kit could be useful. It should contain fishing line, hooks, sinkers, lures, snare wire, compass, razor blades and matches.

A GPS (Global Positioning System) can locate your exact

position on a map or, with a compass, help plan a travel route. But a GPS relies on satellites and only works if they do.

9.   **Light-Heat-Cooking.** A flashlight is a must. Some are available that generate electricity by squeezing a lever or turning a crank. Otherwise store fresh batteries and check them regularly. A good survival candle will burn a long time and even provide a small amount of heat. Other light sources are signal flares (good fire starter, too) and a cyalume light stick that creates a bright fluorescent light chemically for about thirty minutes by simply bending it.

A hot meal might be nice but, if you choose the right foods, it isn't be absolutely necessary. A small backpacking stove and fuel won't add a whole lot of weight, though, and you can use the stainless steel camping cup to cook in. For moderate amounts of heat you could store a catalytic heater with fuel, but they take up substantial space and weigh quite a bit. Have plenty of waterproof and windproof matches stored in a waterproof match safe. You may also want a metal match and a magnesium fire starter. A disposable lighter may come in handy, too, and is small and cheap..

10.   **Personal.** Things like a toothbrush, toothpaste, comb, brush, mirror and personal toiletry items can add a lot of comfort to a bad situation. A watch will help coordinate and paper and pens may be needed for notes and messages. A small amount of cash and change may be useful. Some may want to safeguard personal documents and valuables such as credit cards, securities, deeds, contracts and insurance policies. The best thing for protecting these items is a military ammo can. It is made from heavy-duty metal and is watertight when closed.

You may also desire to have some weapons for protection. A small .22 pistol may serve well but a Charter AR-7 .22 survival rifle or other takedown rifle would be better. Some may prefer a larger caliber weapon. Have a decent supply of ammunition.

Obviously, any vehicle you plan on using should contain a small kit with common repair parts and tools (see Table 27-1 in Chapter 28for a list of the basic on-board tool kit). Also keep it at least half fueled at all times.

If you think you may need to evacuate for a nuclear attack, then plan on taking the items listed in Table 27-1. Also take along instructions for building an expedient shelter, plans for a KAP, a fallout meter or plans and materials for a KFM and potassium iodide. The KAP, KFM and potassium iodide are covered in Chapter 27.

TABLE 20-1. BASIC EMERGENCY EVACUATION KIT (EEK)

Communal Container:

☐ purifying tablets	☐ water filter	☐ collapsible bucket
☐ solar still	☐ dish pan	☐ detergent
☐ G.I. can opener	☐ tarp or tent	☐ portable toilet
☐ toilet bags/ties	☐ toilet paper	☐ hand soap
☐ wet towelettes	☐ facial tissues	☐ first aid kit
☐ first aid booklet	☐ moleskin	☐ transistor radio
☐ nylon rope/cord	☐ cable saw	☐ route maps
☐ tape	☐ folding shovel	☐ flashlight
☐ fresh batteries	☐ matches/lighter	☐ fire starter
☐ mirror	☐ documents/valuables	☐ extra food
☐ plastic drop cloth	☐ plastic/paper bags	☐ paper plates/cups
for solar still	☐ towels	☐ folding stove/fuel
☐ survival manual	☐ sewing/repair kit	☐ scissors
☐ nail clippers	☐ tweezers	

Communal Water Container: (one for every 2-4 people)
☐ 5 gallons of water in poly bucket with handle, lid and spigot

Individual Containers: (each person)   *where applicable

☐ 1 to 2-qt canteen	☐ purifying tablets	☐ food for 3 days
☐ salt tablets	☐ knife, spoon, fork	☐ steel camping cup
☐ plate	☐ G.I. can opener	☐ change of clothing
☐ coat	☐ rain wear	☐ extra socks
☐ extra underwear	☐ work gloves	☐ boots/shoes
☐ hat/cap	☐ emergency blanket	☐ sleeping bag
☐ hand soap	☐ sanitary napkins*	☐ shaving items*
☐ diapers*	☐ toilet paper	☐ medications
☐ insect repellant	☐ survival kit	☐ candle
☐ matches	☐ toothbrush/paste	☐ comb/brush
☐ paper/pens	☐ watch	☐ washcloth/kerchiefs
☐ survival knife	☐ sharpening stone	☐ Chapstick/lotion

21

GENERAL SURVIVAL TOOLS

A number of tools serve a variety of survival purposes. These include firearms, knives, multi-tools, axes and saws.

Firearms

"A well regulated Militia, being necessary to the security of a free State, the right of the people to keep and bear Arms, shall not be infringed."

Second Amendment, The Constitution of the United States of America

We, as individuals, have an inalienable right and the responsibility to defend our lives, our families and our property with whatever force is necessary. The Second Amendment of the U.S. Constitution simply recognizes that right. If a government doesn't trust its citizens with firearms and tries to disarm them, its motives should be questioned.

If the conditions expected by many actually develop, firearms will be vital. Even now, in many instances, you are the only one who can guarantee your safety. Having a defensive firearm and knowing how to use it effectively to protect your family may be of even greater importance in coming times.

The "ideal survival gun" doesn't exist because the answer depends on the specific tasks required. Likewise, an untrained person won't accomplish much with the best gun, while an expert can do a lot with a mediocre firearm. In spite of that, some guns are better than others.

First, choose the caliber. It will be easier to obtain ammunition for the most popular calibers and those used by the military and police. Following those guidelines generally limits you to these calibers:

.22 Long Rifle	.223 (5.56 NATO)	.308 (7.62 NATO)
.30-06	.270	.30-30
9mm Parabellum	.45 ACP	12 gauge
.357 Magnum	.38 Special	.44 Magnum

A .357 magnum also shoots .38 special while the .44 magnum would be a good choice for reloaders. The fewer calibers you choose, the easier it will be to stock and use ammunition without confusion. Limiting the number of firearm models will also make it easier to stockpile spare parts, and non-working guns can be scavenged for parts if necessary.

Survival Battery

Firearms can be divided into two general categories for survival use: defensive and working guns. Defensive means self-defense while working guns are used to provide food, to control predators and pests, and to protect you from dangerous animals like wild dogs and snakes. Pistols and revolvers are limited to about fifty yards or less, while shotguns can be very good defensive weapons at ranges under forty yards (with a rifled slug best over twenty-five yards). A .223 rifle is best used under 250 yards.

The number and type of firearms to stock in your survival battery depends on your budget and the circumstances you anticipate. The Violent Crime Control and Law Enforcement Act of 1994 banned the manufacture and importation of so-called "assault" rifles, pistols and large capacity ammo clips. Although the existing "pre-ban" firearms are still available, this curtailed their supply and dramatically increased their cost. Because of this, the following recommendations only list "non-ban" firearms:

Defensive-	rifle:	.308	
	and/or	.223	Ruger Mini-14
	pistol:	9mm	SIG, Glock, Beretta, Ruger, H&K,
	or	.45	Browning, Colt
	shotgun:	12 ga	Remington 870, Winchester Defender, Ithica 37
Working-	rifle:	.22 LR	Ruger 10/22, Winchester 9422, Marlin 39, Remington
	and/or	.308	
	revolver:	.44 Mag	Ruger, Colt
		.357/38	Smith & Wesson
	and/or	.22 LR	Ruger Mark II, Colt

If you have the money and want an "assault" rifle, you can find them for sale at gun shows, on the Internet or from a local firearms dealer. Have two to six extra magazines for any defensive weapon, and have good holsters for all handguns. Hunting rifles could be scoped, and all rifles should have shooting slings. An extra ventilated-rib barrel with

Ruger Mini-14 .223

Browning Hi-Power 9mm

Ruger .22 Bull Barrel

a variable choke or interchangeable choke tubes would modify the shotgun for hunting. The AR-7 makes an excellent EEK or cache weapons and the Savage 24F is a combination gun—a rifle caliber over a shotgun—you might consider. All firearms would be good barter items with a .22 perhaps the best.

AR-7 .22

Guns can be stored for the long-term by wrapping them in plastic and storing in a waterproof container, perhaps including a desiccant, or by packing all moving parts in a grease like Cosmoline or petroleum jelly and wrapping in a heavy waxed or oiled paper bound with twine. Put a heavy coat of furniture wax on all wood and leave an excess of oil in the bore and on all outside metal. Any guns stored around the house should be locked up for safety and to prevent unauthorized use.

Guns can be hidden either on or off-site in lengths of PVC pipe. Use an auger to dig a deep enough hole, place the pipe vertically in the hole, fill with the guns, keeping all parts together, and cover with at least one foot of soil. Use a rust-preventative on all metal parts prior to placing them in the pipe. Have a method for locating your cache when needed. Additional information on caching of weapons can be found in *Modern Weapons Caching* by Ragnar Benson.

Ammunition

Store at least two hundred rounds per firearm; depending on your budget, one thousand per firearm would be better. Ammunition will make great barter items. Military surplus ball ammunition should be boxer-primed so it can be reloaded. Buy high-base #4 buckshot and rifled slugs for defense and #6 shotgun shells for hunting. Stored in a cool and dry location away from ammonia and oil-based products, cartridges will be useable for decades. Shotshells are more susceptible to moisture and may not last as long; wrap them in plastic and store in airtight containers. About the best container of all is the military ammo can, and you can go that one better by sealing the rounds in plastic before putting them in the can.

Care and Repair

You must take care of your guns if you want them to last. Clean them after every use. Store cleaning kits with rods, tips and brushes appropriate to your caliber choices. Also store plenty of cleaning patches, bore cleaner (solvent) and gun oil. Break Free can be used as a bore cleaner, solvent, gun oil and protective coating. Silicone or teflon lubricants work best in cold weather.

Have a supply of spare parts for each gun to keep it operating. These normally include a spare firing pin, extractor and assorted springs, but get the advice of a competent gunsmith if in doubt. Store the parts wrapped in an oily cloth.

You'll also want a gunsmithing tool kit. Brownells (see Chapter 32) carries a selection of tool kits along with a tremendous parts inventory. Gunsmithing books worth considering include:

Gun Digest Book of Firearms: Centerfire Rifles by J.B. Wood
Gunsmithing (3 volumes) by Patrick Sweeney
Gunsmithing at Home by John Traister

Reloading

The capability to reload could become important. If you plan on doing a lot of practice and/or hunting, it can also save you considerable expense. Many experts recommend that handloads not be used for defense because they may not be as reliable as factory-loaded. But, if you are careful, that shouldn't really be a concern. Handloads also are said to have shorter shelf lives than factoryloads, but this can be overcome by sealing the cartridge around the lead and primer after loading with a small amount of finger nail polish. Cartridges do have longer shelf lives than the individual primers and powders do.

The least expensive way to reload is with a Lee Loader (about $20 per caliber), but it uses different size dies than full-size bench presses do. The HDS Compac Tool, available from Huntington for $80, uses the regular dies and weighs only thirty-seven ounces. The standard of bench presses, the RCBS Rock Chucker, can be bought with a   complete reloading kit (powder measure, scale, funnel, deburring tool, case lube kit, reloading guide, etc.) for about $400. You need one set of dies per caliber at about $30 or so per set.

HDS Compac Tool

Bullets can be cast from scrap lead (e.g. tire weights) with a simple melting pot (even a cast iron skillet will work), a dipper or ladle, a sizer/lubricator, top punches and sizer dies, lube cutters, lubricants and bullet molds. However, solid lead bullets will result in barrel leading, rifling fouling and less reliable automatic feeding.

Swaging (forming bullets inside die and punch sets under pressure rather than casting) allows making jacketed bullets as good as factory-made. Normal bench reloading presses can be used for calibers up to .357 pistol and .243 rifle with larger calibers requiring a swaging press. Also needed are swaging dies, punches, lubricant, a core cutter or a core mold and the lead and jacket material. Lead is handy stored as lead wire. You can buy the commercial gilding metal jackets to store or swage your own from copper and brass tubing. You can even make .223 and .243 jackets from used .22 LR cases. Swaging equipment and supplies are available from Corbin Manufacturing & Supply.

Primers are relatively inexpensive but vital. Store more than you think you need. A selection of basic powders can handle all of your survival reloading needs; choices of one expert are twenty pounds of IMR-4895, eight pounds of Herco and three pounds of Red Dot. That should load around 8,000 average rounds. Unique is another versatile powder.

Reloading components should be stored where it's cool and dry. Lead bullets, brass cases and paper shotshell cases and wadding can corrode and deteriorate from moisture. Primers and powder must be protected from moisture and heat if you want them to last more than a few months. Like ammunition, don't store them around ammonia and oil-based products or flammable materials. They should be left in the original factory containers, wrapped or sealed in plastic and stored in an airtight container for long shelf life. Deteriorating powder forms a fine, brown dust on its granules and develops an irritating acidic odor. Again, the ammo can is hard to beat and desiccants can be used. Rust won't affect the aluminum bullet molds but the more durable iron ones can be stored in a can filled with motor oil.

Other Weapons

Black powder guns compare poorly with modern guns and use dangerous black powder. Muzzle loaders also are extremely slow to load and are single shot. If all the smokeless powder runs out, and you are forced to make your own black powder from saltpeter, sulfur and charcoal, you can still use it in any centerfire gun. Either way primers will still be necessary unless it's a flintlock.

Air guns, on the other hand, have a definite place in survival. The adult spring-piston type is the only type to consider. It is capable of propelling pellets at seven hundred plus feet per second in rifles and over four hundred feet per second in pistols. They seem expensive, ranging into the hundreds of dollars, but are very accurate and powerful enough to quickly and quietly dispatch small game and pests without advertising the fact. They also can be ordered unrestricted by mail. They are recoilless and provide inexpensive practice at about a penny each for .177 pellets, the preferred caliber. That's less than one-third the cost of a similar number of .22 rounds, and they weigh one-fourth as much and take up one-tenth the space. Buy only high-quality pellets for reliability.

Effective air rifle range is mostly in the twenty to fifty yard range but can be up to about sixty-five yards; pistols are limited to the fifteen to thirty-five yard range. Air guns will easily last a lifetime. Stock an oiling needle with some silicone chamber and spring oil. Also have a spare parts kit containing replacement mainsprings, "O" rings, piston seals and breech seals if used for that model.

Bows and arrows could be useful in certain situations, but they are not high on the priority list. You'll need a fair amount of regular practice with either a compound or long bow to hit anything consistently. Crossbows are easy to master and provide high accuracy and power at ranges of fifty-plus yards. For either, store extra strings and quality arrows or bolts.

Slingshots are another item some may want to consider for small game. Store spare sets of surgical tubing bands.

Further Information

This is only a very basic overview of survival weapons. More detailed data can be found in the books listed below. Tappan's is the original classic and contains a vast amount of specific if sometimes outdated information. Cobb's contains some good advice for those on a limited budget.

Survival Guns by Mel Tappan (reprinted 2002 by Delta Press)
The Survival Armory by Duncan Long (Delta Press)
Bad Times Primer by C. G. Cobb
Gun Digest
Shooter's Bible

You might also want to subscribe to The Shotgun News (see Chapter 32) to find mail order sources for guns, ammunition and reloading components at excellent prices.

Knives

Knives are valuable survival tools, and they come in a wide variety of styles for many uses beyond the kitchen, butchering, filleting and skinning mentioned in Chapter 10. Most likely you will want a general hunting and survival knife. A fixed-blade sheath knife is preferred, but a locking-blade folding knife can be handy, too.

The Wyoming field dressing knife is unusual in design, but is small, works very efficiently and has replaceable blades. A Swiss army knife can put a miniature tool box in your pocket. There are many other types you might want to consider including pocket, boot and survival belt-buckle knives. Machetes serve useful purposes for some.

Wyoming knife

There are many good brands to choose from, but be sure to always get quality. Swiss knives should be either Victorinox or Wenger, not some cheap imitation. Custom knives sometimes offer special advantages, but you could get five to ten high-quality factory knives for the same price.

Knives would be excellent barter items. The best buy for the money now is probably Schrade Old Timer knives.

Multi-tools

Multi-tools are a basic tool kit in a pocket-sized package. They usually offer at least one knife blade, pliers, screwdriver blades, can opener, files and other useful tools.

There are many brands and models to choose from, each with its own strengths and weaknesses. Consider the size you desire (make sure they're strong enough), the tools you want, and then compare those models that fit your criteria. Locking blades are a "must have" feature and I would want wire cutters. Brands to consider are the original Leatherman, SOG, Gerber and Victorinox. Again, avoid cheap imitations.

Leatherman Wave

Axes

Axes and hatchets are basic survival tools. A long-handled axe with five pound head (either single or double-bit) is good for felling trees to build a cabin. Shorter-handled axes with lighter heads, such as the single-bit Hudson Bay or the double-bit Cruiser styles, are excellent for homestead chores and general survival. A belt axe or hatchet is also handy.

Saws

Saws can be used for felling and pruning trees, cutting lumber and butchering animals. A good bone saw can make butchering a large animal a lot quicker and easier. Have extra blades. Quality folding saws fit in small spaces and are light-weight. One or two-man crosscut, bow and buck saws are useful for cutting logs.

Sharpening Tools

Knives, axes and saws must be kept sharp if they are to serve you well. Store the needed sharpening accessories and learn how to properly use them. Always use oil or at least water with all sharpening stones unless directions state otherwise.

Get soft and hard whetstones with honing oil for use with knives, axes and other edged tools. A file is used to take out nicks and for rough sharpening. You'll need a saw set tool and a saw gauge for straightening and sharpening saw teeth. As noted in Chapter 10, sharpening steels, ceramic sticks and strop straps are used to straighten the edges on knives.

A useful device to help you get the right angles for correct knife sharpening is the Buck Honemaster, but it is no longer made. There are some rod-guided systems such as the EdgePro Apex Sharpening System and those made by Lansky, Gatco and DMT. EZ Sharp makes a small $13 sharpener many professional chefs like, while the Butterfly and Super Sharpener are handy pocket sharpeners.

Other Tools

This chapter is not meant to be an exhaustive list of all the tools that might be useful for survival but to simply point out some of the more common and necessary. Other tools certainly worth considering are:

☐ rope, cord, twine	☐ pick axe	☐ mattock
☐ binoculars	☐ backpack	☐ compass
☐ woodchopper maul	☐ splitting wedges	☐ adze hoe
☐ sledge hammer	☐ pry-bar	☐ crowbar

22

CLOTHING AND BEDDING

Clothing and bedding are necessary to shelter and protect the body from the environment: cold, heat, wind, rain, sun and injury. Surviving without all the civilized comforts we depend on so much will place a larger burden on the clothes we wear and the bedding we sleep in.

Clothing

I recommend that you have enough ready-to-wear clothing or the fabric and other materials necessary to make them on hand to last at least a year. The advantage of storing ready-to-wear is that they can be used immediately. The advantages of storing fabric and materials is that it costs one-third to one-half as much (but takes time to make) and can be made up as necessary into the items and sizes needed. That can be an advantage especially to those families with growing children. Materials might also be traded for the services of a seamstress. While it is a good idea to always have an extra supply of the clothing you normally wear, we are concerned here with basic survival clothing.

Survival clothing should be durable, warm and comfortable work clothing of various kinds to suit your situation, climate and seasons. Don't worry about the style and appearance but about how well it will function and hold up. Good-quality outdoor clothing is often the best choice (Filson, Pendleton and Woolrich are quality brands). Tightly woven fabric is more snag and tear resistant and wears longer but loosely woven is warmer. Natural fabrics like wool and cotton are more absorbent, and wool retains its insulating properties even when wet. Synthetics, on the other hand, tend to have higher strength, resist abrasion and mildew better, and dry more quickly. Waterproof but breathable Gore-Tex and similar fabrics as well as fleece should be considered for pertinent items.

Table 22-1 is a list of the minimum suggested amounts for various clothing items. Adapt it for your particular situation. Normally, you will have some of the necessary items already on hand. Items used on a regular basis can be stored by projecting needs ahead and purchasing for them on a replenishment basis, rotating just like you do with food. Others you may not normally use can just be stored for the future. Although you usually get what you pay for, the best buys can be the medium-priced, medium-quality items.

A critical item is footwear. Shoes are almost always in short supply during crisis times, and you can't do much without them. Buy only well-fitting shoes and boots with quality leather uppers and heavy nylon hand stitching (not glued). Other features to look for are full bellows tongue to keep dirt out, steel shanks to protect the foot and Vibram soles for long wear. Danner, Chippewa, Red Wing (Vasque), White, Sorel and Timberland are among the better brands. Alternating pairs allows drying out and prolongs shoe life. If you expect to do much work in the cold and snow, you'll probably want some insulated boots or rubber-bottomed boots with spare felt liners. Foam rubber insoles cushion the foot, and thick felt insoles help insulate from cold.

It's difficult to store enough sizes to properly match growing children, but by loosely-fitting them you should be able to get by with two or three different-sized pairs per year. Leather shoes are more protective but not really necessary for children.

You can purchase ready-made shoelaces or purchase nylon or leather shoelace material and cut to fit. The length of shoelace needed for a pair of shoes can be estimated by counting the number of eyelets or hooks on one side and multiplying by six inches. Store plenty of good socks with thin ones next to the skin to avoid blisters and heavy ones on the outside to insulate. Wigwam makes excellent socks but there are other good brands, too. Also store foot powder and moleskin.

TABLE 22-1. BASIC CLOTHING PER PERSON FOR ONE YEAR
Adapt to age, sex, climate and lifestyle

☐ 8 sets underwear (2 long)	☐ 2 pr work shoes or boots
☐ 1 pajamas or nightgown	☐ 1 pr waterproof boots/overshoes
☐ 1 warm robe	☐ 2 pr shoelaces/pr footwear
☐ 2 t-shirts	☐ 12 pr socks (8 light, 4 heavy)
☐ 2 cotton turtle-neck shirts	☐ 4 pr jeans, pants, overalls
☐ 1 straw hat	☐ 1 pr heavy wool pants
☐ 1 knit cap or balaclava	☐ 2-4 work shirts (chambray, etc.)
☐ 1 heavy-duty work belt	☐ 2 cotton flannel shirts
☐ 1 pr suspenders	(chamois, etc.)
☐ 1-2 sweaters	☐ 2 heavy wool shirts
☐ 2 pr leather work gloves	☐ 1 water-repellant windbreaker
☐ 1 pr winter gloves or	☐ 1 winter work coat
mittens, inserts	☐ 1 heavy-duty winter parka

Don't overlook gloves. Have a good supply of leather work gloves to protect your hands, gloves and mittens to keep them warm and reusable rubber gloves to protect you when using caustic chemicals or skinning and dressing animals that may be infected with disease.

Cold Weather Wear

For cold climates, you will most likely want more warm clothing added to the list. You can have heavy-insulated garments or use the principle of layering to keep warm. Down is an excellent insulator when dry but fairly expensive. Thinsulate and similar synthetic insulations retain warmth when wet and are cheaper. Fleece also retains warmth, is light in weight and fairly inexpensive. There are a number of hi-tech underwear fabrics that wick moisture away from your body while providing excellent warmth. Your head lets a lot of heat escape and should be protected by a good hat; a balaclava is a knit hat that can also be used to cover the face and neck in extreme cold. Winter clothing can be improvised from newspapers and other things, but I think I'd prefer to store what I could.

Infants

For an infant, store sixteen to twenty-four plastic pants in assorted sizes through toddler. You can store cloth diapers or make three dozen from twenty-five yards of twenty-seven-inch diaper flannel. Don't forget diaper pins. Disposable diapers would be good for the EEK and water shortages besides being usable as bandages and for the ill. A minimum of ten yards of cotton flannel will make an adequate supply of blankets and baby clothes. You might want to store heavy blankets, blanket sleepers and a snow suit for cold climates and sleeping in unheated homes. Booties, sweaters and caps can be knit from yarn and other clothes can be made from stored cloth.

Cleaning and Care of Clothing

If the power is out, your electric and gas washers and dryers won't do you much good. The dryer can always be replaced by clothes pins on a clothesline or outdoor dryer, but pounding rocks in a stream doesn't seem to be a terrific washing method. If you don't want to use a washboard in wash tubs get a James Washer. It looks like a half-barrel with an attached handle, costs about $500 and is available from Lehman's (see Chapter 32).

Estimate the amount of laundry detergent needed from current usage. You will also want to store bleach and perhaps some blueing. Add a cast-iron flatiron and you can even have pressed clothes! There are also irons that use either gas or propane available from Lehman's.

Footwear will last for years if kept clean and dry. Store leather preservatives and water proofing as well as paste wax for polish. Most footwear is made from chrome-tanned leather and needs a wax or silicone-based treatment like Sno-Seal, Biwell and Leathe-R-Seal. Oil-based compounds are for oil-tanned leather and will weaken the glue on footwear with cemented soles. NeatsFoot Oil and Mink Oil keep leather soft and pliable. Saddle soap cleans and softens leather.

Clothing and Fabric Storage

Clothing, fabrics, boots and bedding should be stored clean in a cool, dry and dark environment. Heat will crack leather, too much moisture may cause mildew, and light deteriorates some materials and fades colors. Moth balls or crystals can be used to protect woolens from moths and other insects and desiccants can be used to reduce moisture. Oiling leather will help it remain pliable, and shoe trees help footwear retain their shape. Acid-free tissue paper should be used for wrapping. Plastic bags can be sealed to keep dust out, and a cedar chest with a tight-fitting top is among the very best storage containers. Label containers with contents. Sleeping bags and down clothing should be stored loose and not all wadded up in a stuff sack.

Making Your Own Clothing

Storing fabric will allow you to make clothing items as needed in the proper sizes. Table 22-2 tells how much is needed to make various items and suggested types of fabrics (check patterns for exact amounts); depending on the pattern it takes two-thirds to seven-eighths as much in sixty-inch widths. Normally woven wools come in fifty-four to sixty-inch widths and cotton and polyester knits are usually sixty inches wide. Patterns can often be arranged with less waste on wider widths of cloth.

Bolts of denim, cotton and wool flannel, broadcloth, corduroy, unbleached muslin and various pants weight cottons could be stored. A supply of leather would also be useful. Babies' sleeper sets take about one yard of sixty-inch stretch terry or cotton knit. Terry is also good for bath towels while muslin is used for dish towels and bandages.

Kits are available from Frostline to make jackets, coats, comforters, sleeping bags and other items. They come complete with all notions and materials including the thread. The fabric and insulation is pre-cut. Fabrics may be bought locally or from mail-order sources (see Chapter 32).

Sewing Equipment and Supplies

Sewing by hand is pretty time consuming and less durable than machine stitching. So, if you are going to sew, you will want to have a sewing machine. An electric one is fine for now, but a treadle sewing machine works when the electricity is off. You might be able to find an old one locally for about $50. Or you can adapt your powered machine with a pulley or even turn it by hand (slowly)!

For heavy-duty sewing with canvas and leather you might want an electric commercial or upholstery sewing machine. Store extra parts, machine oil and a brush.

Store a variety of machine needle sizes (9, 11, 11 ballpoint, 14, 16, 16 jeans, 18, 19 and 21 for heavy canvas and coarse cloths). You'll want some sharps hand needles in various sizes, too. Store thread in various colors and sizes; size 50 general-purpose polyester-core cotton or nylon thread is the best, but you will also want some button cord and heavier thread for denim. Thread is available in inexpensive, large quantities on commercial-sized spools. Have a good supply of sharp colored-ball pins, safety pins, bobbins and some tailor's chalk.

Get a good pair of dressmaker's shears, sewing scissors, pinking shears and a pair of embroidery scissors. Also get a tape measure, sewing gauge, seam ripper, thimbles, pin cushion, darning spool and a tracing wheel with carbon.

You can always make your own patterns by taking apart old clothes, but it would be better to store assorted basic patterns in various sizes. You will also need a good supply of notions to make most items: zippers in a variety of lengths and weights (heavy-duty for jeans and pants, separating for jackets and coats), buttons, snaps, hooks and eyes, rivets, bar tacks, nylon tape fasteners (Velcro), grommets, interfacing, linings, trims and various widths of twill tape, bias tape, seam tape, hem tape, nylon tape, mending tape, bindings, iron-on patches, elastic and t-shirt ribbing.

If you store yarn and the proper needles, you will be able to knit mittens and sweaters. There are also manual knitting machines. Hats, gloves and scarves take about four ounces of a three-ply sport weight

TABLE 22-2. FABRIC NEEDED FOR BASIC CLOTHING

(Approximate yards of 45" width fabric; depending on pattern, 60" requires ⅔ or more as much)

Items of Clothing	Infants	Children			Youth	Women			Men			Suggested Fabrics
	Size 0-2	Size 2-3	Size 4-6	Size 8-10	Size 12-16	Small	Medium	Large	Small	Medium	Large	
Underpants		¼	¼	¼	½	½	¾	1	½	¾	1	cotton knit, tricot
Nightgown (long) or nightshirt	1	2	2¼	3	3¾	3¾	4	4¼	3¾	4	4¼	flannel
Pajamas		1¾	2	2¾	3¼	3¾	4¼	4¾	4½	4¾	5	flannel, cotton blends, prints
Robe (long)		1½	1¾	2	3¼	4	4½	4¾	4	4	4¼	flannel, terry, quilted fabrics
T-shirt (short-sleeve)	½	½	¾	¾	1	1	1¼	1½	1¼	1½	2	cotton blend knits
Shirt (long-sleeve)		1½	1¾	2	2¼	2	2¼	2¼	2¼	2½	2¾	cotton and wool flannels, broadcloth, chambray
Pants	¾	1	1¼	1½	2¼	2½	2¾	2¾	2¾	2¾	3	denim, corduroy, cotton duck, poplin, sailcloth
Overalls	1¼	1¼	1½	2	2¾	3¼	3½	3½	3½	3½	4	denim, corduroy, cotton duck, poplin, sailcloth
Jacket	1	1¼	1¼	1¾	2¼	2¼	2¼	2½	2¾	2¾	3	denim, corduroy, wool, poplin
Coat	1	1½	1¾	2½	3	3½	3¾	4	3	3½	3½	wool, corduroy

yarn while socks take eight ounces and sweaters use four to twelve ounces depending on size.

To put all your tools and fabric to best use, you might want to have the following books:

Complete Guide to Sewing by Reader's Digest
The Complete Photo Guide to Sewing (Singer)

Making and Repairing Shoes

It's much easier to store quality footwear than make it. However, you may want the capability of doing so if the need arises and the same equipment will allow you to repair worn shoes. Table 22-3 lists the necessary tools, supplies and materials for making and repairing shoes and boots. There used to be a couple of books available back from the 1960's but I don't know of any currently. With those tools and supplies you can also make many other leather items like belts, gloves, pouches and jackets. To do these you may want to add the appropriate patterns, leather, lacing of various widths, hardware and a wooden mallet.

Making your own fabric and leather

Although beyond the scope of this book, you can make your own homespun wool with a hand spindle or spinning wheel and wool cards for carding the wool. A loom will make cloth from wool yarn. Plants and minerals can be used to make dyes. Rugs may be woven from cloth

---

TABLE 22-3. COBBLER EQUIPMENT AND SUPPLIES

Tools

Ordinary hardware-type utility knife with blades, sharp small curved paring knife, eight-inch upholstery shears, revolving leather punch, stitching awl with Speedy Stitcher #8 needles, two-inch #00 or #1 harness needles, glue rougher or heavy-grit sandpaper. Handy-to-have: cobbler's or tack hammer, ball-peen hammer, stitching spacer, leather rasp, calipers, pliers.

Supplies

Heavy-duty waxed nylon thread (Nyltex; dental floss or fishing line will do in emergencies), barge contact cement and thinner, shoemaking or clinching nails (⅝" and 1"), eyelets, rivets, buckles and Sam Browne buttons.

Materials

Four to seven-ounce chrome-tanned moccasin cowhide (2-3 square feet per pair shoes), rubber or leather sole blanks, pre-cut heels, one-inch foam rubber for padding.

scraps with no equipment at all. Rope and twine can be easily twisted with the help of a rope machine.

Animal skins and furs may be tanned the old way with the animal's brains, with a commercial tanning solution, or a home-made solution of one and a half pounds of alum, one and a half pounds of salt and five gallons water. Books that may be of interest:

Tan Your Hide! by Phyllis Hobson and Steven Edwards
Home Tanning and Leather Making Guide by A.B. Farnham
Home Manufacture of Furs and Skins by A.B. Farnham

Bedding

Have enough bedding on hand to keep each person warm if there were no other heating. That may be three to four good blankets per bed or more. Bedding includes the following items:

☐ blankets   ☐ quilts   ☐ comforters
☐ mattress pads   ☐ sheets   ☐ rubber sheets
☐ pillows   ☐ pillow cases

Sleeping bags make excellent emergency bedding for family or unexpected guests. You can keep them cleaner, and they will last longer, with liners. Down is warm but expensive and loses its warmth when wet. PolarGuard and Quallofil don't compact as well but are nearly as good, are not bothered by mildew and are easily machine washed.

Quilts and comforters can be made from cloth scraps, recycled clothing and blankets as well as from flannel, cotton and muslin. It takes about three and a third yards for an infant's crib quilt, ten yards for a twin quilt and eleven yards for a double quilt. Store half-inch batts for quilts, one to one and a half inch for comforters. A quilting frame will make the work much quicker and easier. You will also want #5 to #8 quilting and darning needles and thread. Receiving blankets can be made from two yards of forty-five inch flannel. You can also make sheets, but only certain materials come in wide enough widths to make them without seams.

Newspaper can be used for emergency insulation if need be. It's not great but works better than nothing. Spare blankets could be used for warm robes or to line jackets and coats.

23

ENERGY
HEAT, COOKING AND LIGHT

Energy is a critical concern for survival under crisis conditions. If you live in a cold climate, how would you heat your home without natural gas, fuel oil or electricity? Wherever you live, how would you cook your food? How would you see at night? How would you use many of the other things that require energy, like refrigerators, hot water heaters and radios?

Contingency planning for energy shortages or complete unavailability can be very complex depending on perceived needs, circumstances and desires. While some people may feel it is adequate to store a camping stove with a small supply of fuel for short-term emergencies, others may feel it is wise to build an energy-sufficient home complete with solar cells and wind-powered generator. This chapter will point out the possibilities. You will have to decide how far you are willing and able to go. At least one method for each (heating, cooking and light) is recommended but two or three would be preferred. It might be of benefit at this point to refer to Table 23-1 for a comparison of the alternative fuels and see which ones might be best for you.

Heat

First, assess your situation if your normal heating system failed. Realize that most modern systems require electricity to operate thermostats, fans, blowers, fuel injectors and ignition. And, with little or no heat, how would you keep your home's water pipes from freezing?

The best long-term crisis solution for heating a home is an airtight wood/coal stove or furnace for larger areas. Multi-fuel furnaces that use a fossil fuel like gas, oil, or propane combined with a wood/coal capacity allow use of the regular fuel until forced to switch over. A wood/coal forced-air furnace could be used all the time if that is desired, or a wood/coal furnace or stove could be connected up to the normal ducts to serve as a back-up when needed. The same can be done with boiler furnaces for hot water or steam heating. A good wood or coal stove burns with 50-75% efficiency. A Franklin stove burns at only 35-45%.

TABLE 23-1. FUELS

BTU ratings are approximate and variable. Usable energy produced can be found by multiplying the BTU rating by the system efficiency. The normal system efficiency range is given in percentages inside the parentheses. One kilowatt-hour equals 3,412 BTU.

Wood

6500 BTU/lb with 25% moisture content (50-65%). Abundant in some locations, it is scarce in others and may become more so during a crisis. Renewable wherever it grows naturally. A standard cord is 8x4x4 feet of tightly stacked wood; the 128 cubic feet only contains about 80-90 cubic feet of wood. A cord of air-dried softwood weighs about 1¼ tons, while hardwood can weigh over 2 tons. A face cord is 8x4x whatever length it is cut in, making it typically ⅓-½ a standard cord. Softwoods like pine burn quickly and hot and make the best kindling. Hardwoods like oak burn more slowly. Store wood outside, shielded from the weather so it will stay dry. It takes about twelve months to well-season wood. Burning green wood can cut efficiencies by up to 25%. Estimated time needed to chop and split a cord of wood is eight hours. Use a chain saw (Stihl is the best brand), cross cut saw, buck saw or axe to cut and a splitting maul or sledge hammer with wedges to split.

Coal

8,500-15,500 BTU/lb (55-65%). There is more energy stored in the coal reserves of the U.S. than in all the world's known reserves of oil. Coal is mined in 26 states and definitely should be considered the basis crisis fuel in those areas. Anthracite, or hard coal, burns with less soot and smoke than the softer bituminous coal, but is harder to burn and is found almost exclusively in Pennsylvania. Coal burns dirtier than wood, but three to five times as much energy can be stored in a comparable space. A ton of anthracite takes about 35 cubic feet while a ton of bituminous takes about 43 cubic feet. Get the recommended size for your stove or furnace for best results. Store coal in a dark, dry place (e.g. lined pit, coal bin, shed) away from air as much as possible. Use paper and wood to kindle coal.

Kerosene

135,000 BTU/gal, 6.8 lb/gal. Readily available now, like all liquid hydrocarbon fuels, it could be hard to find during a prolonged crisis. It is the most stable liquid hydrocarbon and stores longer without deterioration. It is also reliable and burns hot, clean,"silently and odorlessly in modern, efficiently-designed burners. It's flashpoint is much higher than gasoline, but spilled fuel does not evaporate quickly. Inexpensive when bought in five-gallon or larger quantities. Buy pure "water-clear" 1-K grade white kerosene and store in an opaque container. The 2-K grade has a much higher sulfur content and is for use only in vented appliances.

Gasoline

125,000 BTU/gal (6.1 lb/gal). Used widely in automobiles, generators, chain saws, etc., it will probably be scarce during a serious crisis. Highly volatile, it burns quick and hot. It deteriorates over time unless a stabilizer is added. Spilled fuel evaporates readily. White gas contains 119,000 BTU/gallon. Naptha, sold under the Coleman and Blaze labels, contains 121,000 BTU/gallon, burns a bit cleaner, is less likely to clog burners ,and contains a rust inhibitor, bit it is quite expensive in the small cans. Leaded gas fouls burners.

Diesel

138,000 BTU/gal (6.9 lb/gal). Could be hard to find during a prolonged crisis. Less volatile than gasoline, it is safer to store and deteriorates more slowly. Stabilizers can be added to extend normal storage life. Most automobile manufacturers recommended #2-D diesel fuel with a minimum 40 cetane rating. For improved operation in cold weather and altitudes above 5,000 feet, #1-D diesel fuel can be used. It has added kerosene to make it more viscous and volatile, but it lacks the engine lubricants of the #2-D. Add one quart of lubricating oil per 100 gallons.

Fuel Oil

140,000 BTU/gal, 7.2 lb/gal (70%). Normally #2 domestic heating oil, it may be in short supply during a prolonged crisis. Used in furnaces and heaters, it can also be used as an emergency diesel fuel. Deteriorates over time unless a stabilizer is added.

Liquid Petroleum Gas (LPG)

91,500 BTU/gal propane (4.2 lb/gal), 103,000 BTU/gal butane (4.8 lb/gal) (80%). LPG (propane and butane) is readily available now but would be hard to find during a prolonged crisis. However, methane would work in most LPG equipment. LPG is reliable, easy and clean to use, odorless and fairly inexpensive when used in the 11, 20 and 30 pound or larger refillable tanks. It stores for many years without deterioration. The liquid is stored under pressure and is vaporized to burn. Propane is best for winter use as butane loses its pressure below freezing.

Natural Gas

100,000 BTU/hundred cubic feet (CCF) (80%). Although it may be in short supply during a crisis, it is made up largely of methane gas (850-1,100 BTU/cubic foot) which could be made and used instead. Naturally odorless, gas companies add smell to make leaking more detectable.

Alcohol

65,000 BTU/gal, 6.9 lb/gal. Can be produced at home. Produces little heat and is very expensive for its heat value. Fumes are irritating to some people. Flame can be extinguished with water and spilled fuel evaporates quickly.

Sterno

High probability will be unavailable during crisis. Easy to light, use and reuse, but produces strong fumes and has low heat value, especially considering cost.

Charcoal

12,600 BTU/lb. Readily available now and can be made at home. More heat per cubic foot than wood, but harder to start, especially without starting fluid (needs one quart per five to ten pounds of charcoal). Can spontaneously catch fire if stored wet. Must not be used indoors because produces large volume of odorless but deadly carbon monoxide.

Coal burns about twice as hot as wood and stoves made for it are built with refractory linings and different draft designs and stove pipe installation. Combination stoves for wood and coal are not quite as efficient at burning either one. They should have an interchangeable grate, a removable liner, an ash pan and a larger draft opening than found on wood stoves. Wood may be burned in a stove made for coal, but burning coal in a wood stove will soon burn out the bottom. A wood grate also allows the smaller coal to fall through, and many will not stand up to the heats of coal-burning. If you plan on using much coal, perhaps the best compromise would be to get a coal stove and burn wood in it when you wanted to.

Some wood/coal stoves made basically for cooking also heat up to 1500 square feet of area. A rudimentary wood stove can be made from a 55-gallon steel drum or a used water heater.

Whatever stove you get, be sure to install it properly so it won't burn your house down. Shield it well to prevent children from accidentally burning themselves. Get a poker, an ash pan, a shovel and a metal bucket for ashes and clinkers. Also have a stiff brush to clean soot and a wire chimney brush with extension rods or ropes and scrapers to prevent creosote fires in the chimney.

To preview a wide selection of wood/coal stoves as well as other back-to-basics items, get a copy of Lehman's Non-Electric Catalog. Multi-fuel furnaces are made by Yukon-Eagle. If you plan on heating primarily with wood, you might want a book to learn the tricks of the trade.

Fireplaces are more esthetic than anything else, with typical efficiencies from less than 10% up to about 20%. Heat exchangers help somewhat. Using an insert can raise the efficiency to the 30-60% range, but it now looks much like a stove.

You can also store a large quantity of fuel oil for an oil furnace or space heater but, once used up, you will be dependent on finding a new source.

If you live in a centrally-heated apartment building or only need moderate heating for short-term periods, consider the highly-efficient pressurized kerosene heaters made by KeroSun and Toyostove among others. If they have a flat top you can even do minimal cooking on them. Get one that is UL-approved and use the proper grade of kerosene, or you'll get more than a slight kerosene odor. There are similar propane and natural gas heaters by Rinnai and Suburban. White gas and propane can also be used in flameless catalytic heaters.

Burning any fuel uses up oxygen and gives off poisonous carbon monoxide. To prevent a dangerous buildup of gases or a depletion of oxygen, many believe heaters should only be used in well-ventilated areas or be vented and have a built-in oxygen sensor.

A final option would be a sheepherder stove with pipe. Made from sheet metal, it is heavy but portable, gives off a good quantity of heat and could be used to heat a tent, cabin or similar structure. Cooking can be done on its top.

Pioneer Maid

Cooking

Although some heating options allow limited cooking, most don't have ovens. For cooking and baking, the wood/coal stove with oven offers the most. Lehman's has a cooking stove comparison chart that shows gives details on the heating capacities and cooking surfaces. Lehman's currently offers the Oval, Sweetheart, Waterford Stanley, Enterprise Monarch, King, Savoy, Heartland, and some Amish-made stoves. Many offer

Heartland Oval

water reservoirs or jackets (they call it a waterfront) to heat water as they cook.

Baker's Choice

You can connect them directly to your house plumbing. A double-wall construction will help keep the kitchen cooler in summer.

Cooking and baking with wood or coal is very different from gas or electric. Heat is much harder to regulate. You will need a couple of trivets to raise pans off a too-hot stove, a lid lifter and an oven cleaning rod. Cast iron pots and pans with metal handles that won't burn or melt and some long-handled wooden spoons and forks are necessities. And practice this way of cooking prior to the crisis. If you aren't already proficient at it, it might also be a good idea to get *Woodstove Cookery* by Jane Cooper.

A fireplace can always be used to cook in, but it may leave a lot to be desired. The best way is to have a swinging arm crane or fixed bar and chains to hang cast iron pots from. Tongs and a long ladle will help. A dutch oven can be used for baking, cast iron pans and griddle for frying, and a grill will work if there's nothing else.

Less permanent alternatives are the portable camping stoves that use propane, butane, white gas, alcohol or kerosene. The two or three-burners are adequate for an average family. Coleman also makes a small oven that fits on top of a burner for baking. The obvious disadvantage to these stoves is that they depend entirely on a stored fuel supply.

Stoves using canned heat (e.g. Sterno), heat tabs or fuel bars are strictly for short-term emergency use because of their severely limited cooking ability. A charcoal burner or barbecue grill has the same limitations. Both types should only be used inside when there is sufficient ventilation The Sierra Zip Stove model burns about anything, is portable and would make a good outdoor survival stove. Even better but much more expensive is the folding Pyramid system that uses any solid combustible for cooking, baking and providing hot water. Solar cookers, limited to midday cooking on sunny days, are not adequate.

The final possibility is cooking on an open fire, but be sure you have cast iron cookware. A dutch oven and a reflector oven would help.

Light

A light source can be critical at times, especially when caring for the ill and calming frightened children.

For the long-term without electricity, the Aladdin kerosene lamps seem optimum. They give off a white light equivalent to a sixty-watt light bulb and burn silently with minimal odor for forty-eight hours on a gallon of kerosene. They also give off a small amount of heat, and there is a conversion kit that allows the use of electric light bulbs during normal times. Store extra chimneys, mantles, wicks and a selection of spare parts.

Aladdin brass lamp

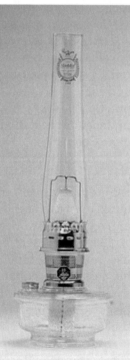

Aladdin Genie lamp

Second choices would be propane lamps and white gas lanterns. Both are brighter than kerosene lamps, hiss and glare when burning and give off light approximately equivalent to 100-120 watts for the single mantle and 150-200 watts for the double mantle. A gallon of propane or white gas will burn about forty hours in a single, thirty hours in a double. White gas is the most dangerous.

Store spare mantles. Cheaper wick lamps and hurricane lamps are much less desirable because they give off an amber light about 10% as bright as the Aladdin, but only burn two to four times as long.

Flashlights and battery-powered lanterns are obvious choices for quick, always-ready portable lighting. Their also obvious limitation is their battery life. Nicad rechargeable batteries only hold about half the energy of regular ones, but they can be charged up to a thousand times. You can store them for long periods of time prior to ever charging them; once they are charged they will develop a "memory" and fail to hold a full charge unless you totally discharge and recharge them three times. Then discharge them varying amounts and recharge on a regular basis. A multi-volt solar array can be used to charge the batteries or run small calculators, radios, etc. directly. Some lights, radios and calculators come with built-in chargers and solar cells. Store spare bulbs and batteries for flashlights and lanterns.

Candles are basically for short-term emergency use only. Although they do give off enough light for some activities and a small amount of heat, their open flame can be dangerous. Keep a supply of them on hand, but don't count on them as your main light source. You may also want to store candle holders or lanterns. Tables supposedly giving the burn times for candles of various sizes are useless because the burn time also depends heavily on the characteristics of the particular wax used, the wick size and the number of wicks.

It's easier to store candles, but if you want to make them later you should store paraffin, wicking and perhaps some molds (you can always make your own molds).

Also store a supply of regular light bulbs for when your normal electric power is on. Nothing seems to truly replace Edison's invention.

Hot Water

Hot water is needed for bathing, cleaning clothes and washing dishes. Water may be heated by your wood/coal stove or even over an open fire but there are better ways if you plan for them now. Solar water heaters work very well on sunny days and can be added to homes without too much effort. There used to be wood-fired hot water heaters imported from Mexico, but they apparently aren't even being made there now. You can make a wood-fired hot water heater out of an old gas one by welding a fire box to its bottom. Be sure to install a temperature and pressure relief valve (available at a hardware or building supply store) on it.

For portable hot water, there are the SunShowers that you simply fill with water and place in the sun. Zodi also offers the Extreme portable propane showers that you can hook to a bulk tank.

Refrigeration

Most people would miss the convenience of refrigeration even more than lighting. What can you do about it? Well, there are refrigerators and freezers that use power sources other than electricity. Dometic offers the Servel Americana series dual electric-LP gas (can be converted to butane or natural gas) or kerosene refrigerator-freezers. Lehman's also sells the Frostek freezer that uses LP gas, kerosene or propane. There are other refrigerator/freezers made for the RV and marine markets (usually 12-24vdc) that operate on electricity or LP gas, including the Explorer, Novakool and Norcold brands. SunFrost, Solarfridge and Polartech refrigerators use one-fourth the usual electricity.

Stockpiling Fuel

The best fuels are those that presumably could always be replenished locally like wood and coal. However, since some choices require liquid hydrocarbon fuels, the only solution is to stockpile a large quantity of it and hope for an alternate source by the time it runs out.

Stockpiling liquid fuel can be dangerous if not done correctly, and storing more than five to twenty-five gallons of gasoline is illegal in most urban areas (check with the local fire department) and will void fire insurance. Nevertheless, it can be done safely (any cars exploding in their garages regularly and they store ten to more than forty gallons of gasoline on a regular basis?) Unless you absolutely have to, though, do not store gasoline in or near your home or attached structures.

The best way to store fuel is underground in properly vented tanks covered with at least four feet of earth. This not only prolongs the life of the fuel, but also reduces evaporation and helps protect it from theft, fires, accidents and gunshots. You can use anything from 55-gallon steel drums to large tanks that hold thousands of gallons. Steel tanks will last more than ten years underground when protected from corrosion with two coats of Rust Not (one gallon per two hundred square feet) or a well-tarred protective wrapping (not simply asphalt-coated). Fiberglass tanks last at least thirty years, tend to be cheaper in sizes larger than 2,000 gallons and can't be located by metal detectors, if that worries you. Be aware that EPA regulations on underground tanks are extremely strict now.

Before burying and filling the tank, check for leaks using air pressure (five pounds) or water, and install and test all fittings. Losing stored fuel could be disastrous, and getting water into it could also be a problem. Avoid copper pipe and fittings. Unless you use gravity feed, have at least one hand pump available (not the same one for water).

For above-ground gasoline storage, the safest method is with ExploSafe cans if you can still find them. Other UL-approved gas cans, five-gallon Jerrycans and drums may be used but are more hazardous. Any fuel container that can't be easily lifted when full should have a hand pump or manual syphon. Never syphon with your mouth because ingested gasoline can cause fatal chemical pneumonia. The vapors can be extremely explosive. To minimize vapor formation keep containers nearly full with only a few inches for expansion (gas expands .06%/^{0} F). Volatile fuels like gasoline, propane and butane have heavy vapors that settle in lower areas and can puddle, possibly causing suffocation or an explosion. Do not store them in basements, shelters or near heat, flame or motors.

Fuels stored above-ground are much more subject to temperature variations, with alternating expansion and contraction, and this must be taken into account in container size and venting. Containers that must be stored directly in the sun can be wrapped with insulation or painted with reflective silver paints to keep variations to a minimum.

Long-Term Storage

All liquid hydrocarbon fuels deteriorate over time (kerosene is by far the most stable). Components of gasoline oxidize to form gums, lacquers and peroxides that reduce performance, cause stalling, clog fuel filters, foul carburetors and spark plugs, and can even damage pistons and valves if extensive enough. Anti-knock compounds in high grades of gasoline decompose. Diesel fuel separates into its various constituents, little streamers of paraffin form in it and bacteria and fungi may pollute it. The resulting sludge and slime plugs filters and strainers, fouls fuel probes and lines, gums up injectors and combustion chambers, and breaks down tank sealants and coatings. Heat is the main enemy of stored fuels, greatly increasing the oxidation rate. Gasoline is presently formulated to be used within six months under normal conditions and may deteriorate in less than two months in a hot garage. Diesel fuel and heating oil deteriorates within a year or so.

Kerosene is more stable.

Fortunately there are stabilizer additives that will retard the chemical breakdown and preserve the fuels for much longer periods for small added expense. Many preparedness sources sell Power Research's PRI-G (for gasoline) or PRI-D (for diesel or kerosene) fuel preservative; a quart will treat 512 gallons of fuel. Fifteen ounces of B.H.T. (butylated hydroxytoluene or 2,6-ditertiary butyl p-cresol) or one gallon of Fuel Mate Plus will treat 1,200 gallons of gasoline. Diesel Plus is used one gallon per 600 gallons of diesel fuel, and contains an anti-gel for winter use and a biocide to prevent algae and bacteria contamination. Two pounds of Ethyl's EDA-2 is recommended to treat 1,000 gallons of kerosene. Storage tanks of all fuels can also be treated every six months with one-third ounce of Angus Chemical Company's Bioban P-1487 per 1,000 gallons to keep fungi and bacteria down.

Treated gasoline will keep about six months in direct sunlight and two to five years underground. Diesel fuel and heating oil keeps about five to ten years when treated. Larger amounts extend the storage life further, and you can re-treat. For even longer fuel storage, use ten grams of disodium EDTA, a chelating agent, per hundred gallons for added protection from metal ions. The anti-oxidants will store indefinitely in an airtight container.

Butane is added to gasoline to ease starting. The loss of this butane is called high-end burn-off and can make starting impossible. This loss is prevented by underground storage or by using expensive vapor recovery systems. Also, try to buy gasoline during the winter months when it has been winterized with extra butane.

Filter any fuel that has been stored for long periods of time through a fine filtering agent like chamois before using. If gasoline smells like varnish, the gums have already formed. It is still usable mixed with two to three times as much fresh fuel. Acetone in a 1:20 ratio can also be added twenty-four hours prior to use to dissolve the gum deposits.

How Much to Store

The amount to store depends on intended uses and expected time period. Some figures are listed throughout this chapter to help you estimate usage. Calculate all usage of a fuel in BTU's and then divide the total by the BTU's given in Table 23-1 to find the needed amount. Remember to take system efficiencies into account.

Other information that may be of help: artificial light is needed about 1,400 hours a year, freezers must operate a minimum of four hours per day to keep food frozen, and a family of four uses about six million BTU's of gas or nineteen million BTU's of wood or coal to cook meals for a year.

You can also estimate heat needs if you know the amount of heating day degrees for your location (a local utility company or architect will probably know; for example, the average is 8200 in Minneapolis, 7383 in Concord, NH, 6052 in Salt Lake City, 4711 in Kansas City and 2773 in Sacramento). An average 1500 square foot two-story home built on a concrete slab with R-30 ceiling, R-20 wall and R-5 foundation insulation, with weatherstripping, caulking, storm windows and doors (.7 air changes/hour) uses 13,300 times the heating day degrees in BTU's per year for heat. A less insulated home could require more than double that amount while a home using passive solar techniques could require a lot less. Estimates can also be made by comparing winter and summer utility bills.

Improvised Fuel

When you run out of stockpiled fuels, or if you simply want to make them last longer, there are a number of fuels you can make from items commonly found around many homes.

Newspapers that are folded, soaked in water containing detergent, rolled and then dried burn as clean and hot as normal wood. Homemade charcoal can be made by cooking pieces of hardwood, black walnuts and fruit pits. Fire starters and fuel can be made by pouring a paraffin and sawdust mixture into paper egg cartons, cupcake papers or tuna cans filled with rolled cardboard. Although they give off a strong smoke and are difficult to control, rubber tires cut into small pieces will burn in stoves. Other things that burn include peat, corncobs, straw, grains, manure and old motor oil.

Producing Your Own Electricity

Electricity is a terrific convenience and you may not want to do without it completely. There are a number of ways you can produce your own.

The most basic methods use your own power. One of the simplest is a bicycle with a small bicycle generator attached to the wheel for powering small lights and recharging batteries.

Gasoline, diesel, LP, natural gas and combination AC generators are excellent for immediate backup power. They will provide large amounts of power but are not really designed for continuous operation. You can greatly prolong their lives as well as cut fuel usage in half and reduce maintenance by running them once a week. During the time they are running, you can do chores such as washing and vacuuming that take substantial power and charge storage batteries at the same time. Expect to use about eight to sixteen gallons of gasoline per hundred kilowatt-hours of power; diesels use about 25% less. Smaller generators tend to use less fuel, but it depends on the particular model and the operating load.

The proper generator size can be determined by adding up the total wattage of all the appliances, tools and lights that will be used at any one time, then adding in the wattage needed to start any motors, compressors and blowers, and finally adding a 25% margin. A battery charger uses about fifteen amps at 110-120 volts. Choose the smallest adequate size. All generators located in enclosed areas should have their exhaust vented to the outside. Store motor oil to keep the generator lubricated.

For planning purposes, the average 1500 square foot home uses about twenty kilowatt-hours per day normally. That's the equivalent of 174 amp-hours at 115 volts. Under survival conditions you could probably get by on half that amount or less.

One of the best ways of providing electricity without reliance on fuels is by photovoltaics (pv). This method uses a photovoltaic cell ("solar cell") array to convert sunlight directly to electricity. Storage batteries are used to store excess power for use during nighttime and other times when sunlight is unavailable. Because of the uncertainty of sunlight, you should not rely exclusively on photovoltaics but have a reliable backup system using another method.

An excellent book on using photovoltaics for your home is *Solar Electric Independent Home Book* by Paul Jeffrey Fowler. You can wire a home with a twelve-volt system that runs off of storage batteries charged by any electricity-generating system. It can also be powered temporarily with your car battery, charging the car battery while driving. A twelve- volt system can utilize the wide variety of equipment and accessories made for use in campers, motor homes and vans. Invertors that convert twelve-volt DC to 110-120 volt DC can be used to power appliances, tools and equipment using induction, capacitor or split-phase motors such as normal refrigerators, air conditioning, electric stoves, appliances and power tools.

You can buy prepackaged pv kits from various sources (see Chapter 32) if you don't want to design your own. They offer intertie systems (you interconnect with the commercial power grid and don't need storage batteries) or stand-alone systems. Other solar devices recharge batteries or power cell phones and laptop computers.

If you have an independent, continuing source of water with enough flow and head (vertical drop), you can use a water turbine and generator to produce electricity. The amount of potential power in kilowatt-hours per month can be estimated by multiplying the average flow in cubic feet per minute (CFM) times the head in feet and then multiplying by the system efficiency factor (.5-.8 is about the range). For example, a four CFM flow with a fifty foot head flowing twenty-four hours per day through a 60% efficiency system could provide about 120 kilowatt- hours each month. You probably wouldn't be interested in producing a whole lot less than that. Hydroelectric power can be the best and cheapest, if you have the water potential.

Wind generators can be used only in those relatively few locations where the average monthly wind speed is at least ten miles per hour or greater. Your local airport, weather station or National Weather Service can tell you. If your location appears to have enough wind , you should check to make sure before buying a thing. Do this by renting an anemometer, placing it on a temporary tower thirty to fifty feet high and recording the wind velocities for a calendar month. Then find a local weather station that records the wind velocities daily and extrapolate to find the wind speed probability. Wind power might be used to compliment solar power.

If you decide you can live without electricity, get a copy of *How to Live Without Electricity—and Like It* by Anita Evangelista or *Living Without Electricity* by Scott and Pellman.

Storing Electrical Energy

You won't want to use all the electricity as it is produced, so you'll need some type of DC storage battery facility. Not only will it provide power at nights and on sunless or windless days, but also it will smooth out power variations. You don't need batteries with intertie systems, but will probably want them in case of grid power failure.

Standard automobile, golf cart or forklift batteries can be used, but stationary service deep-cycle storage batteries are much better as they have a much longer life when deeply discharged repeatedly (can exceed twenty years). Maximum battery life is achieved when prolonged charging and discharging doesn't exceed 15% of the amp-hour rating. This means you should have a minimum of seven times the amp- hours (you may want two to three times that amount) you expect to use in a day. For a minimal five kilowatt-hours per day that would take about 2900 amp-hours of twelve-volt battery capacity. You'll want spare batteries in case of failures. A special high-powered battery charger is necessary and plugs into any AC generator. Invertors are notoriously inefficient, but they will allow you to run AC-powered items from DC battery storage.

Making Your Own Fuel

Stored fuel will eventually run out but there are ways to make your own on an on-going basis. Digesters can make methane that can be used in place of propane and natural gas in lanterns, heaters, water heaters, ranges, refrigerators and furnaces. Alcohol stills can be made and fed with wood products, excess grains and agricultural wastes.

Conserve What You Have

Not to be overlooked in the search for energy sources is the conservation of what you have. Obviously an earth-sheltered home utilizing passive and active solar techniques would be nice, but there are many other things nearly anyone can do around his home to reduce the need for energy.

Begin by making your home as thermally efficient as possible. Be sure you have enough insulation in the ceilings and walls. Insulate heating ducts, electrical outlets, hot water tank and pipes. Have double and triple pane windows or storm windows and doors. Use weatherstripping and caulking to seal leaks and around doors and windows. Cut energy use by cooking with waterless cookwear and using ovens for more than one thing at a time.

If a prolonged crisis comes, you can conserve energy by heating only a portion of your home. The best place is near the heat source and on the south side to get as much solar energy as possible.

Spare Parts

While you're stockpiling fuel and the equipment to use that fuel to provide you all the comforts of civilization, be aware that the equipment can break down at the least opportune time. Store a supply of spare parts to fix at least the most common repairs needed.

Fire Starters

Many of the items mentioned in this chapter utilize a flame of some type. Obviously, to light them you will need matches or other lighter. Store wood friction matches, not the paper safety ones. You could also store other means, such as disposable lighters.

24

MEDICAL AND DENTAL

Being ill or injured is bad enough under normal circumstances, but it could be catastrophic during a crisis when medical assistance may be severely limited or not available at all. You must be ready to help yourself as much as possible.

MEDICAL

Improper nutrition weakens the body's defenses against disease. In addition, during an extensive crisis there almost certainly will be inadequate sanitation and medical care. Taken together, the conditions will be optimum for deadly epidemics of a wide variety of diseases. Dysentery, hepatitis, typhoid fever, typhus, tularemia, rabies, plague, tetanus, diphtheria, cholera and anthrax are diseases that might be expected to proliferate.

Medical Preparation

The easiest and best way to prepare for many possible diseases is to keep immunizations for them current. Children should be routinely vaccinated for diphtheria, pertussis, tetanus, polio, measles, rubella and mumps, and tested for tuberculosis. Adults who where fully immunized in childhood should have a tetanus/diphtheria booster every five to ten years. You may also want vaccinations and boosters as needed for typhoid and paratyphoid, typhus, cholera, yellow fever and plague. Vaccines are also available for influenza, tularemia, tick fever, rabies, type B hepatitis, and types A and C meningococcal meningitis. Smallpox is supposedly eradicated but could make a comeback via terrorism. Consult your physician on the timing for vaccinations and booster shots.

Have regular medical checkups and get preventative or corrective work done as suggested in Chapter 3. Regular eye exams are also important. If needed, store spare eyeglasses in practical frames with a record of the prescription, and have an eyeglass repair kit with nose pads, hinge rings, universal hinge screws and screwdriver. Keep your old eyeglasses; someday they may be better than nothing. Hearing should also be checked with necessary items stored.

It would be wise to take training in basic first aid, advanced first aid and CPR. Definitely consider home nursing, EMT (Emergency Medical Technician) and paramedic courses. Medical instruction is offered through the local Red Cross as well as many colleges and other schools. Your tools will only be as good as your skills make them.

Ignoring modern medicine for home remedies and medicinal plants and herbs is foolhardy. However, there is a place for both when judiciously done, and that may be particularly true in a prolonged crisis with a shortage of modern medicines and personnel. It can't hurt to know what plants and herbs may be used to alleviate common ailments in the absence of more developed medicines.

Medical Kit

Because the circumstances could be much more acute than normally expected in every day life, you will want a much more complete medical kit. Whether you make up your own or buy a commercial kit, it should be adequate for anticipated situations. Even the best commercial kits will likely need augmenting and tailoring to your needs. Store the suggested items even if you don't know how to use them. When the time comes there may be a skilled physician available but a lack of the necessary supplies.

Table 24-1 lists the suggested equipment to store, and Table 24-2 gives the necessary supplies. If the lists look quite long, remember they are capable of doing much more than simple first aid. The amounts should adequately serve up to eight people for a year. Quickly replenish any supplies you may use. A plastic fishing tackle box is an excellent container for your medical kit because it allows instant access, keeps the contents organized and is non-corrosive.

To prepare for emergency childbirth, in addition to the listed items you should store obstetrical pads, sterile cord ties, cord clamps, sanitary napkins, an eight-ounce Peri squeeze bottle, diapers, diaper pins and a receiving blanket. If you don't already have instructions in another good text, get a copy of *Emergency Childbirth* by George J. White, MD.

You should stockpile a good selection and quantity of medicines to meet the anticipated problems. Table 24-3 lists suggested medicines to store, both OTC (over-the-counter) and prescription. Current medicines change over time so get a physician to update those listed with the best and latest available. It's awfully hard to treat many of the life-threatening diseases without prescription medicines, so also try to find an understanding physician that will give you the needed prescriptions. You may also want to store cough syrup and throat lozenges.

Another thing you should be aware of is that many veterinary medicines come from the same drug batches as those sold for human use at much higher prices. They are just as pure and safe but have different labels on them. And they normally can be bought without a prescription, too. Veterinary medicines can be bought from veterinary supply outlets, pet and feed stores, and from the mail order sources listed in Chapter 32. If you decide to cut costs for your medicine storage by buying veterinary medicines, you should also get a copy of *Survivalist's Medicine Chest* by Ragnar Benson. He briefly discusses using veterinary medicines and suggests specific medicines for the treatment of diseases.

If you suffer from a chronic illness or disease, consult with your physician about storing an emergency supply of any special medications. Diabetics should store a two to three month supply of insulin along with instant glucose and syringes.

TABLE 24-1. MEDICAL AND DENTAL EQUIPMENT

☐ 2-3 oral-rectal thermometers
☐ 1 forehead thermometer
☐ angular bandage scissors
☐ operating scissors
☐ suture scissors
☐ splinter forceps (tweezers)
☐ tissue forceps (thumb dressing)
☐ 2 medium hemostats
    (1 straight, 1 curved)
☐ Mayo-Hegar needle holder
☐ urethral catheterization kit
☐ #14 Foley catheter
☐ 1-qt Kelly bottle with tubing
    and #18 needle
☐ #18x4-inch spinal needle
☐ adult/child airway tubes
☐ #16 French stomach tube
☐ #12 French stomach tube
☐ medicine dropper
☐ bulb aspirator
☐ bed pan
☐ graduated plastic cylinder
☐ inflatable leg splint
☐ inflatable arm splint
☐ fingernail clippers
☐ 2-gal plastic garden sprayer

☐ 4 5-cc disposable syringes
    with #22x1½-inch needles
☐ 4 10-cc disposable syringes
    with #18x3-inch needles
☐ 2 3½-cc syringes with
    #25x⅝-inch needles
☐ 10-cc glass or metal syringe
☐ 2 #21-22x1½-inch metal-hub needles
☐ 2 #18x3-inch metal-hub needles
☐ scalpel
☐ 3 #10 surgical blades
☐ 3 #11 surgical blades
☐ 4 single-edged razor blades
☐ exam light (or penlight)
☐ otoscope (ear light)
☐ pocket magnifier
☐ stethoscope
☐ sphygmomanometer
    (blood pressure cuff)
☐ rubber sheeting
☐ enema kit
☐ adult rib belt
☐ stretcher and blanket
☐ snake bit kit
☐ dental kit

TABLE 24-2. MEDICAL AND DENTAL SUPPLIES

- ☐ 10 tongue depressors
- ☐ 1-lb roll absorbent cotton
- ☐ 6 Povidone surgical scrubs
- ☐ 20 Povidone prep pads
- ☐ 4 surgical sponges
- ☐ 1 pt hydrogen peroxide
- ☐ 16-oz Hibiclens cleanser
- ☐ 2 bars/person Fels Naptha soap
- ☐ 8-oz iodine shampoo
- ☐ Seven insecticide
- ☐ Rotenone insecticide
- ☐ 2/person household dust masks
- ☐ assorted Ziploc bags
- ☐ 3 large garbage bags
- ☐ mentholatum
- ☐ petroleum jelly
- ☐ hand lotion
- ☐ olive oil
- ☐ calamine or Caladryl lotion
- ☐ cornstarch
- ☐ 100 grams activated charcoal
- ☐ epsom salts
- ☐ sanitary napkins
- ☐ assorted plastic bandages
- ☐ 10 assorted Telfa gauze bandages
- ☐ 6 5x9 surgipad bandages
- ☐ 2 8x10 surgipad bandages
- ☐ 15 Coverlet fingertip bandages
- ☐ 10 Coverlet elbow/knee bandages
- ☐ 5 Coverlet knuckle bandages
- ☐ 18x22 trauma dressing
- ☐ 2 triangular bandages
- ☐ 12 3x36 Vaseline gauze
- ☐ 2 rolls Kerlix bandages
- ☐ 3 or 4-inch Doma-Paste bandage
- ☐ Spenco Second Skin
- ☐ 60x92 burn sheet or towels
- ☐ roll resin plaster bandage
- ☐ 2 3-inch rolls cast liner
- ☐ 3 elastic bandages
      (1 ea. 2, 4 and 6-inch)

- ☐ Q-tips
- ☐ 20 sterile swabs
- ☐ disposable exam gloves
- ☐ 4-oz tube K-Y Jelly
- ☐ 10 ammonia ampules
- ☐ 1 gal 70% isopropyl alcohol
- ☐ 1 gal concentrated multipurpose
      sanitizer/germicide
- ☐ 2 lb high-test granular
      calcium hypochloride
- ☐ Gatorade or ERG powder
- ☐ assorted safety pins
- ☐ dental floss
- ☐ 2 cold compresses or
      instant ice packs
- ☐ talcum powder
- ☐ baby oil
- ☐ Desitin
- ☐ zinc oxide
- ☐ PABA 15 sunscreens
- ☐ table salt
- ☐ baking soda
- ☐ 4 adhesive eye pads
- ☐ 20 2x2 gauze pads
- ☐ 20 3x3 gauze pads
- ☐ 60 4x4 gauze pads
- ☐ 16 rolls gauze
      (4 each 1, 2, 3 and 4-inch)
- ☐ 4 rolls Gauze tape (2 ea. 1 and 2-inch)
- ☐ 4 BandNet Tapeless Bandages
      (2 hand/foot, 1 ea. finger, head)
- ☐ 4 rolls adhesive tape
      (2 ea. 1 and 2-inch)
- ☐ 10 butterfly enclosures and/or
- ☐ 12 Steri-Strips
      (6 ea. ½x4 and ¼x3)
- ☐ 10 packs nylon sutures with needles
      (2 ea.2-0, 5-0; 3 ea. 3-0, 4-0)
- ☐ 2 packs 3-0 plain gut suture
      (absorbable) with needles
- ☐ rubberized tourniquet

TABLE 24-3. MEDICINES

☐ A & D Ointment, 1-2 4-gm tubes
☐ Acetamine, 100 tablets
☐ *Ampicillin, 200 500-mg tablets
☐   10 500-mg powder vials plus diluent
☐ Aspirin, Datril, Panadol, Percogesic, or Tylenol, 100 tablets
☐ *Atropine sulfate, 4 1-cc ampules (grs 1/150)
☐ *Azo Gantrisin, 100 .5-mg (7.5 gr) tablets
☐ *Benzoin Compound Tincture, 2-oz bottle
☐ Camalox, 2000 tablets
☐   12-fl oz bottle
☐ *Chloramphenicol, 200 250-mg capsules
☐ *Compazine, 100 25-mg tablets
☐   12 25-mg suppositories
☐   10 2-cc (10-mg) ampules
☐ *Cortisporin Ophthalmic Ointment, ⅛-oz tube
☐ Decadron, 1-cc (4-mg) ampules plus diluent
☐ *Demerol, 2 30-cc (50-mg/cc) vials
☐   4 2-cc (100-mg) ampules
☐   100 100-mg tablets
☐ *E.E.S. 400, 250 400-mg tablets
☐ *Epinephrine USP 1:1000, 10-cc bottle
☐ *Furacin Soluble Dressing, 454-gm tub
☐ Hydrocortisone Cream ½%, 2 1-oz tubes
☐ Ipecac Syrup, 1-fl oz bottle
☐ Kaopectate, 12-fl oz bottle
☐ *Lomotil, 100 2½-mg tablets
☐ Neosporin Ointment, 2 1-oz tubes
☐ *Penicillin VK, 200 250-mg (400,000 units) tablets
☐ *Phenergan, 200 25-mg tablets
☐ *Pitocin, 2-4 1-cc ampules (for females)
☐ *Pontocaine HCL Eye Ointment ½%, ⅛-oz tube
☐ *Pyribenzamine, 50 50-mg tablets
☐ *Silver Sulfadiazine Cream 1%, 400-gm jar
        or mafenide acetate cream, 3 4-oz tubes
☐ *Sulfadiazine, 500 .5-mg tablets
☐ *Sumycin, 200 250-mg tablets
☐ Tinactin Cream Ointment, 4 ½-oz tubes and/or 4 ½-fl oz
☐ Triaminic Syrup, 8-fl oz bottle
☐ *Tylenol #3, 100 tablets
☐ *Valium, 2 2-cc (5-mg/cc) disposable syringes
☐   50 5-mg tablets
☐ *Xylocaine 1%, 2 50-cc vials
☐ *Zomepirac Sodium, 100 100-mg tablets

*Usually requires prescription

Proper Storage of Medicines

Most medicines decompose when exposed to heat, light, moisture and air. Store them in the original labeled container in a cool, dry and dark location. Medicines are required by law to have an expiration date stamped on them, but pharmacists may not put it on a prescription container unless you ask them. The expiration date is important because drugs lose their potency, and some like tetracycline even become toxic with age. A few let you know when they are no good (aspirin smells like vinegar, for instance) but others give no clues. Rotate all drugs before their date is up to assure effectiveness. A pharmacist will be able to help you with shelf life and storage condition needs for particular medicines or you can check with the manufacturer.

Medical Library

A medical library is critical for getting the most from your stockpiled medical supplies. See Chapter 32 for a list of books generally in priority order.

DENTAL

Use good oral hygiene to prevent dental problems and visit your dentist regularly to correct any that may develop. Have all preventative and corrective work done. Store soft-bristle toothbrushes, dental floss, toothpaste or powder and tongue scrapers. If you wear false teeth, keep an extra set if possible. Store fluoride tablets for children.

For the dental emergencies that may arise during a crisis, buy an emergency dental kit. There are a number of kits on the market (Stahl, Atwater Carey and Searles) but all of them are pretty sparse and are meant mainly for getting you through a weekend. You could start with one of these and add a few other necessities to it.

A complete kit should contain detailed instructions with at least the following items: a temporary filling kit of a half ounce of zinc oxide powder USP and a one quarter ounce tube Eugenol oil of cloves, a five to fifteen gram tube of Orabase with Benzocaine, a bottle of cotton pellets, a bottle of benzocaine .5% and benzalkonium chloride toothache gel or drops, a bottle of dental wax, dental cement, cotton rolls, a mixing block with spatula and a dental mirror. You might also want *Where There Is No Dentist* by Murray Dickson.

25

SANITATION AND PERSONAL CARE

Inadequate sanitation and hygiene following major disasters is often deadlier than the disaster itself, rapidly producing disease and virulent epidemics. But providing proper sanitation and hygiene without running water, functioning sewer hookups and periodic garbage service can be quite difficult without considerable forethought and preparation.

SANITATION

The sanitation needs during a crisis consist of adequate means of disposing of human wastes and garbage as well as keeping people and living accommodations clean.

Waste Management

Without the three to six gallons of water for each flush and a sewer system to accept it, disposing of human waste can quickly become a considerable problem. A satisfactory solution must not only remove the waste from sight and smell, but must also prevent water contamination and the spreading of disease by insects and rodents.

A short-term solution could be a simple portable toilet using plastic bags or a portable flush toilet with a built-in holding tank. Even a five-gallon plastic pail, bucket, or paint can with a tight-fitting lid could be fitted with a seat of some sort (perhaps an old toilet seat) and used as a toilet. Then you'll need some larger containers to empty the smaller toilets into. You don't want ones too large or heavy to move, so about ten-gallon seems the right size. They should be water-tight and have attached tight-fitting lids. An emergency solution can be made by placing a grocery sack inside one the same size and filling the space between sacks with shredded newspaper or a plastic bag liner. One person will need about five to ten gallons of space per two-week period for waste storage.

Store deodorizer/bowl cleaner chemicals and disintegrating toilet paper for the portable flush toilets or extra bags for the non-flushing type. Store heavy-duty plastic liners, deodorizers and a gallon of bleach or other disinfectant for the cans. A small quantity of the bleach or disinfectant should be added after each use to control the germs and odors. Also store at least a quart of fly and insect spray to control insect problems.

Without better facilities, you will eventually be forced to bury the accumulated wastes. Dig the hole deep enough that you can cover it with at least one foot of earth to prevent insects from breeding and discourage animals from digging it up. The hole should be located at least fifty feet downhill from any water source and where it will be unaffected by flooding or surface runoff. Store a bag of lime and sprinkle some over the waste prior to covering it.

More extended use can be satisfied with a shallow pit or trench latrine. A straddle trench is dug one foot wide, about two feet deep, and two to four feet long with a makeshift toilet seat or a regular wooden chair with a hole cut in it placed over the trench. A larger hole two feet wide, six feet deep, and seven to eight feet long covered with an insect-proof toilet box will provide the average-size family with facilities for a couple of months. Urine soakage pits can also be built to reduce the use of the trenches. As with all toilet facilities, reasonable privacy should be provided for by screening the area from view. As the latrine becomes full it can be covered over and a new one dug.

More permanent solutions could be an outdoor privy or even installing water-less composting toilets in the home. Composting toilets have an aerobic chamber where the waste is turned to safe humus over a period of time. However, they are fairly expensive, the chamber must be almost directly underneath and they do not always function well and without odor. Fans and heating elements are sometimes necessary. A combination composting toilet/outhouse would be a workable backup solution.

Perhaps the best long-term solution is to have a septic tank with leech field to backup the regular sewer system. A properly designed system, given minimal care, will serve for decades. A valve could be installed that could easily switch from the sewer system to the septic system. Another option would be a holding tank, but it would have to be emptied regularly.

Garbage Disposal

Piles of litter and garbage soon attract insects and rodents. Separate garbage into edible garbage that can be feed to animals (pigs, etc.), that suitable for compost piles, garbage that can be burned and the remaining plastic, metal, etc. that must be stored and then periodically hauled away or buried in a deep pit. Have one or more twenty to thirty gallon cans with tight-fitting lids for this storage. Cans can be flattened to reduce bulk. Again, when burying garbage, cover with at least one foot of earth. Garbage that must be stored indoors for some time (such as in a fallout shelter) will keep better if first drained and then wrapped with newspaper and grocery sacks. The can should also be lined with paper. Do not store garbage in airtight plastic bags because the decomposing garbage produces gas that could make the bag explode. Store rat traps and poisons to keep the rodent population under control. Cats would also help.

Wash water containing soap, grease and food particles should be run through a grease trap placed over a soakage pit. The trap can be made from a large box or barrel with adequate filtering. Burlap, straw, grass, or similar material can be used to strain out the grease and particles and should be changed frequently. Wood ashes, sand and gravel can be used to further filter the water. The trap will need periodic cleaning with the accumulated grease either burned or buried.

Personal Hygiene

Personal cleanliness is important to prevent disease and fungus infections. Obvious health practices should be scrupulously observed. Wash hands well before preparing food, eating and after going to the toilet, assisting an ill person, or handling any material that may be contaminated. When running water is not available, baths may be taken by pouring a small amount of heated water into the tub. A sponge bath can be taken with as little as a cup of water and showers can be taken with a SunShower or Zodi propane shower.

Stockpiling

In a crisis it is possible to make many of the items you might need for sanitation, but storing them is a lot easier. Estimate storage needs from current usage or store twenty-six rolls of toilet paper and twelve to eighteen bars of bath/hand soap per person for one year. Bars of soap that are unwrapped so air can get to them will dry out and harden, tending to last longer when used. For women, store sanitary napkins and belts, reusable cloth pads, tampons, or a menstrual cup. Babies need diapers, both disposable and cloth, and towelettes for clean-up.

For the home, store toilet bowl cleaner, drain cleaner, ammonia, detergent cleaners and scouring powders, oven cleaners, cleaning fluids, floor and furniture wax, carpet shampoo, bleach and paper towels. Have floor mops, mop buckets, dustpan, scrub brushes, brooms, sponges, rags, a toilet plunger and a flexible cable clean out (plumber's "snake"). Carpeting could become a tremendous breeding ground for insects if left uncleaned so at least have a manual carpet sweeper or consider replacing your carpeting now with wooden floors and area rugs. Store all cleaning supplies in a dry location away from food stuffs. Liquids should be tightly capped to prevent evaporation.

PERSONAL CARE

Most of these things aren't absolutely necessary but they might be a real help to morale during a crisis:

☐ wash basin	☐ combs	☐ hair brushes
☐ towels	☐ wash cloths	☐ hair cutting items
☐ facial tissue	☐ shampoo	☐ hair conditioner
☐ razor blades	☐ shaving cream	☐ inspect repellant
☐ deodorant	☐ lipstick	☐ cologne
☐ nail clippers	☐ nail files	☐ other beauty aids

A straight razor with strop, stone, brush and shaving soap could replace the razor blades. An average can of shaving cream lasts for about sixty shaves. Having a supply of medicated shampoo with lindane or pyrethrin as the active ingredient will help solve any head lice problem that might develop.

26

PREPARING YOUR HOME

There are many things you can do to better prepare your home for times of crisis. Budget limitations may preclude you from doing all of them, but the more you do the better off you may be.

Repair and Upkeep

There may be extended periods of time when you are the only repairman available when something breaks down. Replacement parts and supplies may not be easy to come by.

The first thing you can do is to keep what you now have in good repair. Do preventative maintenance on all items possible and that especially includes your home. Paint it when needed and have any roofing, plumbing, heating, electrical, or structural problems corrected immediately. Replace worn out appliances with those easiest to repair and requiring the lowest maintenance.

Secondly, you should store tools, spare parts, supplies and repair manuals.

Hand tools are a priority. That doesn't mean you shouldn't have any power tools—they can save a lot of labor—but get the necessary hand tools first so that you can work even without electricity. Buy quality tools that will last. Proto and Snap-On are especially reliable brands.

Table 26-1 lists the tools for a basic tool kit that will allow you to handle basic maintenance, minor repairs and modest building projects. It is assumed that you already have axes, picks, general shovels, wood mauls and wedges. Tables 26-3 through 26-6 lists basic tools that could be added in specialized fields. Other areas you might want to consider include welding and cutting, small motor repair, electronics testing and well-drilling. The lists are by no means exhaustive. There are literally thousands of tools, most with a purpose, and some you may find useful as you get more involved. It's also easy to go overboard in buying "just one more". List your priorities, and buy as you can. Buy tools for the particular skills you have or want to develop that will be useful during crisis times. Avoid any unnecessary redundancy.

Tools that are stored must be properly prepared to prevent rust and other problems that could destroy their usefulness. Coat wood and metal parts with a coat of linseed oil and let it dry for a few days prior to storing. Corrosion Control Grease from Lubrimatic can be used to preserve metal parts that are used more often. Store tools in a dark, dry location where they can remain straight. Hanging them by the handle is best.

Purchase spare parts when you purchase the items. Get any special tools at the same time. Appliances aren't hard to repair if you have the spare belts, bulbs, cords, switches, etc. that they require. Table 26-2 gives a basic supply list while Table 26-7 offers additional items to stock. You may think of others.

Unless you're already expert with all tools and situations, you'll want to have a number of how-to books. Two of general interest are:

Reader's Digest *New Fix-It-Yourself Manual*
Reader's Digest *New Complete Do-It-Yourself Manual*

You may also want some other volumes on basic plumbing, electrical work, carpentry, auto repair, small engine repair, blacksmithing, masonry work and construction. Home Depot and Lowe's have their own repair manuals and specialized instructions, many free.

Home Security

It makes no sense to stockpile large amounts of items to insure your physical well-being only to loose them to fire or theft. It makes even less sense to loose your life or those of your family in the process. Prepare to maintain the security of your home.

Fire Protection

First, make your home as fireproof as possible. Then install a number of smoke alarms, both electric-powered photoelectric and battery-powered ionization. The key to proper location of smoke alarms is to place them between the hazards and people. That usually means in central hallways outside bedrooms. Test all units after installation and at regular intervals thereafter. Carbon monoxide detectors are also worthwhile.

Next get some firefighting equipment. Start with some ABC multi-purpose, rechargeable fire extinguishers with the highest ratings for the heaviest size you can handle (probably ten to twenty pounds of agent). Put one near the kitchen, one in a major hallway, one in the garage and perhaps a smaller one in your automobiles. A home-chargeable water unit would be a good backup. A garden hose and nozzle hooked up ready for use could come in handy. Have fire ladders available for all locations higher than the ground floor. Emergency escape masks and Water Jel Fire Blankets are other precautions. The blanket protects much longer than a regular one soaked with water and is available from Alliance Medical, 8624 Rt. C, PO Box 147, Russelville, MO 65074, 888-633-6908, www.allmed.net.

Without ready access to the services of a functioning fire department, you would need more extensive firefighting capabilities to handle larger fires, accidental and set. In rural areas or even on large suburban lots there is also the danger of forest and grass fires.

Hardening Your Home

Sadly, through necessity our homes are becoming more like fortresses.

Although it's impossible to make your home totally impregnable, you can make it a lot harder to get into. All exterior doors should be of heavy-gauge steel with no glass, mounted tightly in a steel frame with inside or pinned hinges. Install wide-angle door viewers and forged, hardened steel pin, tumbler deadbolt locks with pick-resistant cylinders and at least a one-inch throw on all exterior doors. Mortise and vertical deadbolts are preferred, and Schlage Primus, Medeco and Kaba locks are among the best. Pay particular attention to securing sliding glass doors, outside basement doors and weak garage doors.

All windows should have quarter-inch, case-hardened pins or five-sixteenths-inch eye bolts through both frames. You may want to protect them further with decorative wrought iron, iron rods, or heavy-gauge sliding steel shutters. Regular glass can be replaced with shatterproof glass or unbreakable Lexan. Put heavy wire screen over garage windows and skylights.

Install burglar alarms and other intruder detection devices. Discourage intruders by properly locating and trimming trees and shrubs, using blinds on windows and providing nighttime illumination of your entrances and yard. Engrave or otherwise mark all valuables for identification.

Guard Dogs

A good guard dog provides a substantial deterrent against intruders. Larger dogs are usually more intimidating with German Shepherds, Dobermans, Rottweilers, Airedales, Bullmastiffs, Boxers, Rhodesian Ridgebacks and Bouvier des Flandres among the better breeds. If you spend the money to get one, make sure it is adequately trained and poison-proofed. Also get it vaccinated for rabies, distemper and parvovirus, and store food and medicines for it.

Hiding Valuables

There is nothing like an ostentatious display of goods others may not have to make you the target of the wrong crowd. The old cliche "out of sight, out of mind" is a good watchword for protecting your stockpile and other valuables. You can use hidden rooms, disguised closets, safes and vaults. Safes are rated ABCD for fire resistance and EFGH for burglar resistance with the last rating of each type the best. There are entire books written on how to hide items safely and, if you have a lot to hide, get one of them. Burying things in PVC pipe "safes" works well and, buried about six feet deep or so, even metal detectors have a hard time locating them.

Personal Protection

Besides weapons, there are other things you can do to protect yourself. Modern concealable body armor, made from Kevlar, Zylon and other hi-tech materials, is lighter, thinner and more flexible than ever. It can be worn comfortably for long periods of time in almost any climate. It comes in different thicknesses for different levels of protection, with the heaviest capable of stopping bullets from .357 Magnum and 9mm pistols. Check your local laws to see if you are allowed to purchase and use body armor. Some companies also may only sell to law enforcement agencies.

CS and CN tear gas canisters can be carried in many locations (others restrict them to permit holders or ban them altogether). Pepper sprays come in different sizes and strengths.

Evasive driving tactics can be learned at Bill Scott's BSR driver schools in Summit Point, West Virginia, or Bob Bondurant's School of High Performance Driving near Phoenix, Arizona. There are also armored cars, but they're anything but cheap. Finally, you can learn self-defense skills like karate and take gun training at places like Jeff Cooper's Gunsite Ranch in Paulden, Arizona, or at BSR.

Disaster Preparation

There are also many things you can do to better prepare your home from the physical effects of natural and manmade disasters.

One of the first things to do in preparing for any disaster is to learn how to shut off the utilities. Locate a shut-off tool where everyone in the family can always find it quickly. Ruptured gas lines can explode and burn, severed power lines can electrocute and start fires, and broken water mains can flood. Store sand bags and pumps for floods and sheets of plywood and heavy-duty plastic for tornadoes, hurricanes and nuclear war. Some other preparations you should make for nuclear war are discussed in the next chapter.

Earthquake Preparation

Very few people, even in earthquake prone areas, are prepared for earthquakes. When the inevitable happens, many will suffer. Yet there are a number of simple, low-cost measures that can be taken now that would considerably decrease the possibility of major earthquake damage and injury.

First, learn what to do in an earthquake to best protect yourself. If indoors, don't run outside but get under a doorway or a sturdy piece of furniture, against an inside wall in a central hallway or bathroom, or in a corner. Stay away from windows that may shatter or heavy pieces of furniture that could fall on you.

Think about and discuss the effects of an earthquake with family and friends. Consider how you would react and what you should do to minimize the risk at home, at work and while driving in an automobile. Make your home and its contents as resistant to earthquakes as practical.

What type structure do you live in? A carefully engineered and properly constructed wood frame home is among the very safest due to its built-in give. An unreinforced masonry home can suffer much greater damage. Windows shatter from bending unless the frames have been braced with plywood sheathing. Gas meters are especially dangerous because they rupture, but there are earthquake-proof gas valves (see Chapter 32). Hot water heaters should be bolted down or secured to wall studs with steel bands. This may prevent their tumbling over, breaking water and gas lines (which may be ignited by the pilot light). Do the same with gas furnaces, and use flexible connections on all gas appliances. Bolt homes to their foundations with steel sill anchors. Brace masonry chimneys by tying them to the frame with steel straps and nails.

Use camper-type latches on cupboard doors, store heavy items on lower shelves and secure top-heavy furniture to wall studs. Properly hang heavy mirrors, paintings and light fixtures. Locate beds away from windows and heavy furniture.

The above are but some of the things you can do to prepare for earthquakes. For more information I recommend the following book:

Peace of Mind in Earthquake Country by Peter I. Yanev

Emergency Shelter

In the event that your home is destroyed or made uninhabitable by disaster, you should have an alternate shelter. This could be a trailer, mobile home, camper, tent, or even just a canvas or nylon tarp. One item most never consider but that would make a fairly suitable temporary lodging is a tipi like the Plains Indians used. Even in the dead of winter in a cold climate it can be kept tolerable inside with a small fire. If you are forced to live for any length of time in a tent you will appreciate cots or ground cloths with air mattresses or pads.

Survival Home

As is now obvious, preparing your home for crisis can be quite involved. Space has limited the detail and breadth of preparation covered here. Get a copy of the *The Secure Home* by Joel M. Skousen. It covers not only how to remodel your present home to make it suitable for survival, but also how to build a survival home from scratch. Sections cover planning, integration of security and self-sufficiency systems, construction and implementation, and recommended equipment and suppliers. He also wrote *How to Implement a High Security Shelter in the Home* with a more limited scope.

For thought, extensive research by Brigham Young University has shown that a family of six can be almost completely self-sufficient on two an one half acres of decent farm land with a dozen chickens, a similar number of rabbits and two milk goats.

Retreating

Obviously, some locations will be better than others during any particular crisis. Yet, determining the best areas is not as cut and dried as some seem to believe with their maps of population density, earthquake zones and fallout patterns. Certainly large population centers must be among the worst under any scenario. Small towns away from large urban areas seem to offer the most in all but the worst cases.

However, the vast majority of people desiring to prepare for crisis can not or do not want to move from their present location. From this fact stems the idea of having a retreat located at a substantial distance from the normal habitation as a safe place to go for sanctuary.

The subject of having a retreat is a controversial one. Some feel it is the only viable alternative while others question its value. I find myself among the latter.

If the retreat is located in a small rural community far enough away from your present home to do some good, what is the probability that you will reach it safely in a time of crisis? Will you be able to drive through the roads clogged with frightened, angry and most likely violent people? Is your vehicle capable of making it without any roads? Will there be enough fuel to get to your destination? And will you find someone else already there, willing to fight for what they have found? Face it, getting to a distant retreat in a time of crisis could be difficult at best and depend on a great deal of luck. And making the decision to leave for the retreat would be a most difficult one. On top of that, a working retreat takes years to develop adequately.

What about storing all your stuff in your current home, planning on packing it all up and taking it with you when the crisis develops? I'm afraid that has even less chance of succeeding. The amount of gear you would need to survive when you got somewhere safe is enormous. Thinking that you will have the time to pack it up and the capability to move it ahead of the panicked masses is wishful thinking.

The only safe and sane solution for those living in major metropolitan areas is to decide now, no matter what the resulting difficulties, to relocate to a suitable location as soon as possible. True, it could mean substantial changes in lifestyle. But not anywhere near as drastic as staying put might mean one day. Everything done now will greatly lessen the impact latter.

If you want to learn more about the retreat option, get the book *The Survival Retreat* by Ragnar Benson. He has also written *The Modern Survival Retreat* from a different perspective.

TABLE 26-1. BASIC TOOL KIT

- ☐ 16-oz claw hammer
- ☐ 24-oz ball-peen hammer
- ☐ 6" slip-joint pliers
- ☐ 7" linesman's pliers
- ☐ 10" groove-joint pliers
- ☐ 6" needle-nose pliers
- ☐ 8" and 12" adjustable wrenches
- ☐ combination wrenches, ⅜"-1¼"
- ☐ 10" and 14" pipe wrenches
- ☐ 15" chain reversing pipe wrench
- ☐ 7" and 10" straight and curved Vise Grips
- ☐ socket wrenches, ⅜"-1¼"
- ☐ hex key sets
- ☐ hand or breast drill with bits
- ☐ heavy-duty brace and bits, ¼"-1"
- ☐ wood boring bits, ⅜"-1¼"
- ☐ expansive bit set, ⅞"-3"
- ☐ steel drill bits, 1/16"-½"
- ☐ masonry drill bits, 3/16-⅜"
- ☐ 12" combination square
- ☐ 16x24 framing square
- ☐ 4' spirit level
- ☐ 9" torpedo level
- ☐ 12' to 20' steel measuring tape
- ☐ 50' to 100' steel measuring tape
- ☐ 8" sliding 'T' bevel
- ☐ 5" Vernier caliper
- ☐ 100' chalk line with chalk
- ☐ plumb bob
- ☐ feeler gauges
- ☐ angle or stair gauge
- ☐ 2 pr 4" and 10" 'C' clamps
- ☐ 3" corner clamp
- ☐ manual staple gun
- ☐ non-electric soldering iron
- ☐ propane torch
- ☐ 4" bench vise
- ☐ 7" woodworking vise
- ☐ 30" wrecking bar
- ☐ joining and pointing trowels
- ☐ contractor's wheelbarrow
- ☐ sawhorse brackets
- ☐ manual winch with pulley block

- ☐ 5 assorted slotted screwdrivers
- ☐ 4 assorted Phillips screwdrivers
- ☐ 8-10 pt. 26" crosscut saw
- ☐ 5-6 pt. 26" rip saw
- ☐ hacksaw with 12+ assorted blades
- ☐ keyhole saw with assorted blades
- ☐ coping saw with assorted blades
- ☐ close-quarter saw
- ☐ back saw with miter box
- ☐ 3-5' two-handled crosscut log saw
- ☐ ¼" and ½" wood chisels
- ☐ ¼" and ½" cold chisels
- ☐ ⅜" center punch
- ☐ aviation-type metal snips
- ☐ utility knife with spare blades
- ☐ stockman's knife
- ☐ putty knife
- ☐ 6" wall scraper
- ☐ bolt cutters
- ☐ glass cutter
- ☐ heavy-duty tubing cutter
- ☐ tubing flaring tool set
- ☐ auger-bit file
- ☐ dual-sided wood rasp
- ☐ 12" half-rounded wood file
- ☐ 6" slim taper file
- ☐ 10" round bastard file
- ☐ 10" round mill bastard file
- ☐ 10" flat bastard file
- ☐ warding file
- ☐ cross-cut file
- ☐ needle file set
- ☐ file brush
- ☐ 7" block plane
- ☐ 14" bench plane
- ☐ combination sharpening stone
- ☐ hand grinder with extra wheels
- ☐ grinding wheel dresser
- ☐ saw sharpening & setting tools
- ☐ wire brush
- ☐ assorted paint brushes
- ☐ work apron
- ☐ protective goggles

TABLE 26-2. BASIC SUPPLIES

☐ Assorted fasteners: common and finishing nails, screws, nuts, bolts, washers, anchors, brads, staples, tacks, cotter pins
☐ carpenter's wood glue
☐ epoxy glue
☐ plastic wood filler
☐ solder with flux core
☐ silicone sealant
☐ tube silicone instant gasket
☐ gasket material
☐ faucet washers

☐ 17-gauge galvanized wire
☐ electrician's tape
☐ duct tape
☐ filament packing tape
☐ rope, cord, string
☐ lightweight machine oil
☐ WD-40 or LPS25 spray lubricant
☐ Liquid Wrench
☐ additional oils and lubricants
☐ honing oil
☐ assorted fuses
☐ sandpaper assortment

TABLE 26-3. ADDITIONAL WOODWORKING TOOLS

☐ 14-oz shingle hammer
☐ wooden mallet
☐ ¼" and 1" wood chisels
☐ mortise and marking gauge
☐ 6" dividers (inside, outside, etc.)
☐ adze

☐ 10" to 12" drawing knife
☐ 6" extra-slim taper file
☐ 10" round wood file
☐ 12" miter/try square
☐ froe
☐ peavy (cant-hook)

TABLE 26-4. ADDITIONAL BLACKSMITHING-METAL WORKING TOOLS

☐ bellows or hand-crank forge
☐ 100+ lb anvil on fire base
☐ anvil hardie
☐ hot chisels, cleavers
☐ 32-oz ball-peen hammer
☐ 12-oz ball-peen hammer
☐ 2½ -lb cross-peen hammer
☐ 4-lb sledge hammer
☐ 20" bolt forging tongs
☐ 20" straight forging tongs
☐ welder's gloves

☐ assorted pin and drift punches
☐ ½" and 1" dia. tapered reamers
☐ quench tube
☐ 7" machinist's vise
☐ 20" adjustable wrench
☐ riveting set
☐ ¼-¾ NC and NF taps and dies
☐ screw extractor set
☐ tin snips
☐ leather apron

TABLE 26-5. ADDITIONAL MASONRY TOOLS

☐ additional trowels
☐ cement edger
☐ cement joiner
☐ assorted star drills
☐ 18-oz bricklayer's hammer

☐ manual mortar mixer
☐ tamper
☐ wood float
☐ sand screen
☐ square-point shovel

TABLE 26-6. ADDITIONAL AUTOMOTIVE TOOLS

☐ lever grease gun
☐ oil filter wrench
☐ oil spout
☐ timing light
☐ compression tester
☐ vacuum gauge
☐ automotive analyzer
☐ hydrometer (with numbers)
☐ battery post and clamp brush
☐ batter cable puller
☐ cable clamp spreader
☐ battery terminal lifter
☐ battery charger

☐ antifreeze tester
☐ battery-operated trouble light
☐ hydraulic floor jack and/or
☐ 2 5-ton hydraulic hand jacks
☐ jack stands
☐ ft-lb beam-type torque wrench
☐ bead breaker
☐ 2 pry bars
☐ bubble balancer
☐ ball joint separator
☐ Pitman arm puller
☐ general-purpose gear puller
☐ transmission tools

TABLE 26-7. ADDITIONAL SUPPLIES

☐ additional fasteners: glazier's points
   masonry nails, hooks & eyes,
   hinges, locks
☐ PVC plumbing tape, glue
☐ rubber cement
☐ J-B welding compound
☐ powdered graphite
☐ grease
☐ flux ☐ dimensional and construction lumber
☐ brazing and welding rods
☐ Naval Jelly
☐ tie wire
☐ fencing wire
☐ chain

☐ caulking
☐ putty, wood and glazier
☐ cement and plaster patch
☐ paint, varnish, stains
☐ paint thinner
☐ roofing cement
☐ tar paper
☐ plastic, rolls of black and clear

☐ plywood
☐ #14 electrical wire
☐ aluminum and brass solid stock
☐ assorted metal rod stock
☐ sheet metal

27

TERRORISM AND NUCLEAR-BIOLOGICAL-CHEMICAL (NBC) WARFARE

Terrorism is a method of waging war used by those who are militarily weak or wish to hide their real agendas. The goal of terrorism is to make everyone feel vulnerable every moment and, therefore, capitulate to the terrorists in order to have "peace" or safety.

Because terrorism can be carried out in many ways, it is relatively easy to do and extremely hard to totally prevent. Excellent intelligence is the key to stopping it before it happens. This may or may not be possible given the limitations of an open society. Terrorism has been growing world-wide for some time, and you can expect terrorist acts to increase in the years ahead. This chapter will help you prepare for those potential threats. For much more detailed information see my book *Surviving Terrorism: A Comprehensive Guide to Preparing for and Surviving Biological, Chemical and Nuclear Attacks* (available from www.Cross-Current.com).

Surviving Terrorism

There are three things you can do to increase your chances of surviving terrorism:

1. **Limit exposure to potential terrorist targets.** Don't be in the wrong place at the wrong time. Terrorists like to cause as much havoc as they can with as little effort on their parts as possible. To accomplish this they seek out high-profile government or private facilities, events or infrastructure targets. Airports, bridges, subways, harbors, dams, power plants (particularly nuclear) and water reservoirs are likely targets. You can decrease your risk by not living by or going near these kinds of sites.

Obviously, its not practical nor desirable to always stay away from every potential target. You can't let fear rule. Your life should go on as close to normal as possible. The vast majority of the time no terrorist acts take place at even the most likely targets. You will have to weigh the risks and make choices.

2. **Prepare ahead of time.** Store items that would be useful in responding to terrorist situations and their aftermaths. A list of these items will be discussed later in this chapter. Stay as healthy as possible, keep your immunities up with vaccinations and perhaps take some preventative medications.

3. **Know how to react to terrorist incidences properly.** If you know how to respond to a situation as best you can, you can minimize its affects on you. Know how to best treat the potential diseases, chemicals and radiation sickness. How you should respond will be explained in this chapter.

Assess the Risks

On January 29, 2002, President George W. Bush stated: "We have found diagrams of American nuclear power plants and public water facilities, detailed instructions for making chemical weapons, surveillance maps of American cities, and thorough descriptions of landmarks in America and throughout the world." The threat from terrorism is real as we have become painfully aware. And their targets are not limited to America.

Terrorists can cause extensive destruction. Many of their prime targets are substantially unguarded and easily damaged. For example, all of the electric power in the United States goes through three interconnected power grids and attacks at a few key switching points could entirely shut them down. Over two and a half million trucks in the United States have licenses to carry hazardous materials, and every one of them is a potential disaster. Many uncovered reservoirs provide major cities with water and could be readily contaminated. Things as simple as a small crop duster plane could become the instruments to sow disease and death over wide areas.

Biological Terrorism

There is quite a list of potential germ warfare agents: anthrax, smallpox, bubonic or pneumonic plague, botulism, tularemia, hemorrhagic fever (ebola and Marburg), yellow fever, E. coli, salmonella, foot-and-mouth disease, listeria,, brucellosis and perhaps others. Each differs in how it is contracted, if it is contagious or not, how it affects the body, what its symptoms are, if there are vaccines or other preventative measures that can be taken, how it can be treated and how effective the treatment may be. Some have a mortality rate over 90% if not treated.

Chemical Attacks

The list here too is long: VX , GA, GB (sarin), GD and other nerve gases, cyanide, phosgene, mustard, lewisite, chlorine and many others. Chemical weapons usually act much more quickly than biological weapons and, often colorless and odorless, can be as difficult to detect. Again the effects can be different as can the treatments. Some are designed to only disable, while others can be almost instantaneously lethal. Many work by inhalation, and others attack through the skin.

Nuclear Warfare

Nuclear weapons have proliferated around the world, and nuclear contraband has been smuggled across borders and into unsuspecting countries for years. Not only do the major powers like Russia and China have thermonuclear weapons, but rogue nations and some terrorist groups potentially have access to radioactive materials and even suitcase nuclear bombs. They don't need to be smart enough to actually design and build a real nuclear bomb—all they have to do is pack some high-explosives with a bunch of spent nuclear waste and blow it all over a population center. The resulting radiation could contaminate the entire area for centuries and bring about many deaths.

Other Terrorism

Truck and bus bombs have become a regular fact of life for years in the Middle East. The Oklahoma City bombing showed just how deadly these can be. A cyberattack through the Internet could cripple vital infrastructure such as the 9-1-1 system, the air traffic system and major utilities, disrupting the economy.

Prepare Now

There are a number of things that you can do ahead of time to prepare and lessen the potential harm.

First, keep a low profile. As previously mentioned, avoid high-risk targets and areas or at least weigh the risks versus the benefits. If you live in such an area, you might even consider relocating.

Second, make a family crisis plan covering what you would do if you were forced to evacuate, how you would contact and stay in touch with each other, and where you will meet. Pick both a local gathering site a few miles from your home and one further away that would most likely be unaffected by the crisis. Print out cards for everyone with phone numbers and locations on them; tape 50 cents to the back to be used if pay phones are working when cell phones aren't. If you have children, know what the school's emergency plans are.

Decide under what conditions it would be a good idea to evacuate if asked to and when it might not be best. Consider how well-prepared and knowledgeable local authorities really are. Are you willing to trust their advice in a crisis?

Third, put together supplies and equipment that would prepare you for potential terrorist attacks, a terrorist survival kit.

Terrorist Survival Kit

Although some of the things are items you should already be storing as part of your other preparedness storage, they will be listed here again. Many of the items could just be part of your Emergency Evacuation Kit (EEK).

Water. Store at least a two-week supply of water, a water filter or purifier, and a method of water purification (tablets or liquid bleach). Water filters don't filter out all dissolved chemicals, but the better ones do remove bacteria, many viruses and even some chemical agents. Filters need to be 0.2 micron to filter out bacteria and 0.01 micron to totally remove viruses. Charcoal filters can remove some chemicals.

Food. Store enough nonperishable food to last at least three days. Two weeks would be better while there is the possibility you could be quarantined and forced to remain in your house for up to two months.

Portable radio. You need to know what the authorities are saying, where and what the dangers are, and what to do about them. If you want to know what is going on outside the country, you will need a shortwave radio. Store extra fresh batteries.

First Aid kit. Every home should have one. Make sure you keep it stocked and the items fresh and useable.

Communications. Have cell phones, walkie-talkies, CB radios or other ways of communicating with your family and others that don't depend solely on a traditional phone. Consider using more than one method.

Goggles. These might be necessary to protect your eyes from some biological and chemical agents.

Flashlights and batteries. Potential attacks don't all happen during daylight hours. Keep a couple of flashlights with fresh batteries handy. Store extra batteries and spare bulbs.

Gas masks. Adequate gas masks can protect you from some biological and chemical attacks. The problem stems from the fact that many biochemical agents are odorless and colorless—you wouldn't know you were being attacked—and you would have to be wearing the gas mask when the attack occurred to do you any good. They can filter most radioactive particles out of the air you breathe.

Be careful which gas masks you buy. Some are old with cracked and brittle rubber, don't seal properly, are uncomfortable to wear, and their eyepieces quickly fog up. Gas masks must be individually fit for the correct size to fit snugly and be effective. You also need to have some training so that you will know how to use them properly. Old filters may have soaked up enough moisture and airborne particles to be virtually useless. Low-cost disposable N95-style or HEPA masks can be adequate alternatives to regular gas masks for the short-term. Available from stores like WalMart for less than $2.00 each, they filter down to 0.1 micron and would remove around 99% of biological agents. Paint, dust and surgical masks are not adequate.

Protective clothing. Full haz-mat (hazardous materials) protective suits would be nice, but really effective level A suits aren't sold to the general public and less effective level B suits still cost $50-250 each. You can improvise protective clothing for biological, chemical and nuclear attacks from disposable Tyvek coveralls, rubber, latex or synthetic gloves, rubber over-boots and even rain ponchos.

Cleaners and disinfectants. Store a supply of chlorine bleach to purify water and to make disinfectant solutions. Also store a supply of anti-bacterial soaps, cleaners and detergent with bleach.

Antibiotics and painkillers. You might want to stock up on some antibiotics like Cipro, Doxycycline (fewer side effects than Cipro), Amoxicillin or tetracycline for treating anthrax and tularemia, and streptomycin or gentamicin for plague. Antibiotics are not preventive. Even a 3-day supply would make it more likely you would survive until the authorities could get additional antibiotics to your area. Atropine, an antidote to many nerve gases, is stored at hospitals and carried in ambulances but not available to the general public because it has serious side effects. Botulism antitoxin halts, but does not reverse, the paralytic effects. Painkillers might also be desirable.

Potassium Iodide (KI). Fallout contains radioactive iodine 131. Accidentally inhaled or swallowed, it concentrates in the thyroid gland, destroying its functioning and causing delayed abnormalities and cancer. This is most serious for young children, especially babies. However, you can prevent this problem by storing a supply of stable potassium iodide for use as a blocking agent. You'll need 30-170 130-mg tablets or one ounce of reagent grade crystalline or granular potassium iodide per person. Tablets can be bought from a number of preparedness sources, and the powder can be bought in bulk from a local chemical supply house without a prescription. Directions for making a solution from the powder are in my book *Surviving Terrorism* and in *Nuclear War Survival Skills*.

Realize that potassium iodide can't protect you from the immediate effects of the high-level radiation of a nuclear blast, but only protects one part of the body from long-term effects.

L-Cysteine and Vitamin C may be helpful in preventing radiation damage. L-Cysteine tablets can be bought without a prescription at pharmacies, health food stores and chemical supply companies. Another drug that might be useful in protecting from radiation, but not yet approved by the FDA, is 5-androstenediol, an immune-system booster. Amifostine is also a medication that is currently used to protect the salivary glands of cancer patients during radiation treatment and might be helpful.

Radiation meter or KFM. If you seek shelter from a nuclear attack you need to know when it is safe to go out again. A radiation meter can tell you. You can buy a new one from Ludlum for $1,000 or so, a recalibrated CD V-715 meter for $225-275 from KI4U (see Chapter 32 for addresses), or make your own, the Kearny Fallout Meter or KFM discussed later in this chapter, from common supplies or from a kit for about $20-25. It measures up to 43 R/hour. You might also consider storing rechargeable high-range dosimeters along with a charger so you can tell how much total radiation you have been exposed to. Dosimeters cost about $45-125 with $65-195 for the charger.

Flu and other vaccinations. Beyond these preparations you will want to keep your vaccinations and immunizations up to date. Get flu shots because many of the diseases that terrorists might spread have early flu-like symptoms that might mask their prompt detection. Although not generally available until the summer of 2002, smallpox vaccinations are highly effective. However, about two out of a million people will suffer brain infection and death from the vaccine itself. If you were vaccinated prior to 1972 when the vaccinations ended, you still most likely have some lingering immunity. Research has shown that the disease only kills about 10% of those who have been vaccinated as much as 50 years earlier.

Safe Rooms and Shelters

If your home is in the midst of a biochemical attack you can make an improvised shelter if you have stored a few items before hand. If possible, select an upstairs room to be your safe room because many nerve gases and other toxic gases are heavier than air and settle at ground level. Try to include a bathroom or even a kitchen in your safe area if you can. Store a couple of rolls of plastic sealing (packaging) tape or duct tape and some sheets of clear plastic sheeting or even trash bags. Use these to seal around the doors and windows and to close off heating and air conditioning ducts. Use wet rolled-up towels pushed against the bottom of doors to seal them.

Nuclear Preparations

First, decide if you live in or near a likely target. Targets would include large population and economic centers, military and political command and control centers, major military or missile installations, communication facilities, major ports and transportation hubs, large power stations and distribution points, oil refineries and storage, and certain chemical industries.

If you live near a probable target you can either move somewhere else, attempt to protect yourself against possible blast effects (you can if you are not right at ground zero and are willing to build an adequate blast shelter) or hope you will have enough warning to evacuate the area.

Get a copy of *Nuclear War Survival Skills* by Cresson H. Kearny. It was written by civil defense experts at the Oak Ridge National Laboratories and is available from the Oregon Institute of Science and Medicine, PO Box 1279, Cave Junction, OR 97523 (order at www.oism.org/oism/s32p903.htm or download the free on-line version at www.oism.org/nwss). The book tells you how to survive as best one can when not really prepared. If you do plan on evacuating take the book with you because it contains plans for six expedient shelters. You should also have the necessary tools and supplies to build and equip one of those shelters. The bare minimums are listed in Table 27-1.

If not located in close proximity to a probable target, you could construct a better, permanent shelter. The more shielding between you and the radioactive fallout the better with the suggested absolute minimum a Protection Factor (PF) of forty. That's not very high and my recommendation is a PF of 1,000. This means that only one-thousandth

TABLE 27-1. EXPEDIENT SHELTER TOOLS AND SUPPLIES

☐ 1 or more shovels	☐ pick (for hard-soil areas)
☐ bow saw with extra blade	☐ axe or hatchet
☐ hammer	☐ file
☐ nails, wire, rope, etc.	☐ pliers
☐ 4-mil polyethylene film	☐ work gloves
☐ 4 20-gal poly trash bags	☐ siphon or pliable garden hose
and 2 burlap bags or	☐ KAP
pillow cases per person	☐ fallout meter or KFM
(or other method to carry	☐ potassium iodide (KI)
large quantities of water)	☐ bleach

of the outside radiation will penetrate inside. The 1,000 PF only requires about double the thickness of a forty PF and yet keeps out twenty-five times as much radiation. A 1,000 PF can be provided by two feet of concrete, three feet of dirt or almost anything else with about three hundred pounds of material per square foot of the shelter walls and ceiling. It would be best to build the shelter now.

The KAP

Without adequate ventilation, in warm or hot weather, shelters can get so dangerously hot and humid within a few hours that people will collapse and die from the heat. The Kearny Air Pump (KAP), a homemade shelter-ventilating pump designed by Cresson Kearny when he was at Oak Ridge, can be easily made with a few inexpensive materials. Plans are contained in *Nuclear War Survival Skills*.

The KFM

Once the fallout has arrived, you must stay inside your shelter. But how will you know when it's safe to come out? What you need to tell you is a fallout dose-rate meter. It should be able to measure up to at least twenty-five to fifty roentgens per hour (R/hr) with a five hundred R/hr range even better. This means you can either buy a commercial fallout meter for hundreds of dollars or more, or you can make your own reliable one from common materials. It's called the Kearny Fallout Meter (KFM), and it was

Kearny Fallout Meter

also designed and tested by Mr. Kearny at Oak Ridge. Again, plans for it are in *Nuclear War Survival Skills*. Be sure you have an original copy from OISM because in many other printings the necessary patterns have been reduced to fit the page size, and therefore will not result in an accurate meter. Emergency Essentials sells a KFM kit for $20 while KI4U's version is $25 postpaid (see Chapter 32). You can also download a set of plans free from www.Cross-Current.com and a few other sites such as OISM's listed earlier.

Other Provisions

You must also make provisions for water, food, sanitation, light and a few other needs in the shelter.

Store at least fourteen gallons of water in the shelter per person and enough food for two weeks. The same types of foods used in the Emergency Evacuation Kit (EEK) discussed in Chapter 20 would be appropriate. In fact, plan on taking your EEK with you into the shelter. A portable toilet or hose-vented five-gallon can with heavy-duty plastic bag liners, toilet paper and additional smaller bags, plastic buckets or garbage cans can provide for sanitation. A total waste storage capacity of at least five to ten gallons per person is required. A supply of small long-burning candles, matches and flashlights with extra batteries are good, but additional sustained light is a real advantage. This can be provided with a one-tenth to one-quarter amp twelve-volt light bulb hooked up to a large dry cell or car battery or by making a lamp from a pint glass jar with a cotton wick and cooking oil for fuel.

Also provide a first aid kit with a tube of antibiotic ointment, blankets or sleeping bags for sleeping and a radio with extra batteries. You will want to protect the radio by shielding it from the EMP (Electromagnetic Pulse) that is caused by nuclear explosions and can destroy communications and equipment. Like a lot of the other preparations discussed here, there is not sufficient space to go into any detail about EMP or protecting from it in this short chapter. It is covered in my book *Surviving Terrorism* and there are some sources of EMP protection listed in Chapter 32.

If you evacuate, take the KAP, KFM, potassium iodide and other supplies with you. Otherwise, keep them in the shelter.

Responding to an Attack

Regardless of whether the attack is biological, chemical or nuclear, the first thing to do is to limit your exposure. Get uphill, downwind, or as far away from the problem as possible or seek shelter immediately. Close off air entryways for biological and chemical attacks, and put as much mass as possible between you and a nuclear attack.

A slight "overpressure" can be created in a safe room (not an entire house) by sticking the sucking wand of a regular vacuum cleaner out a window, closing the window on the middle of the wand and sealing around it. When the vacuum is turned on it will pull air through the vacuum into the room, causing some of the air in the room to be pushed out by the pressure. This brings air into the room through the vacuum and pushes contaminated air out. It will only work if the vacuum has a HEPA filter or a very dirty filter bag to trap the contaminated particles. It is also a short-term solution and can burn out the vacuum motor fairly quickly. The air coming in also is at whatever temperature it was outside, and could be too hot or cold for comfort.

Decontaminate yourself and your surroundings as much and as soon as possible. People and animals can be wiped with bleach solutions and then washed and showered with anti-bacterial soaps and cleaners. Mix regular bleach in a 10:1 ratio or the "ultra" at 12:1 for cleaning skin. Wash off within five minutes and then rinse with soap and water. Use the bleach at full strength for wiping off surfaces. Clothes can be sanitized by washing in detergent with bleach or, if too contaminated, should be put in plastic bags and safely discarded. Radioactive dust (fallout) should be washed off and as far away as you can get it.

If you absolutely must leave the safe room or shelter into a still-contaminated environment, wear whatever protective clothing is available. Then, when you come back in, decontaminate yourself and your clothing again.

Any person injured by the attack should receive expert medical attention immediately. If this is not possible, use whatever supplies and knowledge you have at hand to treat the injuries as best you can. You may not know exactly what the agents used were so focus on treating the symptoms and trying to make the victim as comfortable as you can. Seek professional help as soon as it is practical.

28

TRANSPORTATION

Maintaining mobility and the potential to travel relatively long distances could be important in a crisis. This is especially true if you plan on escaping to a distant retreat, but it is also helpful just for doing work and hauling things around the homestead.

Various options for transportation are covered here. In considering them, keep in mind what you will want them to do. What kind of surfaces will they be expected to operate on? During what kind of weather? How many passengers must they carry? And for how far? What type of cargo and what is it's size, shape and weight? You can't expect any mode to be ideal under all conditions, so you need to have a good idea what you will expect it to do.

Vehicles

Rather than try to recommend the ideal survival vehicle for your use in circumstances I couldn't possibly know, I can only give you some general guidelines to follow.

If you are concerned about getting to a retreat, you will want every advantage you can get. The vehicle should be the toughest and most dependable you can find that is capable of carrying the expected load of passengers and gear. It must be capable of traveling off-road in the worst weather imaginable with plenty of ground clearance for rocks and other obstacles. It must also have the needed range under full load with expected road conditions (test to make sure). These criteria virtually eliminate all passenger cars and suggest a sturdy truck-type vehicle. Around the homestead a vehicle is used basically to haul load and do other work, again pointing to some type of truck. The vehicle should still be tough, but fuel economy becomes more important than it is for just getting to a retreat. And, because you may have to service and maintain the vehicle in either case, it should be as simple as possible and easy to maintain and repair with plenty of spare parts available such as would be the case with a fairly common model.

Typically the vehicles that best fit the above criteria are SUVs, full-size pickups and vans. Pick the one that best fits the combination of passengers and cargo you anticipate. A 3/4 ton pickup or van is built much stronger than a 1/2 ton, and the 1-ton is perhaps heavier-duty than necessary.

Although newer models have the advantage of newer parts, they also usually have computer chips that increase complexity and might be hard to diagnose and fix in a survival context. One option might be to rebuild an older model. To rebuild doesn't mean to make cosmetically appealing, but to effectively bring all the components like the engine, transmission, differential, drive line, wiring, suspension, braking and cooling systems to like-new condition. If you have the time to do it yourself you will also become intimately knowledgeable of your vehicle and probably do it for less than half the cost of a new machine.

Options

The engine should be a stock gas six-cylinder or small-block V-8. Why not a diesel? Because their faults outweigh the better mileage and lack of tuneups. They cost more, clatter, stink, are heavier for the power, have poorer acceleration and can be difficult to start on cold mornings. They also require special tools and training for maintenance and repair. But the biggest disadvantage is the fact that they burn diesel. Not only are there a lot fewer diesel outlets now, but during the early stages of a major crisis the probability is high that diesel will be rationed and available only to the truckers that transport vital food supplies and other necessities. Many truck-stop pumps also lack filters—the big trucks have their own—and unfiltered diesel fuel can be destructive to smaller diesels.

What about four-wheel-drive? It would certainly be nice to have in some situations. It also costs more, uses more fuel and is more compli-cated and therefore more likely to break down. Careful driving can often extricate a vehicle without 4WD when those with 4WD, but less care, get stuck. On balance, though, I'd rather have it.

Standard 4-speed transmissions are suggested because they are fairly simple to fix with a few tools. They are also cheaper to begin with and get better mileage. Automatics, on the other hand, require specialized tools and training but are generally more reliable. If you do get an automatic also get a locking-differential and an optional factory-installed transmission oil cooler.

Get the heaviest-duty alternator, cooling system (radiator, water pump, fan), trailering suspension package and gearing, and the highest-rated battery available. A dual battery is recommended to provide backup and to power CB's and scanners without endangering re-starting. You will want a heavy-duty rear bumper, a front brush guard, skid plates, roll bars, cigarette lighter, the standard heater, a trailer hitch and the cold weather package or extra insulation if offered. Also get an oversize fuel tank or have an auxiliary fuel tank installed. Tires should be load-bearing all-terrain type mounted on steel rims. Interiors should be light-colored and the exterior should be a non-conspicuous color. A power-takeoff (PTO) winch is preferred, but an electric one is better than nothing. A steering shock damper can also be added to decrease wear on the steering components.

Avoid all unnecessary power options. With power brakes and steering you must decide whether less fatigue in a heavy loaded vehicle outweighs the additional complexity and failure probability. Obviously fancy paint, heavy chrome and huge tires don't belong on a survival vehicle.

Basic Tools and Spare Parts

The tools and supplies listed in Table 28-1 should be stored on-board your main survival vehicle at all times if you expect to use it to get to a retreat. Table 28-1 suggests the spare parts that should also be stored in the vehicle along with two spare tires. Some of these tools, supplies and parts could be a portion of those stored in accordance with other lists in Chapter 26 if you make sure to keep them in the vehicle at all times. Most of the items would be good to keep in the vehicle even when around home.

At the retreat or at home, you will want to have a larger selection of tools, supplies and parts. The additional tools recommended are listed in Table 28-6. A list of spare parts and supplies is given in Table 28-3. However, to be sure you store the spare parts that commonly break down for your particular vehicle, consult a good mechanic and check the evaluations from off-road magazines. Then make a list of parts that might wear out and any special tools needed. Having two vehicles of the same model and year could simplify parts storage because of common of parts. Old parts that are at all serviceable should also be saved as possible emergency replacements.

Also, get a genuine factory shop manual for each vehicle. The repair manuals by Chilton and Motor are also good. Chances are you'll be doing your own maintenance and repair and you'll want the best instructions possible.

TABLE 28-1. BASIC ON-BOARD TOOL KIT

☐ ½" drive socket set, 7/16-1"
  with 'T' handle, 6" extension
☐ spark plug socket
☐ combination wrenches, ⅜-1"
☐ 6" adjustable wrench
☐ 10" groove-joint pliers
☐ linesman's pliers
☐ Hex key set
☐ Torx key set (if needed)
☐ 4-way lug wrench with breaker bar
☐ tire and tube repair kit
☐ quality air pressure gauge
☐ inflation pump
☐ jumper cables, 4 gauge
☐ can starting fluid
☐ ice scraper/snow brush
☐ siphon
☐ regular gas adaptor (if needed)
☐ can radiator stop-leak
☐ 2-gal water container
☐ duct tape
☐ electrician's tape
☐ safety flares
☐ first aid kit
☐ fire extinguisher

☐ assorted screwdrivers, regular
  and Phillips
☐ ball-peen hammer
☐ 2+ lb short-handled hammer
☐ ¾" cold chisel
☐ mini-hacksaw with extra blades
☐ continuity tester
☐ stockman's knife
☐ can WD-40 or LPS25
☐ 5-ton hydraulic hand jack
☐ 'high-lift' jack
☐ foot-square ¾" plywood
☐ 'come-along' hand winch
☐ nylon tow strap, cable or rope
☐ 60" crowbar
☐ tire chains
☐ shovel
☐ axe
☐ bow saw
☐ bolt cutters
☐ nails, spikes
☐ bailing wire
☐ flashlight, spare batteries
☐ hand spotlight
☐ extra motor oil

TABLE 28-2 BASIC ON-BOARD SPARE PARTS

☐ 2 complete sets of belts
☐ set of radiator and heater hoses
☐ thermostat
☐ radiator cap
☐ water pump
☐ assorted fuses

☐ set spark plugs
☐ distributor cap (if needed)
☐ point and condenser set (if needed)
☐ voltage regulator
☐ fuel filter
☐ fuel pump

TABLE 28-3. SPARE PARTS AND SUPPLIES STORAGE

☐ complete set of belts
☐ complete set of hoses
☐ thermostat
☐ radiator cap
☐ water pump
☐ fuel pump
☐ 4 fuel filters
☐ spare carburetor
☐ 4 air cleaner elements
☐ 2 sets windshield wipers
☐ 5 oil filters
☐ 60 qt motor oil

☐ 4 sets spark plugs
☐ distributor cap (if needed)
☐ 2 sets points and condensers
  (if used)
☐ voltage regulator
☐ generator or alternator with
  spare set of brushes
☐ spare diode bridge for
  alternator (if used)
☐ spare coil
☐ spare starter brushes
☐ set solid ignition cables

☐ wheel-bearing grease
☐ 2-4 batteries
☐ set battery cables, 4 gauge
☐ spare fuses
☐ power-steering fluid (if needed)
☐ 4-6 gal coolant
☐ 2 sets shock absorbers
☐ 2 sets of front wheel bearings,
    seals, cotter pins
☐ spare headlights
☐ other spare lights, bulbs
☐ 2-4 sets of tires
☐ tire and tube patching supplies

☐ clutch plate, pressure plate and
    release bearings (manual)
☐ friction plates, steel plate, rings,
    front and rear seals, complete
    gasket and rubber set
    (automatic transmission)
☐ transmission fluid
☐ spare brake master cylinder
☐ wheel cylinder rebuilding kits
☐ brake pads and linings
☐ gal brake fluid
☐ gal 10% denatured alcohol

Since batteries are responsible for more "no-go" situations than any other component and nearly all are almost impossible to repair or rebuild, store at least two to four spares. They should be stored as cool as possible and recharged once a month with an automatic battery charger with slow-charging capabilities.

Store at least two to four complete sets of tires. They should be a standard mud/snow design in the largest size suggested by the factory for your particular vehicle with the highest load range rating possible (usually C or D on light trucks). Huge over-sized tires shouldn't be used because they greatly increase the stress on wheel bearings, front spindles and rear axles, increasing the chance of failure. Tires should be stored on their side to prevent flat spotting in a clean, dark, cool and dry location, preferably wrapped in heavy paper or burlap. They should not be stored near petroleum products nor around electrical equipment; electrical equipment produces ozone when operating that attacks and cracks the rubber. Ideally, tires should be mounted, inflated to operating pressure, spun balanced, deflated to about 10 psi, and then have new valve stems (or valve cores in tubes) installed and capped prior to storage.

A 3/4-ton or larger vehicle usually has split rims that require tube-type tires. Installing tubes even in tubeless tires on survival vehicles would make them that much more dependable.

If you desire to store a vehicle for the long-term, use a dark, dry and cool but not freezing location. Siphon out as much fuel as possible and run until completely dry, then remove the battery, drain all the coolant from the radiator, flush the cooling system and refill with fresh coolant. Change the oil and oil filter, loosen all belts and place the vehicle on blocks to prevent the tires from flat spotting.

Obviously you will want to store a fuel supply for the vehicles. See Chapter 23 for details. Jerrycans and other portable fuel cans should have adequate spouts.

Trailers can be used to increase the load capacity, but be aware that under even the best of circumstances they can be most difficult to maneuver and turn. Also, their ground clearance is usually poor. If you want a real tough utility trailer for use around a remote retreat, check into the Pack Mule trailers from Helder Manufacturing.

Other Motorized Vehicles

Mopeds, all-terrain vehicles (ATVs) and light scrambler dirt bikes can also be used. Mopeds range in price from $1000 to over $2,000, weigh about an hundred pounds or so, and usually use a one to two horsepower 50cc engine to travel eighteen to forty miles per hour while getting eighty to two hundred miles per gallon. They are no where near as easy to pedal as a decent bicycle. Get one with full suspension, a multi-speed or variable speed transmission and some way to carry items. ATVs cost $1,500 and up, weigh 160 to three hundred pounds, use fifty to 700cc engines, get around fifty miles per gallon and can hit speeds over seventy miles per hour. They go in sand, mud, ice, or snow and can haul loads over fairly rough terrain. Scrambler dirt bikes should be under 250cc so that they won't be too heavy and hard to control in off-road use.

Ultra light planes cruise at thirty to eighty miles per hour with one or two passengers, weigh two hundred plus pounds with a twenty-five to a hundred horse power engine and get about twenty to thirty miles per gallon. They can take off from any reasonably smooth strip a couple of hundred feet long, land at twenty miles per hour in as little as thirty feet and still don't require a pilot's license to operate. Most come in kit form for $3-17,000. There are also autogyros, small helicopters and the larger helicopters and planes.

Motorboats, snowmobiles ,and tracked all-terrain vehicles are other possibilities for transportation in certain situations.

Non-Motorized Transportation

Although it's obvious that transportation modes independent of stored fuel supplies could become very valuable when the stored supplies are all used, they are also valuable before that time as backup systems. There are a number of options to consider.

Bicycles

Bicycles are the most efficient mode of self-powered transportation and would be excellent during a pro-longed crisis if chosen wisely. Get an all-terrain mountain bike. They are wide-ratio, multi-geared and have over-sized brakes, heavy-duty steel frames and usually shocks.

Get a luggage carrier rack, folding side baskets, or saddlebags for carrying loads. Mount a generator with light and store spare brake pads, spokes, rear gear sprockets, chains, tire rims, tires and tubes along with a patching kit and air pump. You'll also want a good bicycle repair manual and a tool kit. For hauling loads up to more than one hundred pounds you can buy or build a two-wheel bike trailer.

Horses and Mules

Horses and mules can be used for riding, packing loads ,or doing work around a homestead like plowing and pulling wagons. A good horse can cover forty miles a day over rough terrain for many days and more than twice that in an emergency. A pack horse or mule can carry one-fifth its weight in gear or supplies, and a team will allow you to farm fifty to hundred acres. Stallions are much more difficult to control than geldings but are more desirable to breed with mares.

A mule has more endurance than a horse, makes a better pack animal and are good choices for draft work. Along with burros, they are more adaptable than horses to drier, less-vegetated areas.

Stalls are usually twelve feet square. Horses also need a minimum of eight hundred square feet of corral and two to four acres for grazing unless supplemented. Plan on two tons of grains, three tons of hay and salt for each horse per year.

For riding, you'll want a sturdy Western roping saddle, a thick saddle blanket, a bridle, halter, ropes and perhaps hobbles. Also get a hoof pick, nail trimmers and grooming equipment. If you expect to shoe your own animals, you'll need horseshoes and nails plus a forge, hammers, tongs and files. If you will want to haul much, you'll need a wagon or cart with harnesses and hitches.

Store worming supplies and other medications to keep your animals healthy and have them properly vaccinated. Daily exercise is important to keep them in shape, too.

Sled Dogs

In areas with lots of winter snow, sled dogs might be a good form of transportation. A good dog is capable of pulling about two to three times his own weight at ten to twelve miles per hour for extended periods of time. You'll need a freight sled, tow lines and harnesses. They can also be used to pull carts when there is no snow and can carry approximately one-third their own weight with a backpack. Real sled dogs eat about 750 pounds of dried fish each per year!

Skis and Snowshoes

Skis and snowshoes can be effective winter transportation. Although regular cross-country skis can be used, the heavier mountain skis allow the use of heavy boots and are preferred. Ski skins give additional traction for mountaineering use. Snowshoes are better in hilly terrain and not as dependent on the snow condition. Have snow goggles or glasses to prevent snowblindness.

Handcarts

Carts can be useful around the homestead for hauling heavy loads of dirt, compost and firewood. They can also be used as a last resort for carrying a sizeable amount of belongings over long distances. Large tires help in rough terrain and a suitable cart can be homemade using twenty-six-inch bicycle tires or the plastic moto-cross bike wheels. A waterproof tarp or other top is a needed addition.

29

COMMUNICATIONS

Having communications before, during and after a crisis can be vital. Before a crisis it can warn of dangerous situations as they develop, keep family and friends appraised, and inform about events either suppressed or ignored by government officials or the media. During a crisis it may be the only way to stay in contact, coordinate activities, know what the present situation is and even call for help. After a crisis has passed, it allows quick assessment and reorientation.

Three types of communications you should consider are radios, cell phones and the Internet.

Radios

The absolute minimum is a battery-operated AM radio. This will allow you to keep abreast of local news and emergency broadcasts Radios using solar cells to power the radio and recharge the batteries for night or overcast daytime operation would save having to rely solely on stored batteries. There are also some radios that use a hand-crank to power the radio, often along with solar cells. All major preparedness vendors listed in Chapter 32 offer these types of radios.

Store both rechargeable batteries and regular ones which you must rotate to keep fresh. Rechargeable batteries generally only have about half the total power of regular and often a slightly lower voltage.

General-Coverage Receivers

If you want to know what is going on outside the country or others' perspectives and interpretations of current events, you should have a quality general-coverage receiver capable of picking up the basic shortwave (World Band) spectrum to 30 mHz (megahertz). This gives access to more than 70 nations and thousands of shortwave broadcasts from around the world, many in English.

The receiver should be AC/DC and have jacks for an external antenna and earphone or headphone, an illuminated display and a good signal-strength indicator. Make sure the radio has a digital frequency readout because it makes locating desired frequencies much easier. Multiple or double conversion is almost a necessity, and synchronous selectable sideband increases adjacent-channel rejection while reducing fading distortion. Direct-access tuning via keypad and preset memories are very convenient. Single side band (SSB) capabilities will also expand your listening options.

The further you are from the places you want to listen to the better your radio should be; if you choose a radio a bit above your perceived needs it has a better chance of being satisfactory in the long run. You'll also want to take into account whether you want a really small radio for travel, a larger and more pleasant to use radio for a fixed base, or both. There are also some in-dash car radios that receive shortwave (i.e. the Becker Mexico 2340 for $460), and other radios can be adapted to run off of the car battery via the cigarette lighter.

Models change and specific recommendations soon become dated; it's well worth the $20 to get the latest edition of *Passport to World Band Radio* and read their reviews before you buy. They also sell in-depth evaluations on their Web site at www.passband.com. Radios in the $150 to $500 range are usually adequate for all but the weakest of stations. Current recommendations are (from good to best) the Grundig Yachtboy 400PE ($150), Sony ICF-7600GR ($170), Sony ICF-SW07 ($420), Sony ICF-2010 ($350) and Grundig Satellit 800 ($500). If you want the very best in sensitivity, selectivity and stability, get the Drake R8B ($1380) or the AOR AR7030 ($2,000) tabletops.

Grundig Satellit 800 Millennium Shortwave Radio

Almost all receivers built since 1980 are solid state and work well even decades after they are built. On the other hand, tube radios tend to loose efficiency with age so buying an old tube set is not highly recommended.

The antenna is even more important than the radio. The built-in antenna portables come with may not be adequate. Outdoor antennas work much better, but if you can't set one up, Sony's AN-LP1 loop antenna (the Sony ICF-SW07 comes with the equivalent AN-LP2) will help. Effective outdoor antennas can be made from fifty to a hundred feet of sixteen to eighteen-gauge insulated copper wire placed between the highest points possible with insulators at each end. Directional dipole antennas and active antennas are other possibilities. Details on building more complex antennas are in sources listed in Chapter 31. Among the best antennas under $100 are the *Eavesdropper* by Antenna Supermarket and those by Alpha Delta Communications.

Develop the habit of listening to shortwave broadcasts now so you'll know how and where to find them when needed. To find out what programs are broadcast when, consult the shortwave web sites listed in Chapter 32. Long-distance reception is best at night and in the winter when radio waves travel much better. Higher frequencies work better than lower ones during the day and in the summer, but they are also most affected by sunspot activity.

Stored radios should have all batteries removed, and protect all radios from moisture, sunlight and freezing temperatures. You should also protect them from the EMP (electromagnetic pulse) likely at the beginning of a major nuclear attack. An EMP with tremendous energy is created by the detonation of a nuclear warhead in space. The EMP induces large currents in conductors, destroying communications components and equipment. Vacuum tube equipment isn't particularly affected by it, but transistorized solid state equipment is highly susceptible. Radios can be protected by leaving them disconnected from electrical outlets, not attached to antennas over ten inches in length and by shielding them inside metal, aluminum foil, or metal window screen-covered boxes that have been electrically grounded. Small battery-operated radios using only built-in short-loop antennas probably won't be affected much by EMP.

Scanners

If you want to listen to local police, fire, ambulance, public safety, aviation, marine, and local, state and federal government transmissions, get a multi-channel programmable AC/DC scanner. To listen in on the many agencies that use trunk tracking (frequency hopping), you'll need a scanner with that capability. My current choices would be the Uniden BC 780XLT ($335) for a base/mobile scanner or the Uniden BC 245XLT ($205) for a handheld. AOR also makes good scanners. Again you can use sources listed in Chapters 32 to help you find your local frequencies.

CB Radios

The most prevalent and most useful two-way radios are those operating on the eleven-meter citizen's band (CB). They operate on forty different channels (channel 9 is the emergency channel) and have a legal maximum four-watt output. Within their normal range limit of a few miles, they are excellent for learning about road and traffic conditions, pileups, road blocks, washouts and other possible problems. They can also function as alternatives to the telephone system if need be.

Cobra makes excellent equipment as do Uniden and Midland. Small 100-milliwatt hand-held CB units with up to one-mile line-of-sight range can be purchased for $40-60. A mobile CB unit is the most versatile choice with a decent one costing $100 or more. Base stations usually cost more than mobile ones, have increased range, but are not normally portable. Single side band (SSB) units are more static free, have half the usual interference and effectively two to three times the power and range of the normal four-watt output.

Although currently illegal, with the proper know-how the power of CB radios can be boosted up to 400 times through the use of linear amplifiers. Illegal frequency "sliders" also allow operating outside normal CB frequencies. While these modifications are illegal to make now, under an extreme crisis they may come in very handy. You might want to locate possible plans for them now.

Other Two-Way Radios

General Mobile Radio Service (GMRS) requires an FCC license (easily obtained) and allows immediate family members to discuss personal or commercial business. GMRS radios operate with two to five watts power, have a range of one to five miles and cost around $150 or so. Family Radio Service (FRS) radios operate on the same frequencies. Strictly non-commercial, they do not require a license, have up to one-half watt power with a range up to two miles and cost as little as $40.

Amateur Radio

The best long-distance two-way communications equipment is the amateur or "ham" radios. To operate ham radios legally you have to be licensed, but with the "no-code" Technician license it's fairly easy to get started. You will have to take a 35-question test on basic electronics and communications rules and are limited to frequencies above 30 MHz. If you want access to all the ham bands then you will need to know how to send messages in Morse code and have the additional knowledge required for the General or Extra class licenses.

The American Radio Relay League (ARRL) is the amateur organization in the United States and annually publishes *The Radio Amateur's Handbook*, the recognized reference work for amateurs, along with other publications of interest (see Chapter 31). Either the *No-Code License Manual* by Gordon West or *Now You're Talking* by Larry Wolfgang (both available at Radio Shack) can prepare you for getting the Technician license.

Ham equipment is again available in hand-held, mobile and base units. Equipment runs from a couple hundred dollars to transceivers costing thousands of dollars, with quality producers including ICOM, Kenwood and Yaesu. Often used equipment can be located through ham organizations or ham retailers (see Chapter 32). This isn't the type of equipment where a few "best buys" can be listed; you'll have to become knowledgeable about it for yourself and the best place to start is talking with other hams.

Emergency Alert Radios

Weather alert radios receive continuous weather reports, forecasts, advisories and warnings from the National Weather Service (NWS). This service also originates the Emergency Alert System warnings heard on the AM/FM public radio frequencies. The NWS broadcasts twenty-four hours per day throughout the United States. Maximum range from a station is forty to fifty miles line-of-sight and reception can be poor in mountainous country. Costs start as low as $20 for a portable, but be sure to get the kind that automatically turns on when a warning is issued and gets your attention with an audible alarm. You'll not only get more current and accurate weather information than possible from the standard radio and TV stations, but you'll be among the first to know of a nuclear attack warning. You might want one where you work, too.

Radios that automatically alert you to emergency warnings on the regular AM/FM dial are fine but not as timely as those using the NWS frequencies.

Cell Phones

Cell phones are extremely convenient and can be used almost anywhere to communicate with anyone connected to the world-wide telephone system. There are even cell phones that use satellites and can place calls from the most remote parts of the world. However, during major crises the telephone system, including cell phones, can become overloaded and make it nearly impossible to get through in a timely manner. Cell phones are basically two-way radios that use local repeaters (or "cells") to function, so they can likewise be disrupted by nearby problems.

Regardless of their shortcomings, cell phones would be helpful in many crises. They can also dramatically increase your safety in situations where you can call for immediate help when needed. Digital cell phones are the preferred option because they offer many additional features over the analog variety.

The Internet

The Internet is the communication medium of choice for sending messages (e-mails and instant messaging) and getting the latest news from just about anywhere in the world. It was designed to work in times of major disaster by routing traffic around malfunctioning sections. You access it with a computer or other Internet device (even some cell phones) and a phone line, cable, or wireless connection.

However, it can be quickly overloaded during emergencies, is subject to hackers and cyber-terrorists, and can be critically damaged by destroying only a few key locations. In spite of that, access to the Internet would be very valuable during and after any major crisis.

For secure messages you will want a good encryption program such as PGP. Download it free at: web.mit.edu/network/pgp.html. With these programs you give your "public" key to whomever you want to send a message to and then encode your message with your "private" key prior to sending it.

30

HOME MANAGEMENT

During or after a crisis there are still basic activities that can or must be done. Not only are the activities useful in themselves, but they also keep minds and bodies occupied and give structure and direction, decreasing the possibility that depression or other psychological problems will develop.

GENERAL FUNCTIONS

Calculations are much easier with a solar-powered calculator. Messages can be produced with a manual typewriter (what's that?) and a duplicating machine or hand-operated press. The typewriter and adding machine will need ribbons and tapes. A wind-up clock will continue to function without batteries or electricity and provide coordination. Knowing the time and keeping track of the days with a calendar will help keep you oriented, too. Other items that could prove useful:

□ paper	□ notebooks	□ note pads
□ pens	□ pen refills	□ pencils
□ erasers	□ manual sharpener	□ markers
□ ink	□ crayons	□ stapler
□ staples	□ transparent tape	□ masking tape
□ paper clips	□ scissors	□ glue and paste
□ posterboard	□ paints and watercolors	

RECREATION AND ENTERTAINMENT

Crises bring tension, apprehension and fear. Normally mature individuals become irritable, loose their tempers and worsen already-bad situations. Young children can become very difficult and unruly. And all these problems are greatly magnified when, for example, you are confined for many days in a shelter. However, some forethought and planning can help avoid many of these problems by providing diversionary activities that help all to relax, release tension, laugh a bit and perhaps temporarily forget their troubles.

Provide a wide variety of board and card games and activities suitable for different ages and social groupings. Small children can be kept occupied with coloring books, puzzles, jacks, marbles, tops and jump ropes. Adults can use arts and crafts materials to build useful items and work on their hobbies. Particularly in confined situations, active games like charades can help.

You can store musical instruments and toys, but both can also be made from odds and ends. Dolls can be made from scraps of wood and bits of cloth and yarn.

Battery-operated tape recorders and CD players can be used with a library of tapes and CDs. When electricity is available, even stereos, televisions, camcorders, DVD players and electronic video games are nice. Sports equipment can provide hours of enjoyment and outdoor "games" can be used to teach about wild plants, trees, birds and other survival skills. Digital or film cameras can be very useful and can provide memories, but you may have to develop the film yourself. Journals for keeping a daily diary may help.

Finally, reading material can take on a whole new light in a crisis. Not only will you want to store plenty of general fiction for escape reading but also a fair amount of educational non-fiction books. The next chapter discusses a survival library in detail. Old magazines and catalogs can be saved and song books can help develop unity.

HOME EDUCATION

A prolonged crisis may mean that children will have to be taught at home. Adults, too, need to exercise their intellectual capacities and develop additional skills. Learning should be a life-long pursuit for all, and a severe crisis may make it even more essential.

Children need to learn basic reading, writing and arithmetic, but there are many other subjects that could be valuable to them like spelling, English, advanced mathematics and geometry, biology, chemistry, physics, history, health, foreign languages and music. Obviously there is a great body of knowledge to learn and storing all the necessary books would be a large undertaking. Keep current textbooks, seek out books thrown out by schools, or buy them inexpensively at a thrift store. Add a good set of encyclopedias, a world atlas and a dictionary. There are also computer versions of these. Pictures, flannel boards and characters, charts, tables and other materials can also be helpful. A selection of decent literature is good, too. See Chapter 32 for a list of books that might be appropriate for you.

31

SURVIVAL LIBRARY

Information can be extremely valuable in times of crises and you should have a good reference library. It's impossible to learn everything now that you may need to know some time in the future, but you can store that knowledge in printed form. Collect all the how-to books, newsletters and magazine articles you can on survival and self-sufficiency. CDs would be a good way to store lots of information if you can guarantee you'll have access to a computer (perhaps a PDA or other hand-held computer?) It can be scanned in or taken directly off the Internet. Read some of it on a regular basis. You probably won't have the time to absorb it all, but know what's in it.

Because of the vast amount of information that might possibly be useful in a crisis situation, this chapter can only point out a small part of the available material. As time passes there will be new books that could be added to these lists. You can find out which books are still available or about new ones on the Internet by searching Amazon or Barnes and Noble. You can also find an updated list of preparedness books at www.Cross-Current.com/bookshelf.html.

Don't think that you absolutely must have all the items listed. Also, in a number of cases, items not listed could readily be substituted for listed ones. You must be selective in your choices so that your survival library is tailored to your individual needs without too much duplication.

The lists of books that follow are generally categorized by topic in the order covered in this handbook.

Sources

You can buy most of the books from the major book sellers such as Amazon and Barnes & Noble or even directly thru www.Cross-Current.com/bookshelf.html. Others are available from the general preparedness sources listed in Chapter 32. However, some of the books you might want can be more easily obtained or are only available from specialized sources. Be aware that some of these sources also sell books on subjects that might be considered offensive. Just ignore those that are distasteful to you. Most have on-line catalogs or order a hard copy.

Loompanics, PO Box 1197, Port Townsend, WA 98368, 800-380-2230, 360-385-2230, www.loompanics.com. Print catalog available for $5 or free with order.

Paladin Press, 7077 Winchester Circle, Boulder, CO 80301, 800-466-6868, 303-443-7250, www.paladin-press.com. Free printed catalog.

Delta Press, 215 S. Washington Ave., El Dorado, AR 71730, 800-852-4445, 870-862-4984, www.deltapress.com. Free printed catalog.

Another source for unusual publications on old-time skills, how-to articles and primitive chemistry are the Survivor series, Granddad's Wonderful Book of Chemistry and CD-ROMs from Kurt Saxon:

Atlan Formularies, PO Box 95, Alpena, AR 72611, 870-437-2999, www.survivalplus.com.

Fiction

If you want to increase your awareness about what could happen you can read speculative descriptions of what conditions might be like under various speculative scenarios:

Lucifer's Hammer by Larry Niven and Jerry Pournelle
Pulling Through by Dean Ing (1987, hard to find)
Alas, Babylon by Pat Frank (1993 reprint)

General References

Besides the books listed, you might want a current world almanac, an authoritative dictionary and a good encyclopedia set (perhaps even a CD-ROM set). Also consider "how-to" books on trapping, tool making, blacksmithing, small appliance repair, motor and small engine repair, water pump repair, plumbing, wiring, carpentry, masonry and small building construction. You should have a good shop manual for each vehicle and a trouble-shooting guide for each piece of electronic gear or appliance. Additional books might be:

Encyclopedia of Country Living by Carla Emery
Back to Basics by Reader's Digest
Foxfire books (first six volumes)
Modern Homestead Manual by Skip Thomson, et al

Cooking and Recipes

Ultimate Food Storage Cookbook by Arlene Michelsen
Catastrophic Cooking by Carol Reid
Woodstove Cookery: At Home on the Range by Jane Cooper
Y2K Survival Guide and Cookbook by Dorothy Bates
The New Cookin' with Home Storage by Vicki Tate
Cookin' with... (series of three) by Peggy Layton
Country Beans by Rita Bingham, et al
The Amazing Wheat Book by LeArta Moulton
Making the Best of Basics by James Talmage Stevens
New Passport to Survival by Rita Bingham
Making Great Cheese at Home by Barbara Ciletti

Growing Food

How to Grow More Vegetables and Fruits, Nuts, Raising Grains...
    by John Jeavons
Mittleider Grow-Box Gardens by Jacob R. Mittleider
Square Foot Gardening and *Ca$h from Square Foot Gardening* by
    Mel Bartholomew.
Backyard Fruits and Berries by Miranda Smith
The Farmer's Wife Guide to Fabulous Fruits and Berries by Doyen
The Backyard Berry Book by Stella Otto
Planning and Planting Your Dwarf Fruit Trees by L. Southwick
Pruning Simplified by Lewis Hill
The Scythe Book by David Tresemer
Seed to Seed: Seed Saving Techniques by Suzanne Ashworth
Seed Sowing and Saving by Carole B. Turner
Five Acres & Independence by Maurice Grenville Kains, et al

Raising Animals

Backyard Livestock by Steven Thomas
Chickens in Your Backyard by Luttmann and Luttmann
Try the Rabbit by S.O. Adajre
The New Goat Handbook by Jaudas and Vriends
Animal Husbandry by Laura Zigman
Merck Veterinary Manual by Susan Aiello
Veterinary Guide for Animal Owners by Spaulding and Clay
Basic Butchering of Livestock & Game by John T. Mettlar Jr.

Wild Foods

Plants of the Rocky Mountains by Kershaw, Pojar and Alaback
Feasting Free on Wild Edibles by Bradford Angier
Field Guide to Edible Wild Plants by Bradford Angier
Tom Brown's Guide to Wild Edible and Medicinal Plants
Guide to Wild Foods and Useful Plants by Christopher Nyerges
Field Guide to Edible Wild Plants by Peterson and Peterson
God's Free Harvest by Ken Larson
Edible and Poisonous Plants of the Western United States
Edible and Poisonous Plants of the Eastern United States
Live Off the Land in the City and Country by Ragnor Benson
Survival Poaching by Ragnor Benson
Cookin' Wild Game by Teresa Marrone
Wild About Game by Jane Hibler and Janie Hibler
Wild Game Cooking Made Easy by John Schumacher
Wild Game Cookbook by Judity Bosley
Wild Game Cookery by J. Carol Vance, et al
America's Favorite Wild Game Recipes (Hunting & Fishing)
Native Indian Wild Game, Fish & Wild Food Cookbook
500 Wild Game and Fish Recipes by Galen Winter

Preserving Food

Root Cellaring by Mike Bubel, Nancy Bubel and Pam Art
Keeping the Harvest by Nancy Chioffi, et al
Stocking Up by Carol Hupping
Putting Food By by Janet C. Greene, et al
The Busy Person's Guide to Preserving Food by Janet B. Chadwick
Ball Blue Book
Kerr Home Canning Guide
The Complete Guide to Home Canning, Preserving and Freezing,
   Bulletin #539 by the USDA is also available from Dover and on
   the Internet at http://extension.usu.edu/publica/foodpub2.htm.
How to Dry Foods by Deanna DeLong and Lara Gates
The ABC's of Home Food Dehydration by Barbara Densley
Dry It, You'll Like It by Gen MacManiman
A Guide to Canning, Freezing, Curing and Smoking of Meat, Fish
   and Game by Wilbur F. Eastman, Jr.
Home Book of Smoke Cooking Meat, Fish and Game by Jack Sleight
   and Raymond Hall

Sausage & Jerky Handbook by Eldon R. Cutlip
Great Sausage Recipes and Meat Curing by Rytek Kutas
Making Great Sausage at Home by Chris Kobler
Home Sausage Making by Charles G. Reavis

Outdoor Survival

Worst-Case Scenario Survival Handbook by Piven and Borgenicht
US Army Survival Handbook
US Army Survival Manual by Dept. of Defense
Collins GEM SAS Survival Guide by John Wiseman
NOLS Wilderness Guide by Mark Harvey
Mountainman Crafts and Skills by David Montgomery
Survival: A Manual That Could Save Your Life by Chris Janowsky
Outdoor Survival Skills by Larry Dean Olsen
Tom Brown's Field Guide to Wilderness Survival
FM-200 200 Military Manuals on CD-ROM by Dept. of Defense

Firearms

Modern Weapons Caching by Ragnar Benson
Gun Digest Book of Firearms: Centerfire Rifles by J.B. Wood
Gun Digest Book of Firearms: Revolvers by J.B. Wood
Gun Digest Book of Firearms: Auto Pistols by J.B. Wood
Gunsmithing : Rifles by Patrick Sweeney
Gunsmithing: Pistols and Revolvers by Patrick Sweeney
Gunsmithing: Shotguns by Patrick Sweeney
Gunsmithing at Home by John Traister
Survival Guns by Mel Tappan (2002 reprint by Delta Press)
The Survival Armory by Duncan Long (Delta Press)
Bad Times Primer by C. G. Cobb
Gun Digest by Ken Ramage
Gun Digest Book of Assault Weapons by Lewis and Steele

Clothing and Bedding

Complete Guide to Sewing by Reader's Digest
The Complete Photo Guide to Sewing (Singer)
Tan Your Hide! by Phyllis Hobson
Home Tanning and Leather Making Guide by A.B. Farnham
Home Manufacture of Furs and Skins by A.B. Farnham

Heat, Cooking and Light

Solar Electric Independent Home Book by Paul Jeffrey Fowler
Solar Living Source Book by John Schaeffer and Doug Pratt
Practical Photovoltaics by Richard Komp
How to Live Without Electricity—and Like It by Anita Evangelista
Living Without Electricity by Scott and Pellman.

Medical and Dental

Emergency Childbirth by George J. White, MD.
Survivalist's Medicine Chest by Ragnar Benson
Do-It-Yourself Medicine by Ragnar Benson
Current Medical Diagnosis and Treatment by Lawrence M. Tierney
Handbook of Current Diagnosis & Treatment by James O. Woolliscroft.
New American Medical Dictionary & Health Manual by Rothenberg
Wilderness Medicine, Beyond First Aid by William W. Forgey
Field Guide to Wilderness Medicine by Paul S. Auerbach
Advanced First Aid Afloat by Peter Eastman & John Levinson
The Merck Manual of Diagnosis and Therapy by Mark H. Beers
Where There is No Doctor by David Werner, et al
Ditch Medicine by Hugh L. Coffee
PDR: Physician's Desk Reference
The Essential Guide to Prescription Drugs by Long and Rybacki
International Medical Guide for Ships: The Ship's Medicine Chest
US Army Special Forces Medical Handbook-Department of Army
Emergency War Surgery-2nd U.S. Revision of NATO Handbook
Where There Is No Dentist by Murray Dickson.

Terrorism and NBC Warfare

Nuclear War Survival Skills by Cresson H.Kearny (OISM)
Life After Doomsday by Bruce D. Clayton
Fighting Chance by Arthur Robinson and Gary North

Survival Home

New Fix-It-Yourself Manual by Reader's Digest
New Complete Do-It-Yourself Manual by Reader's Digest
Peace of Mind in Earthquake Country by Peter I. Yanev
Earthquake Prepared: Securing Your Home by Joel Leach

The Secure Home by Joel Skousen
How to Implement a High Security Shelter by Joel Skousen
Strategic Relocation by Joel Skousen
The Survival Retreat by Ragnar Benson
The Modern Survival Retreat by Ragnar Benson

Communications

Passport to World Band Radio by Larry Magne
Radio Monitoring: the How to Guide by TJ Skip Arey
The World of CB Radio by Mark Long, et al
Guide to Emergency Survival Communications by Dave Ingram
The Radio Amateur's Handbook by ARRL
No-Code License Manual by Gordon West
Now You're Talking by Larry Wolfgang

Home Education

700 Science Experiments for Everyone (UN)
Everyday Science: Fun and Easy Projects for Making Practical Things by Shar Levine and Leslie Johnstone.
Home Learning Year by Year by Rebecca Rupp
Complete Home Learning Resource Book by Rebecca Rupp
Homeschooling Handbook by Mary Griffith
Homeschooling Almanac by Mary Leppert, et al
Saxon math and physics books are available from Saxon Publishers, 2450 John Saxon Blvd., Norman, OK 73701, 800-284-7019, 405-329-7071, www.saxonpublishers.com. Excellent home study series.

Periodicals

The following magazines may be of interest to you. They all have websites where you can take a look at their latest issues. Sometimes they will send you a sample issue or you can pick one up at the store.

Countryside (modern homesteading) www.countrysidemag.com
Home Power (home-made power) www.homepower.com
Backwoods Home (self-reliant living) www.backwoodshome.com
Mother Earth News www.motherearthnews.com

A more specialized bi-monthly covering civil defense is:

The Journal of Civil Defense www.tacda.org

Currently there are no preparedness-specific magazines or newsletters generally being published that I am aware of.

The Internet

The Internet can also be a valuable source of information. Use search engines like Google or Yahoo and look under preparedness, survival, crisis and similar subjects. Be advised that all information found on the Internet is not true so you must use caution and common sense.

Another good way to find useful information on the Internet is to go to www.Cross-Current.com/links.html and try the many links posted there to other preparedness and survival sites. If you come across a book or other publication, as well as Internet sites, that you think might be of interest to readers of *Crisis Preparedness Handbook*, please send it to me at Cross-Current Publications or e-mail me at jspigarelli@Cross-Current.com.

32

SOURCES DIRECTORY

This chapter contains sources for preparedness information, products and training. It lists the major national sources as well as some less-known. You can contact them by mail, phone, or, in most cases today, over the Internet.

The preparedness business is cyclical. Because of this, over time some sources may change names, locations, products, or even go out of business. This list is as current as possible at the time of printing. For an up-to-date list of sources available see www.Cross-Current.com. If you know of any sources that you think should be included or have comments about any of the concerns listed, please email me at jspigarelli@Cross-Current.com.

Just because a particular concern is listed here it is not an endorsement of them or their products. This list is also not exhaustive. You can find other sources, particular items or additional information through the Internet by simply using search engines.

Preparedness Information

CROSS-CURRENT PUBLISHING (publishers of this book), 333 N 425 E, Alpine, UT 84004, 801-756-2786, www.Cross-Current.com. Preparedness books, information, resources, updated sources, web links and free downloads.

General Preparedness Products

EMERGENCY ESSENTIALS, 165 S Mountain Way Dr., Orem, UT 84058, 800-999-1863, 801-222-9667, www.BePrepared.com.

NITRO-PAK PREPAREDNESS CENTER, 475 West 910 South, Heber City, UT 84032, 800-866-4876, www.nitro-pak.com.

MAJOR SURPLUS & SURVIVAL, 435 W Alondra Blvd., Gardena, CA 90248, 800-441-8855, www.majorsurplusnsurvival.com.

C.F. RESOURCES, POB 405, Kit Carson, CO 80825, 719-962-3228, www.cfamilyresources.com.

EPICENTER SUPPLIES, 384 Wallis St. #2, Eugene, OR 97402, 541-684-0717, www.theepicenter.com.

CAPTAIN DAVE'S SURVIVAL CENTER, PO Box 1903, Cranberry Twp., PA 16066, www.survival-center.com.

USA EMERGENCY SUPPLY, 238 E State Rd, Pleasant Grove, UT 84062, 796-1501, www.usaemergencysupply.com.

VERMONT COUNTRY STORE, PO Box 3000, Manchester Ctr., VT 05255, (802) 362-8460, www.vermontcountrystore.com.

Homesteading Equipment

LEHMAN'S NON-ELECTRIC CATALOG, Lehman Hardware, One Lehman Circle, PO Box 41, Kidron, OH 44636, 888-438-5346, 330-857-5757, www.Lehmans.com. James hand washers, wood/coal cook & heating stoves, Aladdin lamps, non-electric refrigerator/freezers, old-time tools and more. Catalog $3.

CUMBERLAND GENERAL STORE, #1 Highway 68, Crossville, TN 38555, 800-334-4640, www.cumberlandgeneral.com. Thousands of old-time products and how-to books. Catalog $4.

Storage Food & Supplies

WALTON FEED, 135 N 10th St., PO Box 307, Montpelier, ID 83254, 800-847-0465, www.waltonfeed.com. Major supplier.

HONEYVILLE GRAINS, 3750 W 7200 N, Honeyville, UT 84314, (435) 279-8197, 11600 Dayton Dr., Rancho Cucamonga, CA 91730, (909) 980-9500, www.honeyvillegrain.com.

READY RESERVE, 800-453-2202, www.readyreservefoodsinc.com.

GRANDMA'S COUNTRY FOODS, 391 S Orange St. Suite C, Salt Lake City, UT 84104, 800-216-6466, 801-886-1110, www.grandmascountry.com.

LONG LIFE FOOD, PO Box 8081, Richmond, IN 47374, 800-601-2833, www.longlifefood.com. Good selection of MREs.

PREPAREDNESS MART, 800-773-0437, www.preparednessmart.com.

Oxygen Absorbers

SORBENT SYSTEMS, online presence of IMPAK Corp., 2460 E 57th St, Los Angeles, CA 90058, 323-277-4700, www.sorbentsystems.com. Oxygen absorbers, mylar bags, desiccants, heat and vacuum sealers.

DESSICARE, Santa Fa Springs, CA & Jackson, MS, 3400 Pomona Blvd., Pomona, CA 91768, 800-446-6650, 909-444-8272, www.desiccare.com. Oxygen Buster oxygen absorbers, desiccants.

Diatomaceous Earth

DIATECT INTERNATIONAL, 875 S Industrial Parkway, Heber City, UT 84032, 800-227-6616, www.diatect.com. Grain protectant.

WHOLEWHEAT ENTERPRISES, 6598 Bethany Lane, Louisville, KY 40272, 800-813-9641, 502-935-8692, www.wholewheat.com. Sells PermaGuard D-10 grain protectant.

Silica Gel & Dessicants

HYDROSORBENT, PO Box 437, 25 School St., Ashley Falls, MA 01222, 800-448-7903, 413, 229-2967, www.dehumidify.com.

Grain Mills & Mixers

COUNTRY LIVING PRODUCTS, 14727 56th Ave. NW, Standwood, WA 98292, 360-652-0671, www.countrylivinggrainmills.com.

K-TEC, 1206 S 1680 W, Orem, UT 84058, 800-748-5400, 801-222-0888, www.k-tecusa.com. K-Tex mills and Champ mixers.

MAGIC MILL, 382 Rt. 59 section 338, Monsey, NY 10952, 845-368-2532, www.magicmillusa.com.

RETSEL CORP., PO Box 37, McCammon, ID 83250, 208-254-3737, www.retsel.com.

COUNTRY BAKER, 8751 N 850 E, Syracuse, IN 46567, 866-843-2253, 219-834-2134, www.countrybaker.com. Bosch mixers , GrainMaster Whisper, Ultra and Family Grain mills.

ATLAN FORMULARIES, PO Box 95, Alpena, AR 72611, 870-437-2999, www.survivalplus.com. The Corona mill.

Cheese Making & Cultures

NEW ENGLAND CHEESEMAKING SUPPLIES, P.O. Box 85CC, Ashfield, MA 01330, 413-628-3808, www.cheesemaking.com. .

DAIRY CONNECTION, 8616 Fairway Place, #101, Middleton, WI 53562, 608-836-0464, www.dairyconnection.com.

Water Purification

GENERAL ECOLOGY, Inc., 151 Sheree Blvd., Exton, PA 19341, 800-441-8166, 610-363-7900, www.generalecology.com. First-Need and Seagull purifiers. Among the best purifiers.

Other water filters are generally available at sporting goods stores.

Garden & Farm Supplies

MOUNTAIN VALLEY SEED, 1800 S West Temple #600, Salt Lake City, UT 84115, 801-486-0480, www.mvseeds.com. Canned seeds..

TERRITORIAL SEED, PO Box 158, Cottage Grove, OR 97424, Fax 888-657-3131, 541-942-9547, www.territorial-seed.com.

HARRIS SEEDS, 355 Paul Rd., PO Box 24966, Rochester, NY, 800-514-4441, www.harrisseeds.com. .

HEIRLOOM SEEDS, PO Box 245, West Elizabeth, PA 15088, 412-384-0852, www.heirloomseeds.com. Non-hybrid seeds.

MELLINGERS, 2310 W South Range Rd., North Lima, OH 44452, 800-321-7444, 330-549-9861, www.mellingers.com. Non-hybrid seeds.

BURPEE, Warminster, PA 18974, 800-888-1447, www.burpee.com.

JOHNNY'S, 184 Foss Hill Rd., Albion, ME 04910, Fax 800-437-4290, 207-437-4301, www.johnnyseeds.com.

GURNEY'S, 110 Capital St., Yankton, SD 57079, 800-824-6400, www.myseasons.com.

GARDNER'S SUPPLY, 128 Intervale Rd., Burlington, VA 05401, 800-427-3363, www.gardners.com.

INDIANA BERRY & PLANT, 5218 W 500 S, Huntingburg, IN 47542, 800-295-2226, www.inberry.com.

MILLER NURSERIES, 5060 W Lake Rd., Canandaigua, NY 14424, 800-836-9630, www.millernurseries.com.

STARK BRO'S, PO Box 1800, Louisiana, MO 63353, 800-325-4180, www.starkbros.com.

RAINTREE NURSERY, 391 Butts Rd., Morton, WA 98356, Fax 888-770-8358, 360-496-6400, www.raintreenursery.com.

SUBMATIC, PO Box 3965, 321 82nd St., Lubbock, TX 79452, 800-692-4100, 806-748-7659, www.submatic.com.

DRIPWORKS, 190 Sanhedrin Circle, Willits, CA 95490, 800-522-3747, 707-459-6323, www.dripworksusa.com.

HIGH COUNTRY GARDENS, 2902 Rufina St., Santa Fe, NM 87507, 800-925-9387, www.highcountrygardens.com.

HIGH ALTITUDE GARDENS, 4150 B Black Oak Dr, Hailey, ID 83333, 208-788-4363, www.seedsave.org.

PLANTS OF SOUTHWEST, 6680 4th St. NW, Albuquerque, NM 87107, 800-788-7333, 505-344-8830, 505-4, www.plantsofthesouthwest.com.

WORM'S WAY, 7850 N Highway 37, Bloomington, IN 47404, 800-274-9676, www.wormsway.com.

A.M. LEONARD, 241 Fox Dr., PO Box 816, Piqua, OH 45356, 800-543-8955, www.amleo.com.

LEE VALLEY TOOLS, PO Box 1780, Ogdensburg, NY 13669, 800-871-8158, www.leevalley.com.

CHARLEY'S GREENHOUSE SUPPLY, 800-322-4707, 360-395-3001, www.charleysgreenhouse.com.

Animal & Veterinarian Supplies

HOEGGER SUPPLY, PO Box 331, Fayetteville, GA 30214, 800-221-4628, 770-461-5398, hoeggergoatsupply.com. Goat supplies.

CAPRINE SUPPLY, PO Box Y, DeSoto, KS 66018, 913-585-1191, www.caprinesupply.com. Goat supplies.

NASCO FARM & RANCH, 800-558-9595, www.enasco.com.

OMAHA VACCINE, PO Box 7228, Omaha, NE 68107, 800-367-4444, www.ohahavaccine.com.

PETCO ANIMAL SUPPLIES, 9125 Rehco Rd., San Diego, CA 92121, 877-738-6742, www.petco.com. Rabbits and other small animals.

SHEEPMAN SUPPLY, PO Box A, Frederick, MD 21702, 800-331-9122, 301-662-4197, www.sheepman.com. Sheep, goats, llamas, horses.

UPCO (UNITED PHARMACAL), 3705 Pear St., PO Box 969, St. Joseph, MO 64502, 800-254-8726, www.upco.com.

Canning Supplies

HOME CANNING & SUPPLY, PO Box 1158, Ramona, CA 92065, 619-788-0520, www.home-canning.com.

Firearms & Ammo

BROWNELLS, 200 S Front St., Montezuma, IA 50171, 641-623-4000, www.brownells.com. Gun parts, tools and accessories. Catalog $5.

CORBIN, PO Box 2659, 600 Industrial Circle, White City, OR 97503, 541-826-5211, www.corbins.com. Bullet swaging equipment.

FIREQUEST, PO Box 315, El Dorado, AR 71731, 870-881-8688, www.firequest.com. Specialized ammo and shooting equipment.

HUNTINGTON, P.O. Box 991, 601 Oro Dam Blvd., Oroville, CA 95965, 530-1210, www.huntingtons.com. HDS compact reloading tool.

MIDWAY USA, 5875 W Van Horn Tavern Rd., Columbia, MO 65203, 800-243-3220, 573-447-5117, www.midwayusa.com.

EAGLE OPTICS, 2120 W Greenview Dr. #4, Middleton, WI 53562, 800-289-1132, www.eagleoptics.com. Binoculars, rifle scopes, spotting scopes, telescopes.

SWFA, 972-223-0500, www.riflescopes.com. Rifle scopes, binoculars.

SHOTGUN NEWS, Box 1790, Peoria, IL 61656, 800-521-2885, www.shotgunnews.com. Ads for guns, ammo, reloading components
RELOADING BENCH, www.reloadbench.com. Reloading powders info.

Airguns

IAR, 33171 Camino Capistrano, San Juan Capistrano, CA 92675, 949-443-3642, www.iar-arms.com. Chinese imports.

Knives, Axes & Saws

CUTLERY SHOPPE, 357 Steelhead Way, Boise, ID 83704, 800-231-1272, 208-672-8488, www.cutleryshoppe.com.
KNIFE PROFESSIONAL, 2527 S White Oak Dr., Shelby, NC 28150, Fax 434-8225, www.knifepro.com. Knives, multi-tools, axes, saws.
BAILEY'S, 44650 Highway 101, PO Box 550, Laytonville, CA 95454, 800-322-4539, 707-984-6133, www.baileys-online.com. Mail order woodsman supplies.

Military Gear

BRIGADE QUARTERMASTERS, 1025 Cobb International Dr. NW Suite 100, PO Box 100001, Kennesaw, GA 30156, 800-338-4327, 770-428-1248, www.brigadeqm.com.
PHOENIX SYSTEMS, 6517 S Kings Ranch Rd. #185, Gold Canyon, AZ 85219, 800-272-2346, 480-474-1226, www.phxsystems.com.
SHOMER-TEC, Box 28070, Bellingham, WA 98228, 360-733-6214, www.shomertec.com.
US CAVALRY, 2855 Centennial Ave., Radcliff, KY 40160, 888-888-7228, 800-777-7172, 270-351-1164, www.uscav.com.
KEN NOLAN, 16901 Milliken, PO Box C-19555, Irvine, CA 92623, 800-972-9280, www.kennolan.com.
SIERRA SUPPLY, P.O. Box 1390, Durango, CO 81302, 970-259-1822, www.sierra-supply.com.

Outdoor Clothing & Equipment

CABELA'S, Inc., 812 13th Ave., Sidney, NE 69160, 800-237-4444, 308-254-5505 in Nebraska, www.cabelas.com. Great selection.
CAMPMOR, Box 700-H, Saddle River, NJ 07458, 800-226-7667, www.campmor.com. Wide selection.
CHEAPER THAN DIRT, 2520 NE Loop 820, Fort Worth, TX 76106, 800-421-8047, www.cheaperthandirt.com. Sporting goods.

DON GLEASON'S, 9 Pearl St., PO Box 87, Northampton, MA 01060, 800-257-0019, 413-584-4895, www.gleasoncamping.com.

EARLY WINTERS,PO Box 4333, Portland, OR 97208, 800-458-4438, www.earlywinters.com. Mostly clothes but some unique products.

L.L.BEAN, Freeport, ME 04033, 800-229-9179, www.llbean.com.

REI, 1700 45th Street East, Sumner, WA 98390, 800-426-4840, www.rei.com. Offers "dividend" on purchases during year for $15 lifetime membership. Good selection and quality, decent prices.

C.C.FILSON, PO Box 34020, Seattle, WA 98124, 800-624-0201, www.filson.com. Some of the best outdoor clothing available.

PENDLETON, PO Box 3030, Portland, OR 97208, 877-796-4663, 503-535-5222, www.pendleton-usa.com. Well-made woolen clothing.

WOOLRICH, One Mill St., Woolrich, PA 17779, 877-512-7305, www.woolrich.com. Sturdy woolen clothing.

Clothing & Bedding Kits

FROSTLINE KITS, PO Box 3419, Grand Junction, CO 81502, 800-548-7872, 970-242-0240, www.frostlinekitsllc.com. Down and other kits.

Leather Goods

TANDY LEATHER, 5882 E Berry St., Fort Worth, TX 76119, 888-890-1611, www.tandyleather.com. Catalog $5 or free with order.

Bullet-Proof Vests & Body Armor

AMERICAN BODY ARMOR, www.americanbodyarmor.com

BULLDOG DIRECT, PO Box 8561, Cincinnati, OH 45208, 513-281-6700, www.bulldogdirect.com.

FIRST CHOICE, www.firstchoicearmor.com.

PACA BODY ARMOR, www.paca-vest.com.

POINT BLANK BODY ARMOR, www.pointblankarmor.com.

SAFARILAND, www.safariland.com.

SECOND CHANCE BODY ARMOR, www.secondchance.com.

US ARMOR, www.usarmor.com.

ZERO G, www.bodyarmor.com.

James Washer

S & H METAL PRODUCTS, PO Box 35, 122 Redman Dr., Topeka, IN 46571, 219-593-2565.

LAKE CITY INDUSTRIES, PO Box 423, Lake City, PA 16423, 814-774-9616 for local source of wringer. www.lakecityindustries.com

Wood/Coal Heating

ALPHA AMERICAN, 10 Industrial Blvd., PO Box 20, Palisade, MN 56469, 800-358-0060, www.yukon-eagle.com. YUKON-EAGLE multi-fuel (wood with gas, oil or electric) furnace.
CHARMASTER PRODUCTS, 2307 N 2 West Grand Rapids, MN 55744, 218-326-6768. Combination wood/oil or gas furnaces.

Fuel Preservatives

YELLOWSTONE RIVER TRADING COMPANY, 800-585-5077, www.yellowstonetrading.com. PRI-G and PRI-D fuel additives.

Non-Electric Refrigerators/Freezers

DOMETIC, 2320 Industrial Parkway, Elkhart, IN 46515, 800-544-4881, 574-294-2611, www.dometic.com.
NORTHWEST ENERGY SYSTEMS, 6791 S Main, Ste. C, Bonners Ferry, ID 83805, 800-718-8816, 208-267-6409, www.nwes.com.
EXPLORER, PO Box 928049, San Diego, CA 92192, 858-587-9766, www.explorerfridges.com. Explorer propane refrigerators.

Alternative Energy

REAL GOODS and JADE MOUNTAIN (Gaiam, Inc., 360 Interlocken Blvd., Ste. 300, Broomfield, CO 80021), 800-762-7325, 800-442-1972, www.realgoods.com, Alternative and renewable energy products.
ABRAHAM SOLAR, 124 Creekside Place, Pagosa Springs, CO 81147, 800-222-7242, Fax 970-731-4675.
ALTERNATIVE ENERGY ENGINEERING, PO Box 339, Redway, CA 95560, 800-777-6609, www.solarelectric.com.
ALTERNATIVE POWER, po Box 351, Ridgway, CO 81432, 800-590-5830, 970-626-9842, www.alternative-power.com.
INTERMOUNTAIN SOLAR, 10288 S Jordan Gateway #D, South Jordan, UT 84095, 800-671-0169, www.intermountainsolar.com.
ZODI OUTBACK GEAR, PO Box 4687, Park City, UT 84060, 800-589-2849, 801-255-6418, www.zodi.com. Zodi Super Shower and Extreme portable propane showers.

Medical

MERCK MANUAL, home edition: www.merckhomeedition.com.
MERCK MANUAL OF DIAGNOSIS & THERAPY, on-line edition, www.merck.com/pubs/mmanual/.

Earthquake Protection

QUAKE PRO, 1073 Hyland Lake Dr., Salt Lake City, 84121, 877-261-3897, 801-263-9600, www.quakepro.com. Water heater braces, gas shut-off valves, quake alarms, shut-off tool, other preparedness products..

QUAKE KARE, PO Box 3152, Thousand Oaks, CA 91359, 800-277-3727, 805-553-0688, www.quakekare.com. Earthquake tie-downs, emergency preparedness products.

SAFE-T-PROOF, 800-377-8888, 818-865-3125, www.safetyproof.com. Commercial earthquake and disaster preparedness.

Nuclear Protection

UTAH SHELTER SYSTEMS, PO Box 638, Heber City, UT 84032, 801-942-5638, www.netoriginal.com/uss. Swiss bomb shelters and filters.

KLEEN AIR TECHNOLOGIES, PO Box 4145, Frisco, CO 80443, 866-528-6537, 970-668-0219, www.undergroundshelter.com. Build underground concrete shelter systems.

RADIUS DEFENSE & ENGINEERING, 222 Blakes Hill Road, Northwood, NH 03261, 603-942-5040, www.radius-defense.com. NBC underground shelters.

ZERO SURGE, 944 State Route 12, Frenchtown, NJ 08825, 800-996-6696, www.zerosurge.com. EMP protection surge protectors.

POLYPHASER, PO Box 9000, Minden, NV 89423, 800-325-7170, 775-782-2511, www.polyphaser.com. Military-grade EMP protection.

KI4U, 212 Oil Patch Lane, Gonzales, TX 78629, 830-672-8734, www.ki4u.com. Sells potassium iodide tablets and radiation meters.

LUDLUM , 501 Oak St., PO Box 810, Sweetwater, TX, 800-622-0828, 915-235-5494, www.ludlums.com. Radiation meters.

Off-Road Trailer

HELDER, 11043 St. Highway 70, Marysville, CA 95901, 530-742-5257. Pack Mule heavy-duty off-road trailer.

Radio Equipment & Supplies

UNIVERSAL RADIO, 6830 Americana Pkwy., Reynoldsburg, OH 43068, 800-431-3939, 614-866-4267, www.universal-radio.com. .

C CRANE, 1001 Main St., Fortuna, CA 95540, 800-522-8863, 707-725-9000, www.ccrane.com.

AMATEUR ELECTRONIC (AES), 800-558-0411, www.aesham.com.

HAM RADIO OUTLET, 800-444-9476, www.hamradio.com.

RADIO SHACK. www.radioshack.com. Stores nationwide.

PASSBAND.COM, Box 300, Penn's Park, PA 18943, 215-598-9018, www.passband.com. *Passport to World Band Radio*, evaluations.

Shortwave Listening Web Sites

Shortwave Listening Guide: www.anarc.org/naswa/swlguide/
Broadcasts to North America: www.triwest.net/~dsampson/shortwave/
Art Bell's Shortwave Radio Guide: www.artbell.com/shortwave.html
Glenn Hauser's World of Radio: www.angelfire.com/ok/worldofradio/
Dxing.com radio resources: www.dxing.com.
DXZone radio guide: www.dxzone.com.

Training Courses

GUNSITE ACADEMY (Jeff Cooper), 2900 West Gunsite Rd., Paulden, AZ 86334, 928-636-4565, www.gunsite.com.

BSR (Bill Scott's driving schools and firearms courses), PO Box 190, Summit Point, WV 25446, 304-725-6512, www.bsr-inc.com

BOB BONDURANT SCHOOL OF HIGH PERFORMANCE DRIVING, Phoenix, AZ , 800-842-7223, www.bondurant.com.

NATIONAL OUTDOOR LEADERSHIP SCHOOL (NOLS), 228 Main, Lander, WY 82520, 307-332-5300, www.nols.edu/NOLSHome.html. Outdoor and survival courses.

OUTWARD BOUND, 888-882-6863, www.outwardbound.com. Five schools across the USA with courses in wilderness skills and leadership.

BOULDER OUTDOOR SURVIVAL SCHOOL (BOSS), PO Box 1590, Boulder, CO 80306, 301-444-9779, www.boss-inc.com.

INDEX

"A first-class book, probably the best available."
Conrad V. Chester, civil defense expert
Oak Ridge National Laboratories

"One of the best—well reasoned and complete—guides to personal preparedness."
Bruce Tippery
Remnant Review

"Excellent over-all book."
Dr. John Sweeney
Public Health Department
New York State

"Many times I have referred to [this] book...one of the few 'normal' books on survival."
George Guillery
Manufacturer of nuclear survival products

"Every family should have—and study—this book...right on the mark."
Survival Guide magazine

"An indispensable guide...money well spent."
Survive magazine

"One of those books that you need to have."
Duncan Long
Survival expert and author

"Everyone needs this book."
Internet site review

QUICK ORDER FORM

E-mail orders: orders@Cross-Current.com

Mail orders: Cross-Current Publishing, 333 North 425 East, Alpine, UT 84004-1427, USA. Telephone 801-756-2786.

Fax orders: 801-756-6360. Send this form.

Telephone orders: Call 801-756-2786. Have credit card ready.

Please send the following:

CRISIS PREPAREDNESS HANDBOOK
    Paperback _____ copies @ $19.95 each
    On CD-ROM _____ copies @ $9.95 each

☐ Please send free information on *SURVIVING TERRORISM: A Comprehensive Guide to Preparing for and Surviving Biological, Chemical and Nuclear Attack*.

Name:_____
Address:_____
City:_____State:_____ZIP:_____
Telephone: (_____)_____
E-mail address:_____@_____

Sales Tax: Please add 6.25% for products shipped to Utah.

Shipping
U.S.: $4.00 for first book or disk and $2.00 for each additional item.
International: $9.00 for first book or disk; $5.00 for each additional item.

Payment: ☐ Credit card   ☐ Check
    ☐ Visa ☐ Mastercard

Card #:_____
Name on card:_____Expire Date:___/___
Signature:_____